MW00776908

THE GREAT JOURNEY

UNRAVELING THE RIDDLE OF REALITY, SELF & SOUL

Garry Appel

Copyright © 2018 Garry R. Appel

All rights reserved. Except for brief quotations in reviews, no portion of this book, including the drawings and photographic images, may be reproduced in any form without the express permission of the author.

Published by Satya Publishing. For reproduction permission or to purchase additional copies of this book, contact the publisher in writing at 2280 South Monroe St, Denver, CO 80210 or the author through his website at GarryAppel.com.

The drawings are by Karen Appel. Other images, including the cover, are by the author unless otherwise stated.

ISBN-13: 978-0-578-43384-4 (Satya Publishing)

ISBN-10: 0-578-43384-2

With deep gratitude.
To all my teachers.

Contents

Chapter 1

Twenty-one Grams

Many eons ago an enormous glacier creaked and groaned as it carved its way through what we now call central New Hampshire. As the earth warmed and the ice slowly receded, what remained in its wake was a shallow basin about twenty miles long, ten miles wide and two hundred feet deep. Runoff from the surrounding hills combined with the melting ice to gradually fill the basin and Lake Winnipesaukee was born. At the lowest spot on its western shore, the cool waters of the lake flow through a channel and eventually make their way to the Merrimack River. The Merrimack snakes lazily south through towns named Concord, Manchester and Nashua before it departs New Hampshire altogether, crossing into Massachusetts, paying little mind to the political boundary. There it turns east as it flows gently past Lowell and Lawrence, eventually offering its waters to the Atlantic Ocean. The penultimate little town along the Merrimack's path to the sea is Haverhill. Settled by Europeans along the river bank more than three hundred fifty years ago, Haverhill is comfortably nestled among the rolling green hills of the New England countryside.

More than a century ago, as the nineteenth century flowed into the twentieth, Haverhill claimed a dozen physicians resident within its borders. Among them was one Duncan MacDougall, native-born in 1866. At the age of thirty-five, in 1901, on April 10th to be precise, Dr. MacDougall, who had become a respected surgeon, and four colleagues whose names are lost to time, acquired by means we do not know six live human subjects, each of whom stood at death's door and was poised to take their final breath. Recumbent on their death-beds, the six – four men, one woman and one person of unspecified gender – had been assembled for the singular purpose of measuring the weight of their souls.

The dubious legacy Dr. MacDougall bequeathed to our world was this somewhat ghoulish undertaking. As a man of science, he believed in objective facts, that is, those facts that could be established through the scientific method – ask a question, form a hypothesis to answer the question, test the hypothesis with an experiment and draw a conclusion from the results. The question that transfixed Dr. MacDougall was whether man had a soul. The hypothesis he carefully formulated was that the soul existed and that its existence could be demonstrated scientifically. The ingenious method he devised to test his hypothesis, his experiment, was to measure the weight of a person just before death and just after, to detect whether their weight measurably declined at the instant of death. If so, he reasoned, the existence of the soul would be undeniably confirmed. Or, as he might have said it more majestically: *quod erat demonstrandum*.

There were some problems with the good doctor's thought process leading to his hypothesis, his experiment and his conclusions. First, his basic premise was that the soul, if it existed, necessarily was a physical thing that occupied space. His explanation for this premise, exceedingly dubious upon retrospection, was that it was "unthinkable that personality and consciousness continuing personal identity should exist, and have being, and yet not occupy space." Thus, spacelessness was unimaginable to Dr. MacDougall and he therefore believed that the soul, if it existed had to occupy space. An option he apparently hadn't considered or couldn't allow to creep into his brain was that the soul existed, but didn't occupy space, like, for instance, the phenomena of light or thought or memory, all of which exist but occupy no space. In any event, MacDougall's reasoning continued, if the soul occupied space, it had to have mass, it had to be, as he called it, "gravitative matter." His hypothesis, then, was that the soul was composed of gravitative matter and one of the properties of gravitative matter was that it had mass that could be weighed. This is the thinking that led to the assemblage of the six hapless folks waiting to die, each reclining supine on specially constructed hospital gurneys in a dark room in Haverhill Massachusetts, along the Merrimack River, on that fine April day in 1901.

Lending an air of credible precision to their plan, Dr. MacDougall and his distinguished medical accomplices had acquired the finest scale, a large one to be sure, able to distinguish increments of weight down to a small fraction of an ounce. The scale was constructed so the gurney with the dying body, presumably complete with soul, could be rested upon it awaiting the fateful moment when the body would breathe its last. At that instant, the collective gaze of five sets of trained eyes would be cast upon the scale to await any change in the reading.

The first experimental subject had the temerity, while the doctors stared intently, to hold out for three hours and forty minutes before he expired. "Suddenly," MacDougall breathlessly recounted in his lab notes, "the beam end dropped with an audible stroke hitting against the lower limiting bar and remaining there with no rebound. The loss [of weight] was ascertained to be three-fourths of an ounce." Three-fourths of an ounce is, of course, 21 grams, more or less. Some years later, Dr. MacDougall recounted the moment for the New York Times in even more dramatic language: "The instant life ceased the opposite scale pan fell with a suddenness that was astonishing – as if something had been suddenly lifted from the body. Immediately all the usual deductions were made for physical loss of weight, and it was discovered that there was still a full ounce of weight unaccounted for."

After the first go, the next victim – excuse me, experimental subject – was wheeled in and placed on the scale and weighed and the death watch began for the second time. Four hours and fifteen minutes it took, but eventually he gave it up and the scale registered a loss of half an ounce. Not sure if the fellow was dead yet, and not wanting to touch him and upset the weighing process, the good doctors waited eighteen minutes more until certitude dawned and then, just for good measure, they waited another forty minutes more, observing no further change in the scale. And so it went with each experimental subject, watching, waiting and measuring the decline in weight. Once all had expired and the day's work done, MacDougall was able to confidently proclaim: "The net result of the experiments conducted on human beings, is that a loss of substance occurs at death not accounted for by known channels of loss. Is it the soul substance? It would seem to me to be so. According to our hypothesis such a substance is necessary to the assumption of continuing or persisting personality after bodily death, and here we have experimental demonstration that a substance capable of being weighed does leave the human body at death."

Presumably to check his results, MacDougall conducted a second round of experiments, this time with dogs as his subjects. Since everyone knows dogs don't have souls, the hypothesis this time was that there would be no loss of weight in dogs at the moment of their death. Sure enough, the death of fifteen canines of different sizes, weights and breeds (this time by poisoning), confirmed no weight loss at all, which must have been the cause of considerable glee as the six jaunty men in starched white lab coats celebrated their scientific breakthrough with a pint of ale or two at Haverhill Inn. To be fair, Dr. MacDougall recognized that his experiments involved a small sample size and "a large number of experiments would" be needed to confirm his results "beyond any possibility of error." But he clearly believed his experiment established the existence of the human soul and that the soul weighed about 21 grams.

After accounts of this experiment were reported in the popular press, counterpoint poured in from doctors and scientists in various fields, who pointed to seemingly important details MacDougall had thoughtlessly overlooked or chosen to ignore. For example, MacDougall excluded the experimental results from two of his six human subjects and he ignored the obvious fact that only the first of the remaining four subjects supported his conclusion, while the other three did not. In addition, there were ample alternative explanations for the weight loss, like the cessation of metabolic function that occurs naturally at death.

MacDougall's soul weighing experiment has never been repeated and is now held up in scientific circles as a shining example of how *not* to employ the scientific method in the conduct of an experiment. His conclusions are regarded as almost certainly not true. And with that, you'd think we could, as it were, bury this small nugget of history. Not quite. It turns out Dr. Duncan MacDougall's legacy is not the daft experiment, but precisely the opposite – the enduring thought in the popular mind that the soul has been measured and that it weighs 21 grams. This misconception has no doubt been buoyed by a successful movie entitled, not surprisingly, "21 Grams" and by countless references to the experiment in film, song and the press.

* * * * * * *

Whether souls exist is an interesting question and we cannot blame Dr. MacDougall for seeking an answer. But whether an answer can be found in the realm of science or whether religion or philosophy would be a better place to look is perhaps open to debate. It seems reasonable to suggest that the existence of some things can be reliably demonstrated through scientific investigation, while others are really just matters of faith. Perhaps then we look in the wrong place if we expect science to prove that God exists and we err in the opposite direction if we expect religion to explain why the earth revolves around the sun.

Some conditions seem obvious and in need of neither rigorous proof nor requiring a resort to faith. A world that has tangible essence seems to exist. It seems to be real. But we might still ask whether this Reality we experience is real. It seems to be filled with things that have substance – that have form and shape and mass and that move in mostly predictable ways. But we can at least ask whether that perception Is true or whether it's an illusion, a trick of some kind. Whatever the Reality, we can certainly ask: How did it arise? Where did it come from? Who created it? Why does Reality seem the way it does?

Like the Reality that surrounds me, I seem to be a Self that exists within this Reality and that interacts with all the other things, including other people like me. But who am I really? What am I? How did I come to be? What is my purpose? Why am I here, whatever "I" may be and wherever "here" is? Where will I go? Is there a creator that created me? Who is that? Does my Self continue after my body dies?

I can ask: do I have a Soul? If so, what is its nature? Where did it come from? Where was it before it became "mine"? How long does it last? What does it do? If this Self has a Soul, did it come into being when my body did or did my Soul exist before my body came to be? What is my Soul made of? Is it matter, pure energy or something else altogether? Can I touch my Soul or see, hear, taste or smell it? Or might I sense my Soul, experience it in some way, using a faculty other than one of the five common senses? What is the purpose of my Soul? Is it even right to ask whether "I" have a Soul? What do I mean by that question? Maybe the Soul is the "real" Me, not this body.

These and others like them are the giant questions we ask in still, quiet, contemplative moments or in moments of tumult or angst. Sometimes these big questions are prompted by a crisis, like the death of a loved one. Sometimes they can be thrust upon us as it becomes clear that our own death lurks in the shadows that shorten day by day. Sometimes we ask these questions when we are young and trying to make sense of the world and our place in it. Sometimes these questions loom larger when the pace of life slows and we find more time for contemplation in our later years. For some, these questions form the backbone of a search for meaning that has been present throughout their life, occasionally at the forefront and sometimes receding into the background. And for others these questions have always been at the forefront, motivating their spiritual, artistic or academic explorations during the whole course of their life.

In their many forms, these big questions, these existential queries, have occupied our collective thoughts and captured our imagination for millennia, probably since the beginning of humankind. These questions are universal. They are at the root of all cultures. We explore some with our science and others through our paintings, our songs, our dances, our literature, our moviemaking, our thoughts and our dreams. Every religion and philosophy that has arisen since humankind began has these questions at its core and each group has offered their own answers, sometimes new and unique and sometimes variations on the theme of a theology or philosophy that preceded it. There is something about these questions that speaks to us both individually and collectively. Each of us answers these questions in some way. We can't really exist as humans without harboring some idea, some conception, of who we are, what this place is and why we are here. Delving into the mysteries these questions lead us to is, in a fundamental way, what it means to be human.

These questions seem to collect around three broad subjects that we can label Reality, Self and Soul. These three spheres are of course not really separate from one another. We can't very well contemplate Reality without also contemplating Self and Soul, we can't understand the Self without having some understanding of the role of Reality and Soul, and we can't go about unraveling the meaning of the Soul without considering the nature and role of Reality and the Self. Think of the three areas as amorphous and often overlapping, like three puffy white clouds floating in the sky, sometimes appearing distinct from one another, sometimes overlapping a little and sometimes so entangled that they appear almost as one.

At its most basic the *Self* is the Me that's posing these questions, the presence that seems to exist in the world, that seems to interact with other people and with other things. I experience my Self all the time. I see my Self in the mirror. I experience my thoughts and emotions. I remember my past and I dream about my future. I am well acquainted with my body, my routines, my accomplishments and my failings. I've been with my Self for a long time and I know it well – or so I believe.

The relationship with my *Soul* is quite different from the relationship with the Self. I don't perceive my Soul in the same way I perceive my body. My Soul is, at least by most accounts, an incorporeal essence, a spirit, a vital force, an unseen is-ness that I imagine to be within or in some other way associated with my Self. I can't see my Soul in the mirror or reflected in a still pond. I don't really know what it's made of, if it's made of anything at all. I don't know my Soul very well, if I even know it at all.

Reality is the tableau upon which my Self lives out its life and, at least in a sense, Reality is also the playground of my Soul. Reality is all that is around me, the world and the universe I perceive with my senses, the container in which I exist. I see Reality all the time. I can't help but be acquainted with it, at least to some extent. At times I may consciously explore Reality and at other times I may just exist within it without particularly noticing much about it at all. Reality has rules that I can observe, explore and try to understand, like gravity, entropy and inertia. I seem to experience Reality as separate from my Self, although my Self seems to exist within the Reality I perceive.

The concept of the Soul has and continues to profoundly shape how each and every one of us views our Self and that Self-view informs our view of Reality, the world around us, and our place in that world. In fact, the Soul and the Self are so central to our understanding of the world, our Reality, that they eclipse everything else. While we seem to have a physical presence that moves through the world from birth to death, it is the Soul – the unseen Self – that our spiritual traditions tell us exists coincident with the physical body and which is immortal or close to it, that truly defines who and what the Self is. Since the dawn of humankind, we have been trying to make sense of our Self and our world and to separate the real from the unreal, the apparent from the enduring. This triumvirate of Reality, Self and Soul, this conceptual trinity, is the bedrock upon which all our beliefs are grounded. When we understand these three, their shapes and contours, their source or sources and how they relate and interconnect with one another, perhaps we can then understand what it means to be human, what it means to be alive. But this is tricky business. It's not a simple thing to do. It's not easy to find firm ground on which to stand to even begin our exploration.

* * * * * * *

I used to have a recurring dream. I didn't have the dream every night. It happened sporadically. Sometimes I'd have it three, four or five nights in a row and then not for a month or two. There were occasions when I'd have the dream one night and then not again for six months or even more. It was about five years from the first appearance of the dream until the last. Although I didn't keep a close count, I bet I had the dream at least two dozen times over the five years. While the little details of the dream varied from night to night, the plotline, the substance of it, was always fundamentally the same. Even though it has now been many years since I last dreamed this dream, it's still very vivid in my memory. The dream always went like this: I'd become privy somehow to the key to the universe – a single thought or idea that explained everything there was to know – where everything came from, why things were the way they were and the purpose of everything. Sometimes the "key" was a mathematical equation so beautifully simple and sublime that I wept in the dream when it became manifest. Sometimes it was just knowledge that entered my brain and gave rise to perfect understanding. In the dream, the appearance of the key to the universe wasn't supernatural in any way. It wasn't about enlightenment in a spiritual sense. It was more akin to putting pieces together that had always been lying around and the assembled picture brought perfect clarity to everything there was to know. It was like a super "aha" moment, a time of boundless clarity and pure understanding.

After the epiphany occurred in the dream there would be a brief interval where I'd just accept what had happened and rest in the joy of perfect understanding. I was always aware in the dream that I was dreaming. But the fact that the key to understanding the universe had come to me in a dream didn't invalidate or diminish the understanding. The initial period of acceptance of the dream as the context within which the understanding arose would then transition into a new phase where the realization I was dreaming gave rise to a deep fear. The fear was always the same – that I wouldn't remember the key to the universe once I awoke. And so I would remind myself I was dreaming and that I needed to remember the key to the universe once I awoke. I'd repeat the key knowledge or thought or equation over and over again in the dream to be sure I would remember it once I transitioned from the sleep-state to wakefulness.

When I'd awaken in the morning with the dream still fresh in my consciousness, the first thing that would come to mind was my apprehension about forgetting the revelation. Then, as I became more and more awake, the key to the universe – the equation or the thought or whatever it had been in the dream – would slowly begin to recede from consciousness, hovering just beyond the grasp of my memory, a little like when you can almost but not quite remember someone's name or the lyrics of a song or some sequence of numbers. It's as though if you just wait for a moment and let go, the information will repopulate your memory and become accessible to your brain. It's like it's somewhere in a temporary cache that will shortly become available to use. In situations like this, at least in my experience, the more you wait, the more the memory slips away and fades. Until eventually you're just sitting there like a dummy, waiting for something that is never going to come.

The dream was like that. I'd lay in bed, waiting for the key to the universe, which I had cautioned myself over and over in the dream not to forget, to return to my memory. But it never did. Then, as I became fully awake, I'd begin to question whether the whole key to the universe thing had actually occurred or whether I had just dreamed that I had dreamed that I learned the key to the universe. Ultimately, I concluded it didn't matter. Whether it was once there and now lost or was never really there at all made no difference. All that mattered was that it wasn't there now.

* * * * * * *

My quest to understand Reality, Self and Soul has been like that recurring dream. I have always sensed that there was a truth, a single clear explanation for my existence and the Reality I experienced. But the truth has been elusive, just out of sight, just beyond my grasp, like I was almost, but not quite smart enough to understand. It was as though if I had just a few million more brain cells or another ten IQ points, it would all fall into place. The truth and I played peekaboo like that for decades. A little glimpse here and a little glimpse there, punctuated by long periods where there were no glimpses at all. I spent a lifetime exploring the religions, cultures and philosophies of the world, both present and historical, learning about each one's explanation of Reality, Self and Soul, then critiquing those explanations, comparing them to my own experiences of the world and testing the logic of their assumptions and conclusions. I always came away dissatisfied and unconvinced, finding each one wanting, flawed in some fundamental way.

Lest you think me a naysayer or an old curmudgeon, that wasn't at all the case. I wasn't looking for reasons to reject beliefs. To the contrary, I dearly wanted to find the truth and it was painful not to. I often questioned my rejection of the verity of these belief systems, wondering what beautiful nuggets I had overlooked in a system of thought or belief that had endured for thousands of years and had attracted hundreds of millions or billions of ardent followers. Many times I asked what these huge flocks of believers saw and felt that I did not. I berated myself: who was I to reject the truths that so many others had accepted? But when I went over it all again, maybe for the tenth time, maybe over a span of many years, I invariably arrived at the same conclusion. The teachings were empty.

Eventually, I just stopped looking. I abandoned the quest. I gave up. And that's when it happened. . . . . .

* * * * * * *

Our experiences of the world sometimes arrive in unexpected ways, sometimes in ways that can't even be said to be perceptual at all in any conventional sense. These non-sensory experiences can become integral to our understanding of the world and can be extremely enlightening, sometimes even life-changing.

I meditate daily and have for a long time. I always set aside at least half an hour first thing in the morning for this practice. One day I sat to meditate as I usually did and had a very deep and peaceful undirected meditation. As my period of meditation came to an end in my usual fashion, with three simulated bells from the meditation timer app on my phone, my mind returned to the phenomenal world and I became aware that three phrases were present fully formed in my consciousness: *All things are one thing; All places are one place; All times are one time.* Nothing like that had ever happened to me before, but the experience nonetheless seemed surprisingly normal and not at all out of place or disturbing. I accepted these three phrases as a gift, one I didn't understand at the time, but one that invited and promised a great deal of future exploration.

Two days later I found myself again sitting in meditation first thing in the morning. It was, like the meditation two days prior, very quiet and peaceful. Again, as I was returning to everyday wakefulness, a new phrase appeared unbidden in my consciousness: *Time, space and matter are One.* I knew instantly, without thought or analysis, that this new phrase was intimately connected to the first three. Later, after some conscious analysis, I noticed that the *time, space and matter* of the fourth verse referred to the same ideas as *things, places and times* in the first three verses. The fourth verse built on the foundation of the first three. Together, the verses seemed to mean that all that exists, all of Reality was indivisible and inseparable. Just as with the first three verses, receipt of the fourth verse, while unusual and out of the ordinary, didn't seem at all disturbing. In fact, it felt pretty wonderful.

In the six days that followed, I meditated as I always did and nothing unusual occurred. Then, precisely a week later I ended my usual meditation and was surprised to find one more phrase, which turned out to be the last, resting front and center in my consciousness: *One is and One is Not.* It was clear now that these five short verses formed a whole. I had a vague superficial sense of what the first four meant, but the last verse was a complete mystery. Initially, I assumed I had heard these phrases which now formed this completed mantra somewhere and that my brain was replaying them for me as if they had sprung fully formed from within. I don't really know why, but after the fifth verse arrived, my initial urge was to discover and expose the external source of these verses. I searched all over to find the source – a translated ancient text, a modern sage or a dharma talk I had attended. I honestly expected to find the source right away, accompanied by an "aha" moment as I recalled where these words had come from. To my great surprise, however, I found nothing. I eventually concluded that the source of the mantra didn't really matter. The point was the mantra had somehow embedded itself in my brain and now I was stuck with it and the journey of discovery it invited me to take.

I don't claim that any of this was a mystical experience or that the verses were revealed from somewhere beyond. Reflecting back, I see they arrived at a time when I had let go of the need to find a single truth and I think it took letting go of the quest for the answer to assemble itself, for all the little bits and pieces gathered over many sources and over many decades to crystallize into a coherent whole. I still can't say where it all came from. But since the mantra found its way to my consciousness, I have spent many years contemplating and studying it. Eventually, I unpacked the mantra and much of its subtle complexity. The result was a clarity of understanding I had never felt before – except in the recurring dream I mentioned before. That understanding and the truth it is based on is what prompted me to write this book – the story of the search for answers to the riddle of Reality, Self and Soul. Join me now as we travel this path of exploration and discovery and embark together on this great journey.

Chapter 2
The Castle Builder

The heyday of Main Street in Florence, Colorado, like most of the seven thousand or so other Main Streets in small towns strewn across the United States from coast to coast, is in the past. Empty storefronts now stand like gravestones, marking dreams come to an unhappy end. Each vacant façade began with an idea, a hope for something more than what was. There's an empty diner. Over there a shuttered clothing store. A few doors down, a ghostly beauty parlor and next to it, a vacant curio shop. Their names in metal and neon still loiter above the empty doorways, testifying each day to the failed dream that died within.

Over one empty storefront the sign says "Rositas." Rosita was his mother and he named the place in her honor. From the time he was sixteen he worked hard pouring concrete, dirty, tiring work, until he built up the courage and saved the nest egg needed to start the place. He would use mostly her recipes and he had lots of friends that along with the townies and tourists in the summer would make the place a success. He spent months planning every detail from the menu to the furniture. He did a lot of the work on the place himself, after twelve-hour days pouring concrete he worked late into the night and early morning painting the walls, installing a new kitchen, refinishing the oak floors and decorating the place with gayly colored Mexican bric-a-brac. One bright and sunny Friday in April the dream was realized. His whole family came to the grand opening, along with many friends from town. Boundless hope accompanied every shake of a hand, every pat on the back, every laugh and every friendly smile.

Business was slow through May, which he expected, but picked up nicely in June as the tourists packed the place from dusk 'til dawn. By July and August, peak tourist time, he was encouraged to be making a little profit, even after paying himself a small salary, although not nearly as much as he made at the job he had forsaken to follow his dream. Autumn saw business decline some and winter was worse, much worse, but he held on waiting for spring and then the Promised Land of the next summer's tourist hoards. Solely on that hope he borrowed money from family and friends, advances they could ill afford. As the finances worsened, he was forced to delay paying some bills. He charged necessities for the restaurant on his Visa and Mastercard and began telling suppliers the lie that the check was in the mail. The hoped-for summer hoards never materialized for Rosita's because by May he was done. The string just wasn't quite long enough to stretch all the way to the start of summer. He closed the doors and turned off the lights for the last time on May 5th, about a year after the place first opened. His dream was now buried under an incomprehensible mound of debt – to the landlord, to the food purveyors, to his family and friends, to the State and the Feds for employment taxes he hadn't paid and to his employees for their last couple weeks of labor. It was a heart-crushing end to his dream. Behind each vacant storefront up and down Main Street in Florence lurked a similar story – boundless and unbridled hope had all come to the same end.

As I turned left from Main Street at the light, just like I'd done at least a hundred times before, I looked ahead as the two-lane Colorado Highway 67 rose gently in front of us.

Jack, my companion on this drive, was more interested in the Carl's Jr. on the corner as his head panned comically to the left, his gaze fixed on the fast food place. His diet tended toward the terrible and I knew he was thinking about asking me to detour through the drive-thru so he could get a bag of tater tots, for which he had an uncommon fondness. I pretended not to notice his transparent interest and for once he didn't protest as we drove on. The Jeep slowly accelerated as we moved through what little remained of the edge of town.

In a few hundred feet we passed the Perlite factory, a weathered concrete building, concrete does weather over time, with a sixty-foot high concrete silo or smokestack – I could never tell which – at least thirty feet in diameter at its base and tapering as it trended skyward. The factory had been there since the depression. It was a family business, still independent of acquisitive conglomerates. They bought alexite ore from a nearby mine and trucked it to the plant. The ore contained a volcanic glass that softened when heated to about 900 degrees. Once it got hot, the water trapped inside the mineral vaporized, causing the stuff to expand about fifteen times its original volume. The process was pretty simple and the raw material – the perlite-bearing rock – was cheap. So the final product, the expanded perlite, was a very cost-effective additive for things like light-weight plaster or insulation or for improving the condition of compacted soil.

The Jeep lurched side to side a bit as we crossed the now little-used railroad tracks and crested the small rise. A Super 8 Motel, painted pink like the dirt it rested on, with a big American flag at the top of a fifty-foot high pole, sat just at the outskirts of town. There were hardly ever any cars parked there and the only business they had were friends, relatives and lawyers visiting the men who had taken up residence in the adjacent Federal prison complex. Called FCC Florence, the sprawling complex in the middle of mostly nowhere includes the minimum-security *Federal Prison Camp* ("Club Fed"), the medium security *Federal Correctional Institution Florence*, the high-security *US Penitentiary, Florence* and the super high-security *US Penitentiary, Florence ADX* ("SuperMax").

"Know what's up there," I say to Jack, pointing to the left up the hill.

"Looks like a prison," I know he's thinking.

"Not just a prison, its Supermax, where they lock up the worst of the worst. I saw a special on TV about it. It's mostly terrorists and mafia. They're in solitary twenty-three hours a day. Concrete beds and tables. Polished aluminum mirrors attached to the wall. That kind of stuff. Moussaoui is there, Yousef too. From 9/11. Ted Kaczynski, the Unabomber, and Timothy McVeigh was there before he was executed. Kinda reminds me of the prison in that movie with Nicholas Cage. I can't remember the name. He and his brother were both in this prison."

"I'll think of it in a minute. John Travolta was in it too. Cage was a bad guy. Travolta was an FBI agent. He had a face transplant – Face Off. That's it. Face Off. Remember. Travolta pretended he was Cage in this max security prison."

"Anyway," I said, "the prison in Face Off was like what SuperMax must be. Oh, and they had to wear magnetic boots that the guards could magnetically lock down to the steel floor."

I let it go because Jack didn't seem particularly intrigued or inclined to much conversation today. From the prisons the highway is perfectly straight for about fifteen miles as it rises slowly out of the Arkansas Valley. But it's hilly, so it's mostly double yellow lines until you get to Wetmore, which marks the beginning of the ascent into the Wet Mountains. The Wet Mountains begin on the north end near Canon City and unfurl south toward New Mexico. Like Florence, prisons, something like nine of them, are Canon City's number one industry and folks are proud of it, proud enough to have erected a big sign in town advertising: "Corrections Capital of the World." The oldest prison was built five years before Colorado was admitted to the union as the thirty-eighth state in 1876. Although not quite true, it seems like there are probably more inmates locked in the prisons than citizens going about their business on the outside. About forty-five miles south of Canon City lies barely-there Gardner, Colorado, home to 574 souls at last count and no one there gives much thought to the obscure fact that Gardner is the southern terminus of the Wet Mountains that Jack and I were driving into.

The Sangre de Cristo mountains, Spanish for Blood of Christ, are referred to locally as the Sangres. They lie just a dozen miles west and mostly parallel to the Wet Mountains. Despite their proximity, the two ranges are about as different as two sets of peaks could be, a little like comparing the Appalachians to the Tetons. The Wet Mountains, echoes now of what they once were, have eroded over the ages into low rolling mounds mostly covered in short western grasses, with a soft green appearance for three seasons and scattered forests of lodgepole and pinon pine mixed with small stands of aspen. The Sangres are majestic peaks, newly uplifted – at least in geologic time – extending seventy-five miles from Poncha Springs on the north to just east of Alamosa on the south. The Sangres include ten peaks that top out over fourteen thousand feet, with some of the most challenging climbing in the Rocky Mountains. Every year a handful of climbers fall to their death from Crestone Needle, a brutal class 5 climb with dangerous exposures for most of the ascent. It's the kind of climb where any little slip will send you tumbling over a sheer drop of a few thousand feet to a certain, quick and ugly death. Methodist Mountain is regarded as the northernmost promontory of the Sangres. At a mere 11,707 feet, its summit is heavily forested and there's a dirt road cut all the way to the top that makes for easy hiking. The views are pleasant enough from the summit, which is probably why you'll be greeted by two communications towers if you should venture there. At 14,351 feet the towering Blanca Peak anchors the southern end of the Sangres. It's a whole different experience. Rugged and isolated, you leave the trees behind more than two thousand feet below the summit. It's a major scramble near the top, with lots of loose rock. Although not a technical climb, it takes your breath away, both literally and figuratively, once you reach the top.

From the summit of Blanca you can see enormous piles of sand spread out below you. The Great Sand Dunes, cresting seven hundred feet high above the valley floor, are the tallest dunes in North America. When you stand at their base in the spring, in the frigid three-inch deep waters of Medano Creek, the sand extends as far as the eye can see. The dunes owe their existence, at least in part, to the peaks of the Sangres. To the west of the Sangre de Cristo range, beyond the Great Sand Dunes, is the San Luis Valley, a flat high desert plain about one hundred and twenty-five miles long from north to south and seventy-five miles wide from east to west. Sparsely populated, with more than eight thousand square miles of mostly treeless ground at an elevation of about 7,500 feet, you could fit sprawling Los Angeles County in the San Luis Valley almost two times over. The winds have blown relentlessly from west to east across the valley for the last half a million years. Had you visited the Valley long ago, you would have been greeted by a vast blue lake lapping the mountain ranges ringing the valley, including the Sangres on the eastern edge. But many millennia ago the ancient lake drained south into what we today call New Mexico, leaving the valley floor filled with fine sand. As the centuries passed, the ceaseless winds lofted the minuscule grains of sand from the valley into the air, carrying them eastward toward the Sangres. When the winds met the high peaks, they were buoyed upward about a mile and the grains of sand, too heavy to rise with the winds, came gently to rest at the western base of the Sangre Range. Over eons, the constant deposition of sand produced the playground we today call the Great Sand Dunes.

As it passes Little Rock on its way to join the Mississippi, the Arkansas River is a formidable waterway, often a half-mile wide. But nearly fifteen hundred miles upstream at its headwaters near the top of the Wet Mountains, the Arkansas is little more than a creek. You can wade across it during much of the year, particularly before the mountain snows begin to melt in the spring and early summer. From the Arkansas River Valley, Highway 67 heads due south out of Florence, where the empty storefronts stand, without gaining much altitude and in a dozen or so miles you arrive in Wetmore. A low and small one-story brick structure, the Wetmore Baptist Church, sits across the road as you pause before rolling through the stop sign and turning right onto Highway 96. Here begins a mostly mild ascent into the Wet Mountains, traversing narrow valleys with names like Bohn Gulch, and paralleling modest waters like Hardscrabble Creek. The road then twists and turns a bit, eventually rising to its zenith before turning due west.

Nestled deep in the Wet Mountains, just past the zenith of Highway 96, is Makinzie Junction. There's no store at this waypoint, only a big red barn marking the spot where you must choose to turn to the right or the left. The turn to the left is far less traveled. It heads south along a steeply descending winding road on the little two-lane Greenhorn Highway. If you follow the Greenhorn Highway along Bishop Creek for twelve miles south of the big red barn at Makinzie Junction, you'll be greeted by a most improbable sight, the kind of scene that makes you wonder whether you're truly awake or trapped in a dream.

As we pulled to a stop beside the road, I said to Jack "OK. Check this out. It's pretty amazing." We got out of the Jeep and both stretched our legs for a minute before coming together on the passenger side. About a hundred feet off the highway sat a stone and iron castle situated on a slight rise, surrounded by mature lodgepole pines and aspens, soaring high up into the cloudless deep blue Rocky Mountain sky. Part Gothic nightmare, part fairy tale dream, Bishop Castle is anchored to the ground by a base of buttressed stone walls three feet thick. Constructed of local reddish-hued rocks of varying shapes and sizes, from fist-sized pieces to hunks as big as a man's torso that must weigh a ton, all held together by mortar hand mixed on site. The main structure is three irregular stories tall, with the top floor coming to a high triangular peak. The front façade, perhaps sixty feet at its highest, is punctuated by three glass-enclosed openings, rounded at the top and filled with colorful panels of stained glass.

Three towering spires of the same mortar and unmatched red stones as the main castle sprout out of seemingly random locations from the main structure, rising at their apex a height of a hundred fifty feet from the ground. Two are round. Of that pair, one seems mostly completed and is topped with a metal dome reminiscent of something you'd see at the Kremlin in Moscow or on a mosque in the Middle East. The other half of the pair is still under construction and sports a giant iron-work ball that will presumably one day be clad in metal like its mate. The third spire, resembling a bell tower, rises the highest by far and has a roughly square shape punctuated on all four sides by tall and narrow pairs of penetrations. At the top of the bell tower are four miniature minarets clad in metal, one at each of the four corners. About forty feet below, another minaret grows from the corner of the bell tower like some enormous mussel clinging for dear life to a rock face on the barren Maine shore.

The three castle towers are connected by hand-wrought iron walkways and railings that dip and loop from peak to peak like a rollercoaster perched precariously high in the sky. The *piece de resistance*, a dragon head clad in hundreds of shiny polished stainless steel scales, emerges from a long neck attached to the apex of the castle's peaked stone and glass façade, just beneath the metal roof. Maybe twenty feet long, with mouth agape, scores of jagged metal teeth and glowing eyes, the dragon can be seen spitting fire to the delight of those watching the spectacle from ground level far below. If you're lucky you might even catch a glimpse of the Castle Builder, as he likes to call himself, standing astride the dragon's head, six stories into the air, holding ropes like equestrian reins anchored to the beast's jaw, with flames shooting from the dragon's gaping maw, echoing images of Captain Ahab riding Moby Dick into the depths of the sea.

No one lives in the castle and no one ever has. It's a work in progress and everything, from the evolving conception of the castle to hand-digging the foundations down to bedrock, to the masonry, the hand-hewn wooden floorboards and ceiling planks, the endless ironwork and the glass glazing, has been produced by one man – Jim Bishop. Bishop is batshit crazy – a bona fide wacko. He rails against the government and asserts his personal sovereignty, whatever that means. Born near the end of World War II, for more than fifty years he's made building the castle his life's work. He's gathered stones from the two and a half acres the castle sits on and from nearby public lands. He's felled trees. He's fought the County, the IRS, the Forest Service and pretty much every other government agency that had the audacity to try to meddle in his castle building enterprise. One of a number of weathered plywood hand-lettered signs on the property lends texture to the experience of visiting the castle. The sign reads:

> THE LOCAL GOVT. DON'T WANT YOU PEOPLE TO ENJOY THIS (FREE) ATTRACTION. FOR MANY YEARS THEY TRIED BUT FAILED TO OPPRESS AND CONTROL MY GOD GIVEN TALENT TO HAND BUILD THIS GREAT MONUMENT TO HARD WORKING POOR PEOOPLE. ALWAYS OPEN FREE! THEY COULD NOT CONTROL WITH ZONING AND OTHER PETTY RULES SO IN AUG. 02 THEY TRIED TO BANKRUPT AND RUIN AND SLANDER THE BISHIP FAMILY NAME BY PURSUING 35 CRIMINAL COUNTS OF FALSE ALLEGATIONS. MY GOD GIVEN UNALLIENABLE RIGHTS SET FORTH IN THE CONSTITUTION HAVE BEEN VIOLATED ARTICLE 8 – NO GUILT TILL PROVEN SO NO EXCESSIVE BAIL. NO CRUEL PUNISHMENT A $50000.00 CASH ONLY RANSOM WAS PLACED ON MY HEAD. I AM

NO FLIGHT RISK. NO COURT CONVICTIONS. I AM NOT A CRIMINAL! AT TRIAL A DOCTOR A FORENSIC PRO TESTIFIED THAT NO GUN SHOTS IN THE CASTLE AND THE PROSECUTER INCOMPETENT. THE JURY RULED — JIM BISHOP <u>NOT GUILTY</u> ON ALL CHARGES. YET WHEN SENTENCEING DAN BISHHIP ON 1 SIMPLE MISDEAMENOR THE JUDGE RULED THAT THE SHERIFF PICK ONE OF JIM'S GUNS — THAT IS COURT ORDERED THEFT! **HELP**

Another sign warns:

ATTENTION READ ALL SIGNS ALL ADULTS MUST SIGN OUR GUEST BOOK. IT IS A RELEASE OF LIABILITY ON THE BISHOP CASTLE. CHILDREN MUST BE WITH AN ADULT — NO CLIMBING ON ANYTHING STAY OFF OF SAND PILE — CONSTRUCTION AREA — PUT TRASH IN BARRELS — KEEP ALL CHILDREN & PETS UNDER CONTROL — NO DRUNKS. **YOU ARE WELCOME** IF YOU AGREE WITH EVERYTHING **IF NOT NO TRESPASSING**! IN MY OPINION, UNREASONABLE & UNFAIR LAWS FORCE ME TO WRITE THIS SIGN BY MY HARD EARNED POWER *Jim Bishop* (CASTLE BUILDER) JIM BISHOP IS CREATING — BY THE HELP OF **GOD** WITH HIS MIND AND BODY THIS MONUMENTAL ART FORM. FOR THE GOOD OF ALL — OPEN ALWAYS ON A TRUE DONATION BASIS

When you visit Bishop Castle, particularly late in the day as the sun descends toward the peaks of the Sangres to the west and the harsh light of mid-day softens into hues of yellow and orange, you can often hear Jim ranting about the government, spouting nonsense about how the IRS is illegal and prohibited from collecting taxes because of some unidentified provision of the Constitution or some treaty with King George. Or maybe he'll be railing against one religious group or another or the rich or powerful. After a nervous breakdown in 2014, he found himself resident in a psychiatric hospital for ten days. He's been prescribed pills to calm the demons. It seems like sometimes he takes the meds. Other times not. He had cancer a while ago and was told he wouldn't survive long. Defying the odds, he continues the work of the Castle Builder. Now he's been diagnosed with Parkinson's Disease. Still he continues to work. Thirty years ago, he was clearing fifty-foot high lodgepole pines on the property to make a place for visitors to park. Severed at its base, one of the tall straight trees came crashing down squarely on Jim's four-year-old son. Little Roy died from his injuries that day. Maybe that made Jim Bishop crazy. Maybe it made his crazy worse. Maybe he would have been as crazy as he is now without the tragedy.

Jim Bishop wasn't anywhere in sight as Jack and I stood on the side of the road and absorbed the scene in front of us. "Pretty amazing, don't you think." Jack was still looking around and didn't respond. "Come on, let's go walk through it." We started forward toward the Castle, past the spot where the lodgepole had killed poor Roy, which was now bare and dusty ground. We crossed over the moat – or at least the beginnings of an eventual moat – and walked a hundred or so feet to what passed for the first floor. The front façade is about forty feet wide and punctuated by two asymmetrical stone arches. The one on the right is about fifteen feet wide at its base and ten feet high and the one on the left is smaller, perhaps ten feet wide. There aren't any doors or windows. The whole space is open, more like a partially enclosed patio with a concrete floor than a room. On each of the two sides of the space is another large rock arch.

It's a big step up from the bare dirt to the first of about a dozen concrete stairs that deliver you to the first floor. Walking through that space, we came to a narrow, steep spiral stairway made of rock and concrete. As we picked our way up the confining stairway we came to the second floor, a space of about twenty by forty feet with a hand-hewn wooden floor. It has five sets of three tall, narrow windows, maybe five feet by one foot each. One set adorns each short side wall and three sets are on the long front facade. The ceiling is low on the second level, not more than eight feet and the space feels dark and crushingly heavy, even in the middle of a sunny day, like the rock and concrete walls were pressing down on your shoulders.

From the second floor, an ornamental wrought iron stairway curves and rises toward the light. The treads of the stairway are open diamond mesh and the straight balusters joining the iron handrail to the stairs are connected by intricate curly-ques. The lightness and transparency of the stairway is such a stark contrast to the heavy rock structure, that it's a little disorienting − almost as though it was designed to make you feel untrusting that it would really support your weight. And I could see in his tentative step that Jack clearly felt that uneasiness. "Come on," I said, "I'll go first. I'm sure it's safe," I lied. "Hundreds of people have walked on this before." First, I rested one foot on the bottom stair, testing the sturdiness of the construction, then brought my full weight to bear. Despite its wispiness, there wasn't any hint the stairway would buckle or sway and so I continued to ascend into the light above. About half-way up I looked back over my shoulder to see Jack still holding tight. "It's fine. Come on. Let's keep going," I said encouragingly. "I'm coming," I thought I heard him say, "just looking around." After a brief pause, Jack followed, tentatively making his way up each riser to the next tread, none of which – I was certain – came anywhere close to complying with even the most lenient of building codes.

Eventually, we both emerged onto the third floor. The steeply vaulted ceiling soared to a height of at least thirty feet above the floor. At the peak was a single skylight from the front of the room to back, forty feet long, extending down the roof about six feet on both sides. It was as if the entire cathedral ceiling was open to the heavens. Three tall gothic openings adorned the front of the room. Into each opening glass panels were set, some composed of individual stained-glass panes. Two glass-fronted gables, one on each side wall, framed the front façade. The space was bathed in light. Luminescence suffused every inch of the room, every little nook and cranny. It was a church. A temple. A sanctuary.

A crazy wrought iron balcony-like walkway wraps completely around the third floor. In places it's four feet wide and in other places as much as eight. It snakes around the uneven castle walls and, like the interior stairway, its bottom is covered in diamond mesh. The construction makes it seem like it's barely there. Contributing to the feeling of distrust is the reality that it's less than clear what force holds the whole contraption up and it definitely felt rickety as we made our way gingerly around the perimeter. From the walkway suspended three stories up you can make your way to the bell tower, the square spire rising a good fifty feet more above the ground. The bell tower has a steep and narrow concrete stairway leading all the way to the top. Access to an exceedingly rickety wrought iron catwalk that leads to the two lower round spires is also possible. "Game to go further," I asked as we clung to the side of the castle on the wraparound walkway. Jack gave me the "I think I'm good," look, which meant he'd had enough. I got it. The place is really overwhelming and hard to really wrap your head around. This was maybe my fourth time here and I was just starting to understand it.

When you first see Bishop Castle, the overwhelming impression it conveys is childishness, like what a four-year-old would create from clay and twigs, only a thousand times larger. It seems an imperfectly rendered emanation of a dream. That initial impression is reinforced over and over again as you explore the labyrinthine innards of the castle, steep winding walkways from one floor to the next, the stairs snaking up the three towers and the external ironworks hanging off the structure and looping between the tower tops a hundred feet in the air. There are no straight lines. There are no stable arcs. Nothing is level. Nothing is even. It is the antithesis of what we would expect a proper building to look like. And that of course is the point. It wasn't planned in advance but has grown as an expression of the whims of the Castle Builder. It has evolved organically with the twists and turns of his brain. It is very literally an enormous manifestation of this man's inner life, rendered in rock, mortar and iron. Since the brain is twisted, the manifestation is too. It's part dream, part penance, part defiance and part insane expression. Above all else, it is most assuredly a clear and accurate image of what lies within the Castle Builder's skull – it is a perfect picture of the inner world he experiences.

Each one of us is like Jim Bishop. We each create our own story about the world, our unique Castle. The Castle we create is based on our perceptions of the world around us and because we all have more or less the same sensory apparatus, we should each share similar perceptions and our individual stories of the world should all be about the same. And in some ways, they are. We all see the sunrise in the morning and set at dusk. We see ourselves existing in a world alongside other beings of our kind. We each recognize the need for food and water so we can continue to exist and thrive. And we all agree that we are born little and helpless and eventually grow to adulthood. We all exist in places around the world, surrounded by physical objects that are separate and distinct and we experience time which points in but one direction.

But there are significant and important variations in the details – the nuances – of our individual stories of the world. The story of the world that we see displayed in Jim Bishop's Castle is very different from mine and I'm sure that mine is very different from yours. Some of us see the world as a happy and welcoming place. For others the world is dark and threatening. There may be as many different stories of the world as there are people inhabiting it. But at least we can take comfort in knowing that the aspects of the story upon which we agree, that we see as the same, represent objective Reality, objective truth. Or can we?

Chapter 3

Is Reality Real?

Eleven hundred miles west of Bishop Castle, the campus of the University of California Irvine is the physical manifestation of the collective mind of its designers. Originally part of the Irvine Ranch, a large agricultural area in Orange County, the campus was founded in the mid-1960s with a donation of 1,000 acres. William Pereira was the "Master Planner." Pereira conceived and designed the physical layout of the campus and most of its extensive landscaping, including tens of thousands of trees perfectly adapted to the Mediterranean climate of the area. At the center of the campus is Aldrich Park which is circumscribed by a pedestrian road, the Ring Mall, which is precisely one mile around. Scores of campus buildings, constructed during the last half century, line the Ring Mall. The buildings are famously connected by subterranean tunnels which have spawned much fanciful speculation by undergraduates about their use and purpose. In truth, they're mostly utilitarian, providing a path for electrical lines and coolant. The campus design is beautifully ordered and sensible. The space is comfortable and, when you see it, is easily comprehended by the brain.

The Department of Cognitive Sciences, part of the School of Social Sciences, is among the many academic departments at UCI. One of the best-known Professors in the department is Donald Hoffman. Hoffman is a theoretician and perceptual scientist. It is a pillar of faith among the world's perceptual scientists that our perceptions, what we see, hear, smell, feel and touch, are accurate re-creations of the world as it exists – objective reality. These scientists reason that evolutionary theory leads ineluctably to that conclusion because our ancestors were naturally selected for accurate perceptions or, more correctly, those with inaccurate perceptions were deselected and perished. Our ancestors, then, according to the theory, were the ones who were best at perceiving dangerous conditions in the world or noticing favorable ones and they acted on those good perceptions. Thus, the best perceivers were the fittest in evolutionary terms and their genes were the ones that were passed on to you and to me. That means, according to the theory, that we can be confident that the way we perceive the world gives us an accurate picture of the world as it really exists. In other words, Reality as we perceive it is objectively true.

The maverick Professor Hoffman disagrees. He espouses the seemingly radical hypothesis that the world we perceive, that which we think we see, hear, smell, feel and touch, is nothing like Reality. His research rests on worlds he creates in the computers in his lab. These worlds are mathematical constructs called interface games that he can model based on rules which he can vary from game to game. In the simplest version, there are two agents and three territories in the world. Each territory has food and water that have a value range from 0 to 100. The first agent picks one territory and acquires its food and water values and the second agent then picks between the two remaining territories and acquires the food and water values from that territory. Hoffman gives the two agents in his mathematical world different perceptual strategies. One perceives the exact value of the food and water in the territories and the other has a simpler perceptual strategy – it perceives only whether the food or water in a territory is greater or less than a particular value – say 50. The simple perceiver sees a territory that has water and food of more than 50 as green and that which has less than 50 as red. So all the simple perceiving agent needs to know to make a choice between the territories is whether they are red or green. The agent that sees the exact value of food and water within a territory has a more complicated cognitive task. To make a decision about which territory to choose, it sees – in effect – just shades of grey. One territory may have a value of 35 and another a value of 70. The agent needs to compare those values and determine which is greater and then choose a territory based on that conclusion.

Performing the perceptual activity isn't free. It "costs" energy to engage in the perception and the costs of the simple perceptual strategy are less than the more complicated, but fully truthful one. In Hoffman's models, the energy cost of perceiving gets deducted from the value of the food and water to get to a net value of food and water that the agent's perception obtains. In addition, the perceptual activity doesn't occur instantaneously. Instead, it takes time to process the perceptual information. The simpler perceptual strategy takes less time than the more complex "true" one and the result is the simpler perceiving agent gets to pick first. The end result is the agent with the simpler perception – the one that isn't "true" – ends up with more food and water than the agent that perceives truth.

Put into evolutionary terms this means the simple perceptual strategy is fitter than the more complex, but truer strategy. When you scale up from the simple model with just two agents and add thousands or millions of agents, the result is the same. The inescapable conclusion, at least according to Hoffman's work, is that the agent with the simple perceptual strategy – the one that sees only red or green – always drives the truth-perceiving agent to extinction. The simple perceptual strategy is, in Darwinian terms, much fitter than the complex one. The result is the same regardless of how you change or add variables to the models, like increasing the number of territories or the number of resources in each territory or adding dangers in addition to resources or randomly distributing the resources and dangers in the territories, to name just a few of the many possible options. This is pretty stunning. Think about it for a moment. What it means is that humans in the distant past who perceived the world in the most accurate way never survived and never became our ancestors. Instead, they were deselected by evolution.

Hoffman's work shows that the fittest actors in these mathematical worlds, those that pass their characteristics to the next generation – the survivors – are those that do not see Reality as it is, but instead see the world in a way that gives them the best chance of surviving to procreate and pass their genes on to the next generation. Hoffman often uses this example to explain the idea underlying his theory. Imagine your computer screen. In the lower right corner of the screen is a blue square which represents a word processing file. If you click on the blue square, the icon, the file will open and you can read it or change it and then save it again. However, the word processing file is not literally a blue square in the lower right corner of your computer and in fact, you don't need to know how the computer creates the word processing file or how it stores it in the machine. All you need to know is if you click on the blue square, the file will open. The blue square on the computer screen is a "hack," a shortcut that allows you to interact with the word processing file. Hoffman proposes that our perception of the world works in an analogous way. When we see an apple growing on a tree, all that matters is that the perceptual hack leads us to eat the apple, providing sustenance for our body. The reality of the apple, what it "really" looks, smells, tastes and feels like or whether it even has any of those perceptual qualities, is irrelevant. On the other side of the spectrum, when we see and smell a rotting carcass on the ground, our perceptual experience warns us against trying to ingest the object. Whether the object actually has the qualities we think we perceive doesn't matter. The perceptual hack has waived us off so we can live to eat another day and find a mate who does the same.

While this hypothesis seems radical, in a broad sense it isn't completely new. Three hundred ninety-five years ago, in the Autumn of 1623, an essay was published in Rome titled *Il Saggiatore,* in English, *The Assayer.* It's author, well known at the time, published the work to propose what would eventually come to be called the scientific method, the same process Dr. MacDougall misused to weigh the Soul. The scientific method was the way to understand the world around us, the author argued, as opposed to spinning yarns based on dogmatic beliefs. Within the essay, the author – a nearly sixty-year-old fellow named Galileo Galilei - observed:

> It now remains for me to tell Your Excellency, as I promised, some thoughts of mine about the proposition motion is the cause of heat,' and to show in what sense this may be true. But first I must consider what it is that we call heat, as I suspect that people in general have a concept of this which is very remote from the truth. For they believe that heat is a real phenomenon or property, or quality, which actually resides in the material by which we

feel ourselves warmed. Now I say that whenever I conceive any material or corporeal substance, I immediately feel the need to think of it as bounded, and as having this or that shape; as being large or small in relation to other things, and in some specific place at any given time; as being in motion or at rest; as touching or not touching some other body; and as being one in number, or few, or many. From these conditions I cannot separate such a substance by any stretch of my imagination. But that it must be white or red, bitter or sweet, noisy or silent, and of sweet or foul odor, my mind does not feel compelled to bring in as necessary accompaniments. Without the senses as our guides, reason or imagination unaided would probably never arrive at qualities like these. Hence I think that tastes, odors, colors, and so on are no more than mere names so far as the object in which we place them is concerned, and that they reside only in the consciousness. Hence if the living creature were removed, all these qualities would be wiped away and annihilated. But since we have imposed upon them special names, distinct from those of the other and real qualities mentioned previously, we wish to believe that they really exist as actually different from those.

Galileo's ruminations, or perhaps they seemed more like ravings by the standards of his day, ran completely counter to the prevailing views in which time had embedded him. What he's saying is that an object has two sets of properties. Some, like shape, size and location, are inherent in the object and others, like color, taste and smell, are qualities that exist only in the inner experience of the person who observes the object. The latter qualities are not inherent in the object itself. An often-used example is a lemon. The lemon has a particular shape, size and location and those characteristics, Galileo argued, are part of what it is to be a lemon. However, the color yellow, the bitterness of the lemon and the scent of the fruit require an observer to exist. There is no yellowness, bitter taste or scent without the one who observes those qualities. Professor Hoffman's hypothesis, that the qualities of objects we think we perceive are not the same as objective Reality, is not dissimilar from the role played by Galileo's secondary qualities, those that require an observer.

Galileo was willing to stand up for his beliefs, even when they were deemed heretical. When he perfected the telescope, some years before publication of *The Assayer,* he used the instrument to make observations about the objects in the solar system. Those observations convinced him to embrace the view that the earth and all the other planets revolved around the sun. He thus rejected the Aristotelian model that the earth was the center of the universe and instead adopted the Copernican heliocentric view. That scientific conclusion brought Galileo into dangerous conflict with Catholic Church doctrine, which had embraced the conveniently egocentric and anthropocentric view that the earth was the center of the solar system. After a prior run-in with the Inquisition in 1615, Galileo was eventually hauled before the Inquisition a second time for his heretical views and imprisoned in

1633, a confinement from which he never escaped, at least not until he died nine years later.

But even Galileo's views, or at least the approach to Reality which they propose, were hardly novel. Two millennia before, the ancient Greek philosophers had trod the same ground, exploring the nature and meaning of Reality – what the world was made of and the ultimate substance of Reality. The Greek views of Reality ranged all over the place, some of which arguably pointed towards the theories that Galileo and even Hoffman later came to espouse.

Professor Hoffman, Galileo, the Greeks and their scores of predecessors and successors in the West hardly had a lock on the examination of Reality. Eastern thought, mostly arising across the length and breadth of India, stretches back at least four thousand years to the Hindus, the Buddhists, the Jainists and others. We'll examine this in more detail in Chapter 11. But for now, suffice it to say that the Indian and proto-Indian traditions ventured deeply into an examination of the nature of Reality and eventually developed systemized ways of unpacking Reality with the goal of finding enlightenment – freedom from ignorance. These ways of envisioning the world predated the Greeks by nearly two thousand years.

The conundrum of Reality is even more fraught than what we've seen so far. Even once we recognize that our senses may deceive us, giving us a false view of the way Reality really is, there's another whole layer of problems. These deeper problems are the result of how our brains work. Researchers have shown in countless studies in numerous different fields, from psychology to neuroscience to magic, that in lots of situations and circumstances our brains incorrectly process sensory input and lead us to false conclusions. So, we can't even be sure that what we think we are seeing, the subjective experience we seem to be having, is accurate.

One category of processing errors are visual illusions, things we think we see that just aren't so. The following are a few common examples to illustrate the point. The first one is called the Muller-Lyer illusion. To most people, the bottom line seems longer than the top one. Actually, both lines are exactly the same length. Our brains process the visual input incorrectly, leading us to falsely conclude that the lower line is longer.

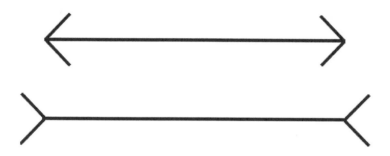

An even more striking illustration of visual misperception, at least to my eye (or brain), is shown in the next picture. This is called the Café Wall illusion. To nearly everyone the horizontal lines appear not to be parallel to one another. Actually, they are. You can tell by measuring the vertical dimension of the rows. It's the same on the right and left of each row. But of course it doesn't look that way to us.

And here's one more, just for fun. This is called the Penrose Stairs illusion. Start at any spot and imagine ascending the stairs. You can keep going perpetually, always walking up. How is that possible? It isn't. Our brains don't process the visual data correctly.

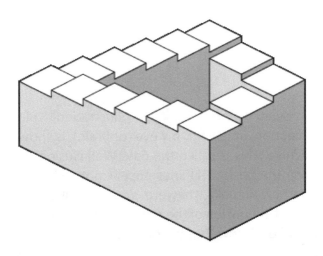

In addition to the perceptual processing errors our brains make, as illustrated by the last three images, we also make thinking errors that are induced by a cluster of processes psychologists call cognitive biases. With these kinds of errors, it isn't the brain's misinterpretation of sensory data that causes us to arrive at an incorrect conclusion. Instead, the incorrect conclusion comes from thinking that isn't rational. A classic example is said to have had its genesis at the Casino de Monte-Carlo. The Belle Epoque-style Casino, coincidentally the location of scenes from the James Bond films, *Never Say Never Again, GoldenEye and Casino Royale*, was the site of a most unusual event. On Monday, August 18, 1913, at a particular roulette wheel in the large gambling hall, the little white ball (probably carved from ivory at that time) settled into a black pocket – not such an unusual circumstance since the chance of it doing so was one in two. On the next throw, a black pocket was again the resting place of the ball. The same result obtained for the next throw, which was somewhat unusual, but certainly not unknown.

Patrons of the casino, though, began to take note and started to crowd around the wheel. They of course placed their bets on red, reasoning that the odds of the ball falling into black again were low and that the streak of black had to end. Amazingly, with continuing successive drops of the ball, the wheel came to a stop with the ball again on black. The more this unlikely result continued, the more patrons gathered around the roulette table and laid increasingly larger bets on red. The total run of black falls by the ball finally ended at twenty-six and the Casino is said to have made millions that day from this most unlikely streak. Although the probability of a streak like this is something on the order of 1 in 136 million, the mistake the betting patrons made was in misjudging the odds for each throw, which remained at one out of two each time, regardless of what color had been selected on the last throw or the prior 26. In other words, whether the prior throw produced red or black had no effect on the likelihood that red or black would be the result on the next throw. This error in rational thinking is commonly called the Gambler's Fallacy and we see it play out in our lives all the time. If we've had a string of mishaps in our life, we think good things must be on the horizon. If a couple has given birth to three boys in a row, the next child is sure to be a girl. If our baseball team has lost the last ten games in a row, they're bound to win the next one. If the stock market has lost ground the last five trading sessions, it will certainly regain its losses the next trading day.

Confirmation bias is another example of how our brains can function in a way that is less than fully rational. Proven over and over again in numerous research studies, it's clear that we all tend to discount or ignore information that runs contrary to the beliefs we already hold and credit information that supports our views. Here's a good example from *Research in Psychology: Methods and Design*, by C. James Goodwin.

> Persons believing in extrasensory perception (ESP) will keep close track of instances when they were 'thinking about Mom, and then the phone rang and it was her!' Yet they ignore the far more numerous times when (a) they were thinking about Mom and she didn't call and (b) they weren't thinking about Mom and she did call. They also fail to recognize that if they talk to Mom about

every two weeks, their frequency of "thinking about Mom" will increase near the end of the two-week-interval, thereby increasing the frequency of a 'hit.'

Confirmation bias works not only with the interpretation of information you receive. It also applies to the type of information you seek out and it affects what information you remember. I heard the following example a little while ago. You're ready to attend your first public yoga class, but you're feeling a little nervous about what others may think of you. As you walk into class, it seems like everyone else knows exactly where to go and what to do. Everyone looks more fit than you are and you're wondering whether this was the right choice to make. As the class begins, you see others doing the poses perfectly, while you feel wobbly and unsteady. You're having trouble keeping up, while everyone else seems to be breezing through. Other students seem to be smirking at you. So what's going on here? Your insecurity about the situation led to misinterpreting information about what was happening in the yoga class. Objectively, some of the other students were more advanced than you were, but others were at your same level and were also struggling. But you registered only the information that confirmed your initial bias – that you were in over your head and going to have a hard time.

There are many of these types of cognitive biases and they bring us to the same place – our brains often think in a way that's not consistent with the way the world really is. In other words, we seem predisposed to draw incorrect conclusions from the sensory data that reaches our brain.

Because the Reality we each experience arises from sensory data in the form of perceptions and from the processing of that data by our brain, we are compelled at a minimum to entertain some doubt about the truth of our Castle — our individual story of the world, the nature of Reality. In a strange way, that conclusion is somewhat comforting because it implies the existence of an objective Reality. While we may be drifting off the shore in a metaphorical boat, at least there is a shore we might one day make our way back to.

Unfortunately, the whole notion of objective Reality is troublesome. We each experience a Reality that is molded and filtered by our perceptual senses and shaped by our cognitive apparatus. For an objective Reality to exist, there would have to be something, a consciousness of some sort, that would perceive it, something we could all agree was perceiving Reality in an unfiltered, unadulterated, unbiased way. Yet, by conjuring such a consciousness into existence, a consciousness capable of perceiving the "real" and "true" Reality, we necessarily endow such a consciousness with its own perceptual and cognitive machinery and the existence of that machinery negates the objective perceiver we had hoped to create. In other words, the very notion of perception necessarily carries with it the particular biases of the perceiver and because of that, all perception of Reality must be subjective. Hence, the notion of an objective Reality is an empty concept. It is meaningless. We need to accept that Reality is inherently, of its nature, subjective. We need to abandon permanently the quest for an objective Reality and recognize that the gentle comfort the idea of a Reality that is "real" provides is not to be.

When you peruse the history of our species, you see a continuous chain of inquiry into the nature of Reality and our role in that Reality, stretching backward in time, all the way from the present day to the very dawn of civilization.

We might even characterize this, not unfairly, as a human preoccupation or compulsion. This exploration of Reality leads us first to wrongly conclude that we perceive Reality as it is. We eventually realize that we only perceive Reality as it *seems*, that our experience of Reality is necessarily subjective. We also learn that both our perceptions and our arrangement of those perceptions into a subjective Reality in our brain is subject to lots of errors, introducing even more uncertainty into the conclusion about what Reality is. Finally, through the work of scientists like Don Hoffman and many others, as well as the deep thoughts of scores of philosophers, we come to recognize that our imperfect experience of a subjective Reality may be all there is, that the world we think we know, the world we think we experience with our eyes and ears and nose and mouth and skin, the world we accept as true and that we rely on as the bedrock of our Reality – is probably not as it seems and that a Reality that is objectively true doesn't exist at all.

Can we at least take comfort in our imperfect subjective experiences, recognizing them as the admittedly shaky foundation for our actions in the world? I'm afraid not. We turn now to the exploration of another nettlesome problem, the troubling propensity of our species to arrive at conclusions and hold onto them tenaciously, even when they are utterly inconsistent with the experiences we think we've had and which should be forming the basis of our conclusions about the world. You'll see what I mean by that in the next Chapter.

Chapter 4
Grandpa's House

I knew my father's father only when he was an old man in his seventies and eighties. His name was Walter Appel. I called him Grandpa. It seemed like everyone in the city knew him. He practiced law for more than sixty years, beginning in 1902. Even at eighty-one, old for someone in mid-century America, he walked a mile to the office five days a week and retraced his steps on the return trip home. I vividly remember his house on Steele Street, just a half-block south of City Park, across 17th Avenue. A two-story red brick structure, it had a large covered front porch that sported a hanging wooden swing that my sisters and cousins and I played on. The sturdy front door was crafted of white oak, stained a light brown so you could still see the prominent straight grain of the wood showing through. The front door opened to a large foyer. Hugging the right wall of the foyer was a broad stairway that rose to the second floor. At the top of the dark-stained wooden staircase on the second floor were three bedrooms and a single bath. The stairway was interrupted by a little square landing three stairs up from the main floor. Inset into the exterior wall at the landing was the highlight of the house – a large stained-glass window about three wide and seven feet tall of an apple tree. It was a joke, of course, a play on our family name.

Along the wall below the staircase was a long, dark carved wooden table. The table always attracted my interest, not because of anything inherent in the table itself, but because of what sat atop it. Grandpa loved chocolates and on this particular table there always rested a little cut crystal bowl invariably filled to the brim with chocolates. The chocolates came from Bauer's, a famous chocolate shop downtown on Curtis Street. Although the type of chocolates varied from time to time, my favorite by far – and I think Grandpa's too – was honeycomb, certainly one of the great culinary wonders of the world. Bauer's was the kind of old-fashioned candy store where you could watch them make what they sold. They had a crazy old contraption with long rotating arms that pulled taffy and another that spit out spice drops of different flavors and hues. But what I most loved about Bauer's was watching them make honeycomb. It was wonderous to see white sugar granules turn molten when heat was applied to the large copper pot. With the addition of corn syrup, honey and a touch of vanilla, the mixture burped and gurgled as it heated past the boiling point of water. When the candy maker added baking soda, a magic ingredient, the concoction began to bubble like crazy. It took two of them to lift the big copper pot from the heat and pour the now-golden mixture onto a tray to cool. As it cooled, air pockets formed, like the holes in swiss cheese but far more plentiful. When the mixture became solid, the large sheet of honeycomb was broken into randomly sized and shaped pieces and each unique piece was dipped in the darkest and smoothest semi-sweet chocolate I had ever tasted. Once the chocolate coating hardened, the honeycomb was ready to be dispensed to devotees like Grandpa and me. To this day, I struggle to resist the lure of honeycomb chocolates.

The front room to the left of the foyer in Grandpa's house was what we would today call a living room. Back then it was called a parlor. Behind the parlor was a large dining room where we often gathered for family dinners, which began precisely at 6:00 o'clock, not a moment sooner or later. Behind the foyer was the kitchen, sealed off from view of the rest of the house. It was a grand house, suited perfectly to the family patriarch.

Grandpa was a leading citizen of the City – or so I inferred from what I saw and the many stories I heard about him. He was born in Denver in 1879 and attended the University of Colorado in Boulder and then law school after that. He and a law school classmate started a law firm in 1902 that bore his name for more than a century. Grandpa wasn't much concerned with the accumulation of wealth. Like other lawyers, he'd dictate client bills to his secretary once a month and she'd type them up and return them to him for review. Unlike other lawyers, word was the bills weren't put into envelopes and mailed to clients on any regular basis. Instead, his habit was to stuff the newly-prepared bills into his desk drawer. When the need arose, he'd reach into the drawer and withdraw a few bills to be mailed out to cover whatever his current fiscal needs might be. Grandpa spoke Latin and ancient Greek fluently, the product of a late-nineteenth-century classical education. The problem was hardly anyone else did. So he became friends with priests from the local archdiocese who shared his facility with ancient languages and they'd get together every week or so – just to gab in languages long deceased to the populace at large.

While Grandpa's house was in the central part of town, I lived with my Mom and Dad and two sisters in a suburb that had sprouted just within the southern boundary of the city after the war. Those suburbs came to be filled with "modern" houses, mostly one-story ranch-style affairs, with attached garages and large yards to accommodate growing families. Originally treeless, the diligent original homeowners quickly planted trees that slowly grew to maturity long after the original families, like ours, had moved on to other quarters. Our house on Josephine Street had three bedrooms, two baths and a basement to boot.

In those days, phones were tethered to the wall by a wire. The wire, made of copper and covered with insulation, conveyed oscillating electric currents generated by talking into the handset. The electric currents traveled by some magic means from the phone on the wall, through wires hanging above the streets and eventually made their way to a phone tethered to someone else's wall on the other end of the conversation. Wireless phones were a thing of the far distant future. With their physical connection to the house, phones in those days were thus associated with a household instead of a person, as they are today. Because of that, the ringing of the phone was an event of importance in the household. What caused a phone to ring was an internal mechanism, a little piece of metal that alternatively struck two little metal half-spheres in quick succession. The clanging was always loud enough for everyone to hear and prominent enough to command a response, which was usually that someone had to answer it. It was extremely rare that a ring would be ignored since there was no voicemail for the call to divert to. Kids didn't answer the phone, at least not unless invited by a parent, usually because their hands were occupied with some activity that prevented picking up the handset. The frequency of phone calls received in the household followed a predictable cadence throughout the day. Calls were few in the early hours, built to a peak that stretched from mid-morning into the mid-afternoon, and then trailed off through the dinner hour. I had never heard our phone ring before breakfast or after bedtime.

It was therefore jarring to hear the phone ring at 7:00 a.m. one Friday morning in the early spring of 1961. I was eating Wheaties at the kitchen table and Dad, sitting with me, was drinking his second cup of coffee. When the mechanical ringing of the phone began, he hesitated for a moment, as if questioning whether the clamorous intrusion at this uncharacteristic hour was real. Apparently satisfied that it was, he turned his head in the direction of the ringing, stood and walked to the phone that was hung on the wall a few steps away. Observing this drama unfold, I heard him say "hello." Then he fell silent, listening to the voice on the other end, which I couldn't hear. After what seemed like a long time, but was probably about thirty seconds, all Dad said was "I'll be right there." Hanging up the phone and avoiding eye contact with me, he headed to the bedroom where Mom was still in bed. I didn't hear what they said to each other, but the next thing I knew Dad was dressed and leaving through the garage door.

When I went to find my Mom, she was dressed, unusual for her at this hour, sitting on the bed and talking on the pale blue Princess phone by her bedside. I lingered, waiting for her to finish the call. When she finally hung up the phone, I asked her what was going on. She put me off, saying she had a few more calls to make. When she finished the calls, she told me Grandpa was in the hospital and she was going to meet Dad there now. I later learned Grandpa had a heart attack during the night, about 11:00 p.m., after he'd removed the uniform he wore every day, a suit, white shirt and a tie, and dressed in his white pajamas and tucked himself into bed. As he lay in bed, he knew something had gone wrong with his body, but didn't want to bother anyone until the morning. After the sun rose and he deemed it a reasonable hour to phone, he called an ambulance (this was long before 911), which took him to Rose Hospital, where he had been on the Board of Directors for many years. One of Mom's calls before she left was to our regular babysitter, Mrs. Whitehead, who came to stay with me and my two sisters, Susan and Cindy.

I don't think I really knew what a heart attack was, but I surmised it was some sort of serious medical condition that involved the heart. Both Dad and Mom were clearly upset by the events that transpired that morning and we kids absorbed their emotions, even without fully understanding the cause. At about 8:30 Mrs. Whitehead ushered me and Susan out the door and we walked off to school. Slavens Elementary, built about the same time as our house, served the children of the neighborhood and was just two blocks away. In the fourth grade, I was able to walk to school on my own since there weren't any busy streets to cross and I was in charge of conveying Susan, who was in the second grade, to school as well. I was relieved to be occupied with school that day so I didn't have to keep wondering how Grandpa was doing.

When we walked home for lunch, something we did every day, Mrs. Whitehead had made us Campbell's soup, Chicken and Rice I believe, and a bologna sandwich with French's mustard. Cindy, my other sister who was two at the time, had already eaten and was down for a nap. I asked Mrs. Whitehead if she'd heard from Mom or Dad and she demurred. After lunch, we made the return walking journey back to school for the afternoon session of learning.

When school let out at 2:30 I was surprised to see Mom and Dad in the car waiting for us. After brief hugs with Mom and Dad, Susan and I got in the car and were chauffeured the short distance back to the house. When we got home, I asked: "How's Grandpa?" Dad said, "let's all go sit down." We never had family meetings and I was filled with a deep sense of dread that I didn't get an immediate answer to my question. We sat in the living room. Mom was somber but not crying. Dad spoke slowly, as he almost always did: "Your Grandpa got sick last night. He had a heart attack. He went to the hospital this morning and then he died this afternoon." Little Cindy was still with Mrs. Whitehead and didn't hear our conversation. At seven, Susan understood the message and started to weep. I felt sad and my first thought was this meant I wouldn't see Grandpa again. He wouldn't bounce me on his knee. We wouldn't have dinner together anymore. We wouldn't share holiday meals at the house on Steele Street with the apple tree stained glass window. We wouldn't sit together in the seats reserved for him at temple on Rosh Hashanah. And most of all, there wouldn't be any more honeycombs in that little crystal bowl on the long table in Grandpa's front hall. I understood Grandpa was gone, I wouldn't see him again and he wouldn't return.

This was my first personal experience of death. Sure, I'd been to the cemetery before and seen the gravestones of my Dad's mother, Rose, my great-grandfather, David, my great great grandfather, Simon, along with their wives. And I knew my Mom's grandmother, Goldie, had died right before I was born and that I was named after her. I'd seen (or seemed to see) people die on TV shows, mostly westerns, like Gunsmoke, Wagon Train and The Lone Ranger, and watched as the consequences of death were dealt with on shows like the Twilight Zone.

I remember a particular Twilight Zone episode in 1961, the same year Grandpa died. It was called *The Long Distance Call*. Little Billy was turning five and his grandmother came for a visit. She gave him a toy phone as a birthday present and told Billy he could always call her on the toy phone. Grandma died shortly after the birthday party, but Billy continued to converse with her on the toy phone, much to the consternation of his parents. Billy seemed to understand that Grandma was gone and wouldn't be returning, but he also easily accepted that he could still talk to her via the toy phone. In fact, he was consumed with talking to her and it took up more and more of his waking hours. Eventually, dead Grandma invited Billy to drown himself in the garden pond and his parents found him there in the cold water, unresponsive, but still clinging to life. Emergency personnel showed up, examined the lifeless boy and somberly told his parents that Billy was probably a goner. That news prompted the Dad to take a trip to Billy's room to call Grandma on the toy phone and urge her to let Billy live. She of course relented and Billy revived as the episode came to a close. The story is an interesting one. Grandma had died and her physical presence had vanished, but she was still able to communicate with little Billy by means of the magical phone. The phone somehow bridged the divide between the physical world, where we all reside, and an unknown and unseen world were people go, or at least where Grandma had gone, following the decease of their physical body. Implicit in the narrative was the assumption that the essence of Grandma continued after the death of her physical body, as we'll see later on, a common belief among the people of earth. The twist here, which makes for an enjoyable tale, is that the essence of Grandma, that which persisted after her physical demise, was able to communicate with little Billy from the "beyond."

At the age of nine, the subject of death or what it meant to die was certainly something I knew about, even before Grandpa died. But my knowledge of death was as abstract as the deaths themselves. I read about them in books or the newspaper, saw them in shootouts on TV westerns or heard about deaths from friends who reported when a loved one was lost. All of those accounts were experiences of someone else that were shared with me, not my own first-person experience. The people who were reported to me as having died were in a sense historical figures – images on a screen that I'd heard stories about but had never experienced first-hand. Experiencing death in real time was different. It was more – well, it was more real.

After Grandpa died, many other deaths followed over the extended years of my life. Friends died and I attended their funerals. Colleagues died and I saw them off at wakes, memorial services or, later on, the ever-popular celebration of life party. My secretary was murdered by her deeply disturbed ex-husband, who stalked her, laid in wait, eventually accosted and then shot her with a handgun and then repented his sin by turning the gun on himself. Grandparents, aunts, uncles and cousins died and I sat with family to mourn and celebrate the departed. My Mom died from lung cancer about fifteen years ago. Near the end of her life, a hospital bed had been set up for her in the living room. When I got the call that she was near death, I rushed to her side and arrived shortly after she died. She was the first dead body I ever saw, which seemed simultaneously fitting and ironic when you realize that hers was the first body I saw when I came into this world. I regretted seeing her dead because it was that memory that bubbled up when I pictured her. For many years after, I didn't' see her preparing dinner in the kitchen or sitting in the front passenger seat of the family Ford station wagon on camping trips throughout the West. I didn't see her comforting smile as she band-aided my scratched knee. I didn't see her tenderly holding her first grandchild. Instead, it was the facial features of her lifeless corpse that I mostly remembered – the tortured look of the lower jaw jutting forward and down. The tightly drawn skin around her mouth. It didn't look peaceful. It looked pained and strained. I wished I hadn't ever seen her that way.

Dad died a few years after Mom. He had moved into hospice care just a few days before. He was tired of fighting – fighting – emphysema and he was ready to surrender to death. I spent a lot of time with him in those last days before he died. But I wasn't there when he took his last tortured breath. I didn't see him die and I didn't go see his body when the hospice nurse called to say he had "passed." I didn't want to. I didn't need to. We had said our goodbyes. After Dad died, I disposed of his possessions, accumulated over nearly eight decades, and wrapped up his worldly affairs. His house was sold and someone else moved in. His car was sold and someone else began to drive it. At the garage sale, someone bought his bed and took it to their home so they could sleep on it. We kids took some things, things that were meaningful to each of us, things we thought we should have, or things we could use in our own homes. The remaining physical remnants of Dad's long life were sold or sent to the landfill for burial.

When I trained as a yoga teacher, we studied human anatomy. To advance my anatomical knowledge, I found myself one Saturday morning about 9:00 a.m. waiting outside a rather nondescript warehouse in North Denver, with twenty other yoga teachers-to-be. Our anatomy teacher arrived and led us into the cadaver lab where six bodies (coincidentally, the same number as in Dr. MacDougall's soul-weighing experiment) rested on gurneys, covered in white sheets, awaiting the lessons we were about to learn. My feelings in advance of this field trip were decidedly mixed. I was, on the one hand, interested to see first-hand the inside of the human body. On the other hand, I was a little freaked out by the thought of seeing dissected strangers and touching their fileted bodies. It turned out to be a very illuminating experience. It was valuable to see the major muscles of the human body, where and how they were attached to the bones, and how they laid over, under and between one another. More surprising was the fact that I felt little humanness about the bodies. I didn't feel attached to them at all. They were inert machines, beautiful, complex and miraculous in their own way. But they were inoperable, not conscious or animate and they clearly lacked the prospect of re-becoming human. Whatever it meant to be human had left them, even though I knew not where it had gone. They were now inanimate. Former humans. It was a fascinating experience.

The only other dead body I've personally experienced was my wife of thirty years. She died in our bed, probably about mid-day and I discovered her lifeless body when I came home from work. The look of the corpse was similar to my Mom. It showed deep pain, almost torture. It's still hard not to remember her that way.

Birth is often seen as the counterpart of death and I have experienced at least as many new humans coming into existence as I've seen leaving this world. When I was two, my sister, Susan, was born. Prefatory to her birth, I'm sure I saw my mother's belly grow and I was probably told a sibling was on the way and I wouldn't be the only child in the family any longer, although I doubt I had much comprehension of the whole thing at that age. I have a vague recollection of Susan being brought home from the hospital, although my memory may be of photos I saw later and not of the actual events. I am sure I saw that she was small and helpless and needed the constant attention of my parents to attend to her needs. I got that she was a baby and the state of babyness required care from others to ensure her needs were met. I also observed directly that she grew and her abilities expanded as time marched on. She was eventually able to walk and talk and feed herself, go to the bathroom on her own and so on, until she was mostly self-sufficient. When my second sister, Cindy, arrived about five years later, I was old enough to experience the whole process again with the more developed understanding of a seven-year-old. By then I surely understood that we all begin as helpless babies and eventually grow and mature through toddlerhood, adolescence and young adulthood, into fully mature persons. I also probably had at least a rudimentary understanding that adults progressed into middle age, then old age and then died.

I experienced little humans from a different perspective with my children. After conception, I saw ultrasonic pictures of a little being moving about in my wife's abdomen and eventually the little being emerged into the world and grew and grew and grew into adulthood. I saw this same pattern repeat over and over again with the children of friends and family.

From my indirect experiences, like reading books and stories about birth and death, I understood that each of us was conceived and born into this world in about the same way, that we matured, both physically and mentally, and barring disease or accident, arrived at old age. In old age the body wound down and eventually stopped working and the person died. These indirect experiences were confirmed by my direct personal observations. And my conclusions about how this process worked were affirmed by the parallel perceptions and conclusions of others.

My experiences of birth and death were of course not unique. In fact, although the details of these experiences certainly vary from person to person, the essential information each of us receives is completely uniform – people are born, they live and they die. And it's not that the majority of people follow this pattern or even that most do. Our experience, that of all seven billion people currently resident on this planet and the one hundred billion or so that have preceded us, is universally the same. It doesn't matter which culture you're from, what language you speak, what part of the planet you call home or even whether you were born today or ten thousand years ago. The experience is consistent from person to person and throughout time. There are no outliers. This is not a bell curve. Everyone is born, lives and then dies and each one of us, without exception, observes and learns the lesson of this cycle of life.

How then can we explain the nearly universal rejection of these facts and the experiences they generate by humankind and each of its individual members? Every culture, every belief system, including all religions, which together are subscribed to by the vast majority of the people on earth, tells us the story that the death we all experience in life as inevitable and invariable is really just an illusion and that there is a Soul beyond the physical body that continues after the apparent death, decay and demise of the body? For some of those belief systems, the story is that the unseen Soul pre-exists the physical body, settling into it at some point along the continuum from gestation to birth. For other belief systems, the Soul arises at the same time as the body and joins with it afresh to create the pairing. The specifics of each of these religious and cultural stories vary, but all hew to the common thread of an unseen Self, the Soul, separate from the physical body, that persists after and despite the death of the body.

The enormous variety and range in the specifics of each of these stories and the belief systems which undergird them is remarkable and we'll explore those in modest detail in Chapter 11. But what's even more remarkable than the details of each of these various stories is the homogeneity – the sameness – of their central tenet. How can it possibly be that over the entire span of time of *homo sapiens* on earth, at least that which is known to us today, all the varied, manifold and complicated stories man has invented about humankind reject the one truth our experience tells us we should all agree upon – the finiteness of our existence? Does the homogeneity of this central principle suggest, as many would argue, that the central principle of all these stories – that man has a Soul – must be true? Or does it suggest some other force at work that we have not yet thought about deeply or clearly enough to identify?

As we've already seen, the way we see the world is a reflection of our experiences and perceptions. However, the assumption that our perceptions give us an accurate, in the sense of objective, description of the world, is probably not true and, at the least, open to serious question. And leaving aside the question of whether our experiences and perceptions are accurate, we routinely – in matters of the greatest importance – ignore those perceptions when framing and adopting our worldview. What good then are those perceptions and experiences if, when it comes time to apply them to important questions, like who we are, where we come from and where we're going, we toss them overboard and instead subscribe to stories based on beliefs that aren't supported by what we see, hear, smell taste and touch? Even that is too mild. What really happens is the stories we adopt are not just unsupported by our perceptions – they're the opposite of what we perceive!

To unravel this mystery, we need to have a deeper understanding of what our brains do – of what our physical Self, or at least the physical Self we seem to be, is and how it works. The science of the brain has in many respects advanced quite far. We know that chemicals in our brains, neurotransmitters like serotonin, norepinephrine, acetylcholine and dopamine, facilitate electrical connections between neurons and that these connections result in the various activities and functions of the brain. We know the brain is involved in perception, motor control, waking and sleeping, body systems control (like breathing and heart function), motivation, learning and memory. We even know that various brain functions are localized in different areas of the brain and we can measure electrical activity in specific areas to determine – at least to some extent – whether a particular activity is occurring in the brain. For example, when a person is feeling pain, scientists can determine the level of pain by examining the level of activity in a brain region called the dorsal posterior insula, a small part of the cerebral cortex.

While the enormous amount of work being done in this field is fascinating and helpful in understanding how the brain works, it's a side road we do not need to travel in our current explorations. Instead of looking at *how* the brain does what it does, which is what science is capable of investigating, what we need to examine more carefully is *what* the brain is doing. We need to look at questions like: What does it mean to sense? What does it mean to have an experience? What does it mean to think? We need to understand our inner life. These are the topics we begin to explore in the next Chapter.

Chapter 5

The Red Ball

Jack sits beside me on the sofa. Actually, he's not sitting but sacked out on the sofa, lying on his back with his hind legs splayed apart in a posture of submission. This is his reclining position of choice. Jack is my beloved Australian Labradoodle. His chocolate brown coat is curly, but not nearly as tightly wound as a poodle. It's also not quite wavy, but somewhere between the two states. A Labradoodle is the result of mating a Poodle and a Labrador Retriever and produces a dog of unusual intelligence that's generally pretty mellow, loyal and loving. Jack's particular breed, and it has now become a breed, was created by a fellow named Wally Conron. To the original mix of Lab and Poodle, Wally added a dash of English and American Cocker Spaniel, a pinch of Curly Coated Retriever and a little sprinkling of Irish Water Spaniel. The combination resulted in a dog with a beautiful coat of hypoallergenic hair that typically weighs about thirty-five pounds. Wally was an Aussie, which is why the breed now has the "Australian" moniker. Jack is a multigenerational Doodle, which means both his parents were Australian Labradoodles, as were their parents and so on backward in time for more than three generations. Genetically, multigenerationals produce offspring like themselves. First, second or third generation Labradoodles, on the other hand, may produce Labs or Poodles or a mix of the two.

Jack suddenly rouses from his slumber and pauses for a moment as he rights himself onto all fours. He looks at me for a few moments and then decamps from the sofa. He walks directly over to the teal colored plastic bin that's nearly overflowing with his many toys and seems to be peering into the bin. After pausing for a few moments in front of the bin, he backs away, wheels around and trots off for parts unknown. About twenty seconds later he returns with a ball in his mouth, one of several balls he counts among his play toys. This is the red ball, his clear favorite. It's a lattice of soft and pliable plastic in the shape of a sphere, about seven inches in diameter, with lots of open

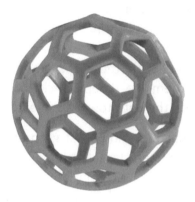

spaces that make it easy for him to grasp. Jack moves closer, drops the red ball at my feet and looks up at me with wide and expectant brown eyes. I remain motionless. After about ten seconds he lets out a gentle "Ruff." I know exactly what he's communicating. He wants me to throw the red ball. It's time to play fetch, an activity I will tire of long before Jack does. In fact, I've never seen him give up on a game of fetch, despite my occasional and futile efforts to outlast him. He is always willing to retrieve the ball for another throw.

What's going on here? Specifically, what's going on in Jack's brain? It's not very difficult to retrace his mental steps. First, Jack formed a goal – to engage me in a game of fetch. He had a memory of the game from the many times we had played it before and he had become conscious of that memory, aware, at some point after he awakened from his nap on the sofa. The memory probably took the form of a mental image – like replaying a movie or a series of still pictures. The memory of the game of fetch allowed Jack to re-live the game in some way in his brain. Next, he had to work backward from his goal of playing fetch to figure out what steps were necessary for him to achieve that goal. That regression would have gone something like this: get up, get off the sofa, go get a toy and bring it back to Garry. And notice that the planning – yes, planning – all probably took place while he was sitting on the sofa looking at me. He also had to remember the plan, keep it in his short-term memory, and check off the steps along the way as he accomplished them to keep track of how he was progressing along the path toward achieving his goal.

Notice too that Jack didn't just grab whatever random object might have been closest at hand, like a pillow or the apple sitting on the table in front of us. His plan required a *specific* object – the red ball. That was probably because he knew from experience, that is, he *remembered,* that from all the possible objects to play fetch with, the red ball created the best experience of the game. And it may be that when Jack evaluated which object would produce the best experience, his evaluation, his judgment, wasn't limited to his own experience of the game. It might also be that he took into account which object would produce the best experience *for me* too. Right. It could well be that he was considering my experience in choosing the red ball, as well as his own, because my experience of the game directly affected how long I'd be willing to engage in the game and the longer I would stay engaged, the more Jack would get to play. This is discriminative behavior. Jack was making a conscious choice among objects to employ in the game of fetch and the choice was governed by a specific criterion: which object would produce the most enjoyable outcome?

Neuroscientists would tell us that Jack's behavior was governed by a chemical stimulus and response. The experience of playing the game of fetch is enjoyable for Jack because it stimulates the production of chemicals in his brain, Dopamine, Serotonin, Oxytocin, and Endorphins, that produce a feeling – yes, feeling – that when it occurs in humans we call pleasure. That's why he wants to play the game over and over. It feels good. But let's not get bogged down in the specific electrical, biological or chemical process or processes that are creating this feeling or where in his brain the processing occurs. Instead, let's just stop for a moment and realize the undeniable fact that Jack feels and thinks. He sets goals, figures out how to accomplish them and then embarks on a course of action involving multiple steps in order to achieve the desired end. Moreover, Jack has learned how to do this. While playing fetch might be instinctual for him, it wasn't instinctual for him to initiate the game, chose the red ball or go find it and drop it at my feet. He learned how to do all that.

Let's dive a little deeper so we can understand in more detail exactly what Jack's brain is doing. Jack's goal was to get a buzz from playing fetch and the first step in the chain of actions needed to achieve his goal was to bring me the ball. Jack decided to use the red ball and so he had to go find it. His first stop in locating the red ball was his toy bin, the place where most of his toys could be found. But the red ball wasn't in the toy bin. This presented a new choice for Jack: modify the plan and choose a different object that was less satisfactory than the red ball or try to find the red ball somewhere in the house other than the toy bin. You can't ignore the complexity of the decision-making. The first choice, picking a different toy to play fetch with, would sacrifice long-term satisfaction for short-term gain. Jack knew, because he'd already made the judgment, that the red ball would produce the most pleasurable game of fetch and that's why he chose it in the first place. If he accepted another object to retrieve, he'd get to play fetch right away; but the buzz he'd get from playing fetch would be less than if he had played with the red ball. Alternatively, he could forego his immediate satisfaction and go find the red ball at the cost of delaying satisfaction but knowing the amount of satisfaction eventually received would be greater. Also, by forgoing whatever object was at hand for the game in lieu of searching for the red ball, he'd also be taking the risk that the effort would be for naught if the red ball couldn't be found. The old bird in the hand/bird in the bush dilemma. All this is pretty complex decision-making!

Having made his choice to look for the red ball, Jack backed away from his toy bin and left the room. What was his brain telling him about where to go and how to get there? This becomes even more complex. Jack didn't roam around the house randomly looking for the red ball. Instead, Jack's brain had constructed a map, an internal model, of the house. Psychologists call this cognitive mapping, a term coined by Edward Tolman in 1948. Back in the mid-1900s, behavioral psychology was ascendant and it was an article of faith of the behaviorists that animal behavior was a response to some stimulus. Tolman rejected the stimulus-response model and believed instead that behavior resulted from cognition. Specifically, he proposed that animals acquired spatial knowledge – knowledge about the things in their environment – and were able to apply that knowledge to construct a mental map of their environment.

The cognitive map is an internal picture, a symbolic representation, that tells Jack the location of the objects that make up his current environment – the house. In the picture that assembles in his brain are objects like walls and floors and sofas, tables and chairs. But his picture isn't just in two dimensions. The house has a vertical element too because there are stairs up and down from the main floor – a total of three main levels for Jack to consider, with the stairs joining one level to the other. In addition, there are more subtle vertical elements to the map. The floor on the main level of the house is the most accessible and often used vertical element. But there are other horizontal surfaces, like the couch, the bed, and the seat of the overstuffed chair in the bedroom, which are all at additional vertical sub-levels.

Once Jack determined the red ball wasn't in the toy bin, his brain was able to construct the three-dimensional map. Also, incredibly, notice that his brain surely tells him where *he is* located on this map because without that information, he would have no way other than random movement to go and get the red ball. Because his movement is directed – he is clearly moving from point A to point B with intentionality – he must know where he is when he begins the movement in order to figure out the path from A, where he is, to B, where he expects the red ball to be.

After six years of playing fetch with Jack, I know that about half the time he heads directly and immediately to where the red ball is located, snatches it up and returns it to me to throw. While that may not seem particularly remarkable, you need to know that the red ball ends up all over the house and is rarely in the same location from one day to the next. In fact, it gets left all over the place. Sometimes it's in the bedroom; sometimes in the family room; sometimes in the library or my office or the basement or even the back yard. The fact that about half the time he successfully navigates directly to the red ball wherever it is resting tells us something important. It means he *remembered* where it was the last time he saw it, which might have been earlier the same day or several days before, and he was able to access that memory on demand and plug the memory into the cognitive map.

When Jack is wrong about where the ball was last abandoned, he'll usually come back to me on the sofa, the place where his plan was first hatched and the steps mapped out, and begin again, setting out to a different room. Notice that this is probably an ad hoc modification of his original plan. He doesn't plan for the contingency of not finding the red ball. Instead, this is a strategy Jack employs off-the-cuff when the original plan, the steps he mapped out to follow at the beginning, don't produce the desired result. If he had anticipated that possibility, then he'd continue the search in some way. But that isn't what he does. Instead, he comes back where he started, adopts a new plan for finding the red ball and then executes the new plan. Sometimes he doesn't find the ball after searching various places where it might be. When that happens, he invariably comes back to me, stands or sits, and lets out another "Ruff." There is no ambiguity about what he's communicating – "can you please help me find the ball?" When this happens, he is abandoning his internally directed effort and asking for help. Typically, I'll then alight from the sofa, join the search and help him find the red ball. When we finally figure out where it is, the game of fetch is ready to begin.

Once Jack acquires the red ball through any of the strategies I've described, he drops the red ball at my feet so

I can pick it up and toss it somewhere for him to retrieve. I'll often throw it down the long hall, banking it off one wall so he'll have a longer run to retrieve it. When I do that, the red ball disappears beyond Jack's view and he tears off in the direction I tossed the ball. How does he know where the ball has gone? How does he even know the ball still exists as it disappears from his view and what does that tell us about how his brain is processing the information? What does that tell us about Jack's inner life?

Babies love to play peekaboo. The way the game usually works is the baby covers their eyes with their hands and then moves their hands away from the eyes – peekaboo! Seeing the other game player – often a parent or other caregiver – the baby erupts in peals of laughter at the appearance of the other person. Give it a try. Look at someone in front of you, cover your eyes and then quickly move your hands away. What's so funny about that you might ask? Well, we need to look at it from the baby's perspective to find out. Until six or eight months (or perhaps as early as 3 or 4), babies don't understand the concept that objects continue to exist when they can't see them. Instead, they believe an object exists only as long as they can see it. When the object is out of sight, it is, to a baby, out of mind. In the middle of the twentieth century a Swiss psychologist named Jean Piaget observed and studied this phenomenon and dubbed it "object permanence." Piaget concluded that the game of peekaboo illustrated that babies lacked the concept of object permanence and the game worked – it was funny – because the baby was surprised by the sudden and immediate appearance of an object that to the baby had ceased to exist. Object permanence became a foundational principle of psychology and, although there is today some dissent about elements of the concept, it is still widely accepted.

The capacity for object permanence emerges when the baby's brain finally becomes able to form a mental representation of an object. The mental representation is a symbolic image of the object. When the actual object is out of the baby's view, they can still imagine the object – they can see it internally – and their symbolic image tells them the object doesn't cease to exist when they can't see it. The ability to form mental images of things is thus essential to object permanence. A child's grasp of object permanence emerges over time instead of all at once. Although the age range varies, it is generally observed to begin at about six months (or even earlier) and to become complete by about eighteen months.

The phenomenon of object permanence applies to people as well as to inanimate objects. When a person moves beyond the field of view of the baby, the baby believes the person has ceased to exist. Some research suggests that babies don't understand people permanence until after they understand object permanence and that people permanence therefore develops later than object permanence. An interesting twist on this is children's belief about invisibility. Recent work in this area, particularly by James Russell at the University of Cambridge in England, delves deeply into the inner workings of the toddler brain. Russell's research shows that 2-4-year-olds think they are invisible when they cover *their* eyes. At its most basic, this means toddlers think if they can't see someone else, the other person can't see them either. I see echoes of this in my own mental processes. We have a hot tub in our small backyard. The yard is surrounded by a high fence. My preference is to hot tub in the buff, which I have done for many years, knowing that the high fence shields my body from the neighbors' view. Recently, two houses across the alley, both one-story ranches, were knocked down to make way for bigger and better ones. The new houses are two-story structures. Once construction of the new houses was complete, I found myself standing naked next to the hot tub thinking: "Whoops. The new neighbors will be able to see me and I will need to modify my hot tubbing behavior." My thinking process was: "I can see them and so they can see me." Then I realized it didn't matter what I could see. What mattered was what they could see and the two viewpoints weren't necessarily the same. So I kneeled down to get a different vantage point and confirmed that all the new neighbors would be able to see from their second story windows when I got into or out of the hot tub was my head. My incorrect initial reaction was a vestige of my early childhood thinking.

If Jack's mental processes were at the level of human babies or toddlers, he wouldn't chase the red ball once it passed beyond his vision because he would have thought it ceased to exist once he wasn't able to see it anymore. That means Jack's cognitive process, at least in this particular regard, is more advanced than a young human because for Jack the red ball has object permanence – Jack realizes the red ball has merely moved beyond his present field of vision, but still exists, and he constructs a cognitive map from present sensory input and stored memory in order to predict where the red ball has gone and plot a path to locate and retrieve it. Jack has people permanence too. Sometimes I tease him by standing in the kitchen behind the waist-high center island, let him see me clearly and then crouch down quickly so I disappear from his view. He'll come tearing into the kitchen and around the island to find me. If he didn't have people permanence – if he thought I ceased to exist when I couldn't be seen anymore – he wouldn't bother and it wouldn't be a game. It's only because he knows I still exist that he runs to find me.

Jack isn't alone in his capacity for object permanence and cognitive mapping ability. The more we study the behaviors of our fellow planetary residents, the more insight we gain about the depth of their cognitive processes – their inner life. The lowly ground squirrel is a good example. The idiom "squirrel away" has been around for more than a century and refers to the squirrel's propensity to gather nuts in the fall when they're plentiful and store them for retrieval during the winter when food is scarce. Researchers have begun to examine how the squirrel is able to find the food they've buried. It was originally supposed that they searched it out using their sense of smell. But that doesn't seem to be the case. Instead, recent research demonstrates that squirrels remember where their precious caches of nuts are buried and their recalled memories lead them to their winter food. This is a variant of the cognitive map Jack employs. The squirrel stores a memory of the location of their buried winter meal and then recalls the memory when it's time to find the food. To be successful with this strategy, the squirrel must create an internal map of its environment, then locate the food on the map. But the hidden food is outside the squirrel's sensory awareness. So the squirrel's brain must be working with the *idea* of its food, a symbolic representation, in creating the cognitive map. This suggests that squirrels, at least to some extent, utilize symbolic thinking in their activities and that they have the capacity for object permanence. The depth of their inner life seems much greater than we ever suspected.

Jack has likes and dislikes. That is, he makes choices and judgments. His judgments aren't necessarily limited to tangible things, like preferring the flavor of one brand of dog food over another or preferring chicken to carrots. He makes judgments about activities and even about the *prospect* of engaging in activities in the future. Jack also has a vocabulary, words he understands. That is, he has a modest command of language or, at least, certain aspects of language. This is momentous because it reinforces what we saw with all that led up to the game of fetch – he thinks symbolically. Here's another example. Jack loves to ride in the car. Sometimes the ride has a reward – like going to the car wash where he'll receive a treat from the cashier. But sometimes the car ride *is* the reward. Here's how it works. I'll head to the bedroom and as I'm retrieving a pair of shoes from the closet, Jack shows up to see what's going on. He sees the shoes and recognizes from prior experience that when I put on my shoes it means I'm preparing to leave the house and he becomes much more alert – excited. His excitement response isn't instinctual. It's learned. And it tells us that he is accessing stored memories of prior instances in which I have put on my shoes. He knows from comparing his current experience to those stored and now-retrieved memories that my putting on shoes is normally the first step in a process that leads eventually to my leaving the house, often through the garage door, getting into the car and heading off somewhere. He also is aware, because he is accessing all those memories, that sometimes the process that begins with putting on shoes and eventually results in leaving the house through the garage door involves him; specifically, that he gets to come along and ride in the car.

My shoes tied, I begin to leave the bedroom and walk toward the door to the garage at the back of the house. Jack is literally at my side, searching and alert to further cues about how my actions are going to affect him. If I walk toward the front door instead of the garage door, he'll recognize that probably means no car ride. If I keep moving toward the garage door, his excitement level grows as the probability of his getting to go for a ride in the car increases. And now verbal communication comes into play. That is, Jack employs the language he understands to assist him in perceiving how this scenario is going to play out. One of the verbal cues I might give him is: "OK, Jack, you can go." Maybe it's the inflection in my voice or the volume or maybe the words themselves – I don't really know – but he clearly understands from the communication what's happening and leaves my side, bounding ahead of me toward the garage door, where he'll wait to be let into the garage and be ready to jump up into the back seat of the car.

Or, I might give him a different cue: "No, Jack, you can't go" or "No, Jack, you have to stay home." When these words are spoken, Jack's excitement level diminishes noticeably and he stays by my side, probably recognizing there won't be a car ride in his immediate future but remaining ready for the possibility that he didn't get the information right or that I'll change my mind. Again, I don't know whether it's the words I've used or the tone of voice or my attitude or something else. And for our purposes here, it doesn't really matter. What does matter is that we have had a conversation. I've made an effort to convey information to Jack and he's comprehended that information and is acting on it. If I don't indicate a change of heart after telling him he doesn't get to go, Jack stays by my side until the last moment as I exit the house through the garage door. If I do change my mind, which happens occasionally, and say something like "OK, you can go," then he squeezes in front of me as I open the door, heads for the car and waits patiently as I open the car door and invite him up and in.

Let's return to the nature of my communication with Jack and see how it demonstrates his ability to think symbolically. There are specific words he understands, like "walk" and "park." The words "walk" and "park" stand for activities that are off in either the near or somewhat more distant future. Jack reacts differently to the spoken words "park" and "walk." His level of excitation is noticeably different in response to the two words. He's far more excited about "park" than he is about "walk." In fact, he goes pretty bonkers at the word "park." Both words result in a stroll for him, but the words have distinct meanings. "Park" means we get in the car and drive to Wash Park, about two miles away. Wash Park has a two and a half-mile pedestrian road running around it where Jack can interact with lots of people and lots of other dogs. It also has two lakes, Smith Lake on the north and Grasmere Lake on the south, and a canal that feeds into and out of each lake. From early spring until the late fall, the canal is filled with water to a depth of a foot or two. Jack loves to jump into the canal and play in the water, which he regularly does when we go to the park. It's one of his most favorite things to do.

"Walk" means something different. To "walk" is to amble around our neighborhood. To get to "walk," we go to the laundry room, which is also where the garage door is located, and retrieve a leash from a drawer, then walk back through the house to the front door, where we exit, walk down the steps from the front door to the street and take one of several routes for a stroll through the neighborhood. Sometimes the neighborhood walk takes us to a local park, where there can be some dogs and people for Jack to interact with. When I say: "Jack, let's go for a walk," his excitement level is noticeably lower than when I say: "let's go to the park." For a "walk" he doesn't bound toward the garage door or the front door for that matter. He doesn't even follow me to the laundry room where I'll retrieve the leash from the drawer. Instead, Jack hangs back, without showing much outward appearance of excitement. Eventually, I have to call him over and attach the leash to his collar before we leave through the front door.

What can we conclude about the workings of Jack's brain, his inner life, from this example? First, notice that Jack's brain is processing cues. Some of the cues are non-verbal, like when I put on my shoes. Other cues are verbal (or at least accompanied by words), like when I say: "do you want to go to the park." "Park" and "walk" are symbolic words – they stand for something that is not within Jack's current perception. He can't see, hear, taste, smell or touch the "park" from inside the house when I say that word. Instead, the word "park" triggers a memory or an amalgamation of memories from prior experiences Jack has had and he associates those memories with the word. It is as if the word "park" causes Jack's brain to replay a movie of his prior experiences in the park. His brain evaluates those experiences as pleasurable, something he would like to repeat, and that evaluation either took place at the time of the experience and was stored in his brain with the experience, or it built up over time and was stored or associated with a series of experiences, or his brain retrieved the visions of "park" experiences and evaluated them at the same time I said the word. We don't know which option his brain actually executes and I don't think an understanding of the specific mechanism is essential for our purposes. What is important to recognize, however, is the fact that Jack is recalling the prior experiences, evaluating them and acting based on that evaluation.

"Walk" is also symbolic and Jack distinguishes between what a "walk" involves, versus going to the "park." He must be recalling memories of "walk" when I say the word. But there's more going on here. Not only does he associate "walk" with one set of memories and "park" with another, but he must also be comparing one set of experiences to the other and after evaluating the experiences, he expresses a *preference* for one (the "park") over the other (the "walk"). His preference then finds expression in his differing levels of excitement.

Sometimes Jack rejects "walk" as an option. I'll get the leash and summon him to my side so I can attach the leash to his collar and he won't come. Or sometimes he'll retreat to where he was laying before the hoped-for adventure was launched. It's tempting to conclude this behavior shows Jack was disappointed and it may look like that from the outside. But we should resist the temptation to label it with emotional content because we really can't know exactly what Jack is feeling as a result of these events. What we can conclude, however, is that Jack had a preference for one activity over the other and that his preference was expressed outwardly in his level of excitement. And in the example I just mentioned, his preference was so strong that he made a choice not to accept the disfavored activity ("walk") if his preferred activity ("park") wasn't available. Let that sink in for a moment: Jack made a choice about a future activity presented to him on a symbolic level! In a human we might say the behavior exhibited petulance. But for Jack, let's just say that the return he anticipated receiving from "walk" wasn't sufficient to motivate him to engage in that activity. Lest you think his response of rejecting "walk" was due to some other cause, like not feeling well or not wanting to go out at all, I can dispel that pretty easily. In all cases, if Jack rejects "walk," and I then say, "how would you like to go the park instead," his excitement level increases tremendously and he bolts for garage door, clearly ready to embark on the activity of "park."

There's a lot going on in Jack's brain. He's aware that communication is taking place, he's perceiving information that is available to him, including indirect cues and symbolic ones like words, he's evaluating the data, including the symbols, drawing on memories of his prior experiences, he's forming preferences – making value judgments – comparing one activity to another, and he's acting on those preferences. Apart from the quantitative aspect of Jack's inner life, there is an important qualitative element. There is an amazing depth to his inner life. Even though "park" involves delayed or postponed satisfaction and "walk" would involve immediate satisfaction and reward, Jack is apparently able to compare the two types of satisfaction and chose the delayed satisfaction over the immediate reward. Wow!

There's no question that Jack is quite remarkable. But is he a wonder dog? Does he do more cognitively than other dogs or do it so much better that he's on a whole different level? I don't think so. Jack is by no means unique and if you have a dog of your own or have been around them enough, you'll recognize behaviors like what I've described in Jack in your own companion, although they may vary by degree from one doggie to another. What is amazing is the degree of sophistication involved in their inner life. So how do we characterize that inner life? What words can we use to talk about the quality of the cognitive experience and the activity that's taking place?

Our language has a whole host of words we might press into use when talking about the inner life as a whole or various aspects of that inner life. *Consciousness, awareness, intelligence, sentience, intentionality, self-awareness* and *mindfulness* are a few that might have occurred to you. We might ask whether Jack exhibits consciousness or whether he is aware or whether his actions exhibit intentionality. You've heard these words and probably used them before in various settings and you might feel like you know what each of them means. But these words don't actually have very stable or fixed meanings. For example, psychologists mean one thing by consciousness, while neuroscientists mean something else and philosophers would define it in yet a different way. We run into the same problem with the rest of our word list. These words describing the quality or nature of an inner life tend to mean one thing in one context and something quite different in another. For example, consciousness might mean wakefulness in one context, like to a medical doctor, and it might be used to connote self-awareness when used by a philosopher. Due in part to the contextual dependence of these words, the definitions tend to overlap to such a significant degree that distinguishing one from another becomes nearly impossible. By the time we get to Chapter 10 we will be far enough along in our explorations that we will be able to identify words that describe various states of inner life and we'll be able to define those words. For now, let's not attach labels to that inner life. Instead, let's just recognize an inner life exists and that the nature of that inner life probably varies from creature to creature, extending along a spectrum that ranges from no inner life at all to a deep and complex one.

You may have noticed that for the most part, I haven't used the word "mind" in this book. Instead, I have referred to activities taking place in the "brain." I want to explain why. The brain is an easily definable physical organ that can be located in the body of all animals, both vertebrates and invertebrates. You can hold a brain in your hand and you can examine it with your senses and with instruments. You can even observe electrical and chemical activity within the brain. It's clearly and unequivocally a "thing." The brain is substance. We know what we mean when we talk about the brain.

But what is the mind? In the Beatles song, A Day in the Life, we find this lyric: "He blew his mind out in a car." Aristotle wrote: "It is the mark of an educated mind to be able to entertain a thought without accepting it." Shakespeare penned the phrase: "Suspicion always haunts the guilty mind." In Stanley Kubrick's 2001: A Space Odyssey, the computer HAL 2000 famously says: "I'm afraid. I'm afraid, Dave. Dave, my mind is going. I can feel it. I can feel it. My mind is going. There is no question about it. I can feel it." In each of these illustrations, even though the word mind is used, what is really being referred to is the physical organ, the brain (or, in HAL's case, the synthetic brain).

We have Rene Descartes to thank for much of the confusion about brain and mind. In the mid-seventeenth century, he introduced dualism, where the mind was regarded as something separate from the physical body and the brain. This schism, the division of brain and mind, has led to a sort of fuzzy popular conceptualization of the mind as something mysterious, ghostly, not directly observable and therefore the seat of the spiritual essence. Mind becomes divorced from substance and becomes evanescence. The mind expands beyond the skull and becomes a mystical magical object that can't be located in space. Once freed from the physical realm, the mind can be imagined as not obeying the laws of time and space. It is the freedom from physical laws and the properties of matter that allows us to ask the question: where does the mind go when the body dies?

The so-called mind-body (or brain) problem has been the subject of an enormous amount of research by scientists and thought by philosophers. Scientific researchers have searched within the physical body, usually the brain, looking for physical correlates of the mind – attempting to find the precise location of the mind within the brain. Volumes and volumes have been written about the nature of the mind – whether it exists independent of the body and, if so, how it arises. This has produced some interesting theories, both on the scientific front and within philosophy. But the truth is no one really knows the answers to these questions. It's all just speculation.

What we do know is that all thoughts, sensations and feelings are generated or interpreted by the nervous system, of which the brain is a part. When the brain dies and all the chemical and electrical activity ceases, as it eventually will with each of us, what happens to the thoughts, sensations and feelings, the stored memories, and the personality – the person's inner life? Is it like a television? When it works it generates pictures and sounds we can see and hear. When it breaks and stops working, it doesn't produce the pictures and sounds anymore. No one asks where the TV pictures and sounds have gone. They just can't be produced by that object any longer. Or does our inner life stick around somehow, somewhere, in some way, in a mind that transcends the physical brain? Well, we don't know.

Because of all this uncertainty, I have two problems with using the word "mind" at this early stage of our explorations. The first is that it is really ambiguous. It isn't clear when we use the word "mind" whether we are talking about the brain, something more than the brain or both. "Mind" is thus a very imprecise word. The second reason is that the word "mind" has, at least in one sense, taken on a property of incorporeality that assumes a conclusion that short-circuits the exploration we have set for ourselves in this book. It simply assumes the conclusion that there is more to the Self than the physical part and by doing so, it presupposes the end of our story – and I'm not ready to cast my lot there. At least not yet. So, let's stick with the word brain when talking about mental activities, at least for the time-being.

* * * * * * *

Pet Rocks were a brilliant marketing scheme that hit the stores in 1975, just in time for Christmas commerce. They were smooth round rocks sold as pets. Each one had a name, came in a little cardboard Pet Rock Carrier and was accompanied by a 32-page training manual that was titled "The Care and Training of Your Pet Rock." The Pet Rock was obviously a gag, but it allows us to ask an important question: do Pet Rocks have an inner life? Nearly everyone would agree the answer is clearly no, a rock doesn't have an inner life – even if it's a pet. A rock doesn't perceive in even the slightest degree. It doesn't process sensory data. It doesn't see or hear or taste or smell or feel. While the photons emitted by the sun may warm the rock and the vibrations of a thunderclap may cause the rock to vibrate sympathetically, the rock has no sensory system to receive sensory input about sunlight or thunder. The rock also has no mechanism to process the sensory data it doesn't receive, and it doesn't have a brain to direct its movement in response to sensory data. If the rock gets hot enough, it will eventually liquify and melt away. It won't jump into the pond to cool off. When the vibrations of a clap of thunder reach the Pet Rock, it won't run into the closet like Jack does to escape the sounds. So, Pet Rocks don't have a way to process external data, interpret it or to shape their behavior in response. The Pet Rock is, for our purposes, inert, not unlike the corpses I saw in my anatomy lab. I feel confident in concluding that Pet Rocks don't have an inner life and that, of course, is precisely why the concept of the Pet Rock is funny – it pretends that something that's inert is actually animate.

Unlike the Pet Rock, Jack clearly does have a very active inner life. As we've seen, he formulates goals. In fact, he formulates multiple goals and is able to choose between them. He plans the steps needed to achieve his chosen goal and then implements those steps by selecting among different strategies. He has a mechanism that allows him to store and retrieve memories – to replay prior events on demand. He is able to construct a symbolic representation of his environment from his memories and perceptions and to project the location of objects within that symbolic representation. Finally, Jack is able to communicate his inner life to others, at least in some degree. He can clearly convey to me in terms I well understand, his desire, his wish, his intention, that we play fetch together. By finding the red ball and dropping it at my feet, he tells me without any ambiguity exactly what he wants to do as clearly as if he'd vocalized the words: "Garry, let's play fetch." So, it seems undeniable that not only does Jack have an inner life, but it is an inner life that is deep, very rich and multi-faceted.

Is an inner life confined to higher vertebrates like Jack or does it extend more broadly into the animal kingdom or even beyond? That is the next turn our story takes.

Chapter 6

Darwin's Worms

My wife and I have a vegetable garden in our front yard that seems intent on expanding year after year. The house and the garden face a moderately busy street and the garden began as a small social experiment occasioned by the presence of a bare patch of ground about ten feet square. The bare patch had formerly, for at least sixty years, been the location of an enormous cottonwood tree, with a trunk at least three feet in diameter, that stood nearly seventy-feet tall. Cottonwoods are members of the poplar family and grow very quickly. Because of their quick growth, their wood is soft. As the tree aged it weakened and the larger limbs hung perilously over the street, alley and sidewalk, threatening to come crashing down on cars, bike riders and pedestrians. At no small expense, we had the arborist support the most imperiled limbs by attaching metal cables, supporting the limbs against the insatiable tug of gravity and keeping everyone safe. The poor tree subsisted on life support in this condition for several years and then one day the City left a little note – actually, an official Order – in our mailbox, commanding that the stately but sickly cottonwood be removed.

Not long after, the same arborist who had prolonged the life of the gentle beast arrived with all the equipment needed to bring the giant thing down. In less than a day the tree was gone, except for a network of large roots that snaked underground from where the tree's gigantic trunk had once stood. What had once been a prominent feature of our little lot was now a void, an empty place where nothing stood. We let it remain that way for a while –

actually, a couple of years. Then one day it dawned on me. This was the one spot on our little city lot where the sun shone nearly all day long from spring to fall. It would be a wonderful location for a vegetable garden. The only counter-argument was that the now-bare patch was directly adjacent to both the alley and the somewhat busy street and we wondered whether the frequent pedestrian by-passers wouldn't be so tempted to pilfer the bounty of our prospective vegetable garden that there would be little left for us as a tasty reward for our gardening labors. After a period reflecting on this dilemma, we decided to create the garden anyway, at least in part as an experiment to see how much of the expected pilferage would actually come to pass.

The garden started life as a small plot, perhaps five by ten feet. In that first year we grew a couple of tomato plants, a zucchini, some radishes and a small patch of different kinds of lettuce. The first summer produced a nice crop of salad makings and it turned out that our fears of passers-by absconding with the produce were greatly exaggerated. In fact, no one ever took anything, even when we encouraged them to, particularly due to the ridiculous over-abundance of the zucchini plant. By mid-summer, the zucchini produced fruit which escaped our notice under the large green leaves, growing to truly Bunyanesque proportions – like fifteen pounds and thirty inches long. Far too much for us to eat, we foisted the over-sized squash upon all takers. I'm sure we lost some friends that way.

Because of the success of the little garden in its inaugural year, we doubled its size for its second season. With the increased area, we were able to add carrots, eggplant and winter squash to the plantings and, over my wife's mild objection, a couple of additional tomato plants. This pattern of expansion replicated itself year after year until after about five years we had what can rightly be called an urban farm that had overtaken most of the yard. It produced numerous varieties of every garden veggie imaginable and we shared the bounty with family and friends and pretty much anyone who didn't run away when we approached them with the bright, beautiful produce in countless shapes, colors and sizes.

The madness that drove us to expand the garden thus had one further inevitable step: because the squashes, particularly the winter varieties, took up too much real estate with their vines crawling everywhere, wouldn't it make sense – we asked one another – to expand into a third dimension by building a large arched arbor that the squash could grow up and over, saving valuable ground-space? That question, rhetorical as it was, is why I found myself one warm March morning at the lumber yard acquiring pressure treated 4x4 timbers for the arbor/arch. As I loaded the heavy timbers into the Jeep, my thoughts turned to the stately cottonwood that had been felled some years before and I was struck by the irony of having paid handsomely to remove the ancient wooden giant, only to pay again for wood to create a structure in its place. Relieved of $134 by the lumber yard, I returned home and in the space of a few days transformed the timbers into a very sturdy garden feature about seven feet high, four feet wide and five feet long, covered in steel mesh on the top and sides to support the squash vines and allow the fruit to hang down for easy picking.

Erecting the arbor/arch required that I excavate four holes in the ground for the main posts of the structure to a depth of about eighteen inches. In the third week of March, I extracted a hefty shovelful of dirt from the first of the four holes-to-be and, to my surprise, I also unearthed a whole colony of worms. One I had clearly sliced in half with the shovel. Seeing the worms in the fertile soil and realizing I had killed at least one and disrupted the lives of the others left me recognizing that I knew little about these little critters. That lack of knowledge triggered a series of thoughts: did the worm I killed feel pain? Did the worms have brains? Were they social? Did they mate? How did they move through the soil? These questions and others they spawned led me to a study of the features, characteristics and behaviors of the creatures and that eventually brought significant clarity to my understanding of the world of the earthworm. By the way, the arbor/arch eventually got pulled and tugged into place and stands there to this day.

Earthworms don't play fetch like Jack does or build castles like Jim Bishop, but I was surprised by how sophisticated they are. Charles Darwin was fascinated with earthworms for most of his life. After his five-year voyage on the HMS Beagle that ended in 1836, Darwin returned home to England and following a chance encounter in his Uncles' garden, he began to study the behaviors of the lowly earthworm. In 1837, his studies had sufficiently progressed to the point that he presented a paper titled "On the Formation of Mould" to the Geological Society of London about the profound effect worms had on the landscape and soil. The paper was published in 1838, apparently drawing yawns from Darwin's colleagues. We can surely forgive that Darwin's study of earthworms then took something of a back seat, delayed by other work, including the accounts of the HMS Beagle expeditions, published between 1838 and 1843, The Origin of Species, published in 1859, and The Descent of Man, published in 1871, all of which literally changed the way we see the world. But, curiously enough, as he approached his final years, Darwin quite intentionally returned to what he regarded as terrifically important, his work on earthworms, and it was in October of 1871, barely six months before his death, that he published his final book, *The Formation of*

Vegetable Mould, Through the Action of Worms (I'll refer to the book as *"Earthworms"*). In its more than three hundred pages, *Earthworms* describes Darwin's many observations of the little creatures, including their anatomy, senses, behaviors, intellectual prowess and his conclusions about their contributions to humankind and civilization.

On the very last page of this marvelous volume, Darwin concludes:

> "When we behold a wide, turf-covered expanse, we should remember that its smoothness, on which so much of its beauty depends, is mainly due to all the inequalities having been slowly levelled by worms. It is a marvelous reflection that the whole of the superficial mould over any such expanse has passed, and will again pass, every few years, through the bodies of worms. The plough is one of the most ancient and most valuable of man's inventions; but long before he existed the land was in fact regularly ploughed, and still continues to be thus ploughed by earth-worms. It may be doubted whether there are many other animals which have played so important a part in the history of the world, as have these lowly organized creatures."

Earthworms includes three discussions relevant to our present inquiry. First, Darwin describes in beautiful language and some detail, which is worth quoting here at length, the anatomy of the earthworm so that his readers would understand how they worked their magic upon the soil.

Structure. A few remarks must be made on this subject. The body of a large worm consists of from 100 to 200 almost cylindrical rings or segments, each furnished with minute bristles. The muscular system is well developed. Worms can crawl backwards as well as forwards, and by the aid of their affixed tails can retreat with extraordinary rapidity into their burrows. The mouth is situated at the anterior end of the body, and is provided with a little projection (lobe or lip, as it has been variously called) which is used for prehension. Internally, behind the mouth, there is a strong pharynx . . . which is pushed forwards when the animal eats, and this part corresponds . . . with the protrudable trunk or proboscis of other annelids. The pharynx leads into the œsophagus, on each side of which in the lower part there are three pairs of large glands, which secrete a surprising amount of carbonate of lime. These calciferous glands are highly remarkable, for nothing like them is known in any other animal. Their use will be discussed when we treat of the digestive process. In most of the species, the œsophagus is enlarged into a crop in front of the gizzard. This latter organ is lined with a smooth thick chitinous membrane, and is surrounded by weak longitudinal, but by powerful transverse muscles. Perrier saw these muscles in energetic action; and, as he remarks, the trituration of the food must be chiefly effected by this organ, for worms possess no jaws or teeth of any kind. Grains of sand and small stones, from the 1/20 to a little more than the 1/10 inch in diameter, may generally be found in their gizzards and intestines. As it is certain that worms swallow many little stones, independently of those swallowed while excavating their burrows, it is probable that they serve, like mill-stones, to triturate their food. The gizzard opens into the intestine, which runs in a straight course to the vent at the posterior end of the body. The intestine presents a remarkable structure, the typhosolis, or, as the old anatomists called it, an intestine within an intestine; and Claparède* has shown that this consists of a deep longitudinal involution of the walls of the intestine, by which means an extensive absorbent surface is gained.

The circulatory system is well developed. Worms breathe by their skin, as they do not possess any special respiratory organs. The two sexes are united in the same individual, but two individuals pair together. The nervous system is fairly well developed; and the two almost confluent cerebral ganglia are situated very near to the anterior end of the body.

Based on Darwin's observations, you can see that earthworms have anatomical features that are not terribly dissimilar from Jack's, yours and mine. They have a mouth and an anus and a rather sophisticated digestive tract connecting the front and back portals. Food enters through the worm's mouth and is digested by various enzymes along the path to the back end, which makes the food usable as energy to sustain the worm's body. The digestive system has a distinct pharynx, esophagus, gizzard and intestine. Earthworms have a circulatory system that includes a series of blood vessels and a mechanism for pumping the creature's blood through its body. Although the packaging is different from ours, the worm's anatomical features and the processes those features support are not unlike our own.

Second, Darwin discusses the Earthworm's sensory capabilities. Earthworms have the ability to sense their environment. In the following passage, Darwin describes his observations of the worm's senses and the remarkable conclusions he draws from those observations. Keep in mind as you read through this that we're talking about worms:

> Senses.—Worms are destitute of eyes, and at first I thought that they were quite insensible to light; for those kept in confinement were repeatedly observed by the aid of a candle, and others out of doors by the aid of a lantern, yet they were rarely alarmed, although extremely timid animals. Other persons have found no difficulty in observing worms at night by the same means. Hoffmeister, however, states† that worms, with the exception of a few individuals, are extremely sensitive to light; but he admits that in most cases a certain time is requisite for its action. These statements led me to watch on many successive nights worms kept in pots, which

were protected from currents of air by means of glass plates. The pots were approached very gently, in order that no vibration of the floor should be caused. When under these circumstances worms were illuminated by a bull's-eye lantern having slides of dark red and blue glass, which intercepted so much light that they could be seen only with some difficulty, they were not at all affected by this amount of light, however long they were exposed to it. The light, as far as I could judge, was brighter than that from the full moon. Its colour apparently made no difference in the result. When they were illuminated by a candle, or even by a bright paraffin lamp, they were not usually affected at first. Nor were they when the light was alternately admitted and shut off. Sometimes, however, they behaved very differently, for as soon as the light fell on them, they withdrew into their burrows with almost instantaneous rapidity. This occurred perhaps once out of a dozen times. When they did not withdraw instantly, they often raised the anterior tapering ends of their bodies from the ground, as if their attention was aroused or as if surprise was felt; or they moved their bodies from side to side as if feeling for some object. They appeared distressed by the light; but I doubt whether this was really the case, for on two occasions after withdrawing slowly, they remained for a long time with their anterior extremities protruding a little from the mouths of their burrows, in which position they were ready for instant and complete withdrawal.

When the light from a candle was concentrated by means of a large lens on the anterior extremity, they generally withdrew instantly; but this concentrated light failed to act perhaps once out of half a dozen trials. The light was on one occasion concentrated on a worm lying beneath water in a saucer, and it instantly withdrew into its burrow. In all cases the duration of the light, unless extremely feeble, made a great difference in the result; for worms left exposed before a paraffin lamp or a candle invariably retreated into their burrows within from five to fifteen minutes; and if in the evening the pots were illuminated before the worms had come out of their burrows, they failed to appear.

From the foregoing facts it is evident that light affects worms by its intensity and by its duration. It is only the anterior extremity of the body, where the cerebral ganglia lie, which is affected by light, as Hoffmeister asserts, and as I observed on many occasions. If this part is shaded, other parts of the body may be fully illuminated, and no effect will be produced. As these animals have no eyes, we must suppose that the light passes through their skins, and in some manner excites their cerebral ganglia. [20th Century research showed that earthworms have photosensitive cells distributed around their body that sense light and darkness and it is the distribution of these cells on the body that controls how they react to light.] It appeared at first probable that the different manner in which they were affected on different occasions might be explained, either by the degree of extension of their skin and its consequent transparency, or by some particular incidence of the light; but I could discover no such relation. One thing was manifest, namely that when worms were employed in dragging leaves into their burrows or in eating them, and even during the short intervals whilst they rested from their work, they either did not perceive the light or were regardless of it; and this occurred even when the light was concentrated on them through a large lens. So, again, whilst they are paired, they will remain for an hour or two out of their burrows, fully exposed to the morning light; but it appears from what Hoffmeister says that a light will occasionally cause paired individuals to separate.

When a worm is suddenly illuminated and dashes like a rabbit into its burrow—to use the expression employed by a friend—we are at first led to look at the action as a reflex one. The irritation of the cerebral ganglia appears to cause certain muscles to contract in an inevitable manner, independently of the will or consciousness of the animal, as if it were an automaton. But the different effect which a light produced on different occasions, and especially the fact that a worm when in any way employed and in the intervals of such employment, whatever set of muscles and ganglia may then have been brought into play, is often regardless of light, are opposed to the view of the sudden withdrawal being a simple reflex action. With the higher animals, when close attention to some object leads to the disregard of the impressions which other objects must be producing on them, we attribute this to their attention being then absorbed; and attention implies the presence of a mind. Every sportsman knows that he can approach animals whilst they are grazing, fighting or courting, much more easily than at other times. The state, also, of the nervous system of the higher animals differs much at different times, for instance, a horse is much more readily startled at one time than at another. The comparison here implied between the actions of one of the higher animals and of one so low in the scale as an earth-worm, may appear far-fetched; for we thus attribute to the worm attention and some mental power, nevertheless I can see no reason to doubt the justice of the comparison.

In the previous passage, Darwin is saying something most momentous: worms do not react simply out of reflex or instinct. Instead, he concludes (and correctly so as many subsequent studies have confirmed) that worms have a brain and the ability to think. Sensory input to the brain of the earthworm comes not just – and not even primarily – from their ability to sense light and darkness. As Darwin discovered, worms sense vibrations, which we might call a type of hearing.

> When the pots containing two worms which had remained quite indifferent to the sound of the piano, were placed on this instrument, and the note C in the bass clef was struck, both instantly retreated into their burrows. After a time they emerged, and when G above the line in the treble clef was struck they again retreated. Under similar circumstances on another night one worm dashed into its burrow on a very high note being struck only once, and the other worm when C in the treble clef was struck. On these occasions the worms were not touching the sides of the pots, which stood in saucers; so that the vibrations, before reaching their bodies, had to pass from the sounding board of the piano, through the saucer, the bottom of the pot and the damp, not very compact earth on which they lay with their tails in their burrows. They often showed their sensitiveness when the pot in which they lived, or the table on which the pot stood, was accidentally and lightly struck; but they appeared less sensitive to such jars than to the vibrations of the piano; and their sensitiveness to jars varied much at different times. It has often been said that if the ground is beaten or otherwise made to

tremble, worms believe that they are pursued by a mole and leave their burrows. I beat the ground in many places where worms abounded, but not one emerged. When, however, the ground is dug with a fork and is violently disturbed beneath a worm, it will often crawl quickly out of its burrow.

Worms also possess the sense of touch, which Darwin believed was their most developed sensory faculty:

> The whole body of a worm is sensitive to contact. A slight puff of air from the mouth causes an instant retreat. The glass plates placed over the pots did not fit closely, and blowing through the very narrow chinks thus left, often sufficed to cause a rapid retreat. They sometimes perceived the eddies in the air caused by quickly removing the glass plates. When a worm first comes out of its burrow, it generally moves the much extended anterior extremity of its body from side to side in all directions, apparently as an organ of touch; and there is some reason to believe, as we shall see in the next chapter, that they are thus enabled to gain a general notion of the form of an object. Of all their senses that of touch, including in this term the perception of a vibration, seems much the most highly developed.

What Darwin implies by "general notion of the form of an object" in the last passage is that the lowly earthworm was able to generate a mental image, however rudimentary, of objects in its environment – in the worm's world – and then to act on that mental image. Remarkable. It sounds a lot like the cognitive mapping ability we discovered in Chapter 5 was part of Jack's inner life. In subsequent passages of *Earthworms* Darwin describes the senses of smell and taste exhibited by the worms and then he sums up with the third point of interest to us, concluding that worms exhibit signs of intelligence

> Mental Qualities.—There is little to be said on this head. We have seen that worms are timid. It may be doubted whether they suffer as much pain when injured, as they seem to express by their contortions. Judging by their eagerness for certain kinds of food, they must enjoy the pleasure of eating. Their sexual passion is strong enough to overcome for a time their dread of light. They perhaps have a trace of social feeling, for they are not disturbed by crawling over each other's bodies, and they sometimes lie in contact. According to Hoffmeister they pass the winter either singly or rolled up with others into a ball at the bottom of their burrows.* Although worms are so remarkably deficient in the several sense-organs, this does not necessarily preclude intelligence, as we know from such cases as those of Laura Bridgman; and we have seen that when their attention is engaged, they neglect impressions to which they would otherwise have attended; and attention indicates the presence of a mind of some kind. They are also much more easily excited at certain

times than at others. They perform a few actions instinctively, that is, all the individuals, including the young, perform such actions in nearly the same fashion. This is shown by the manner in which the species of Perichæta eject their castings, so as to construct towers; also by the manner in which the burrows of the common earth-worm are smoothly lined with fine earth and often with little stones, and the mouths of their burrows with leaves. One of their strongest instincts is the plugging up the mouths of their burrows with various objects; and very young worms act in this manner. But some degree of intelligence appears, as we shall see in the next chapter, to be exhibited in this work,—a result which has surprised me more than anything else in regard to worms.

In the years since Darwin's work, we've discovered that worms breathe air, just as we do, although they don't have lungs. Instead, they breathe through their moist skin, which allows oxygen to be exchanged within what passes for earthworm blood and releases carbon dioxide back into the environment. Earthworms also have a complex reproductive process. They are hermaphrodites, with both male and female sex organs. Their mating ritual takes them to the surface of their environment where they couple, spooning we might call it, and exchange sperm with one another. Sometime after copulation, long after the worms have separated, each worm secretes material which forms a ring around its body. The worm then backs out of the ring, injecting its own eggs and the other worm's sperm into it.

When the worm has left the structure, it seals up the end and the whole thing acts as an incubator for the baby worms to hatch and grow.

In Chapter II of *Earthworms*, Darwin begins an exhaustive description of his investigation of how the worms plug their burrows. His experiments demonstrated that the worms have an *instinct* to plug their burrows, but the manner in which they go about implementing that instinct betrays an undeniable intelligence:

> Intelligence shown by worms in their manner of plugging up their burrows.—If a man had to plug up a small cylindrical hole, with such objects as leaves, petioles or twigs, he would drag or push them in by their pointed ends; but if these objects were very thin relatively to the size of the hole, he would probably insert some by their thicker or broader ends. The guide in his case would be intelligence. It seemed therefore worth while to observe carefully how worms dragged leaves into their burrows; whether by their tips or bases or middle parts. It seemed more especially desirable to do this in the case of plants not natives to our country; for although the habit of dragging leaves into their burrows is undoubtedly instinctive with worms, yet instinct could not tell them how to act in the case of leaves about which their progenitors knew nothing. If, moreover, worms acted solely through instinct or an unvarying inherited impulse, they would draw all kinds of leaves into their burrows in the same manner. If they have no

such definite instinct, we might expect that
chance would determine whether the tip,
base or middle was seized. If both these
alternatives are excluded, intelligence alone
is left; unless the worm in each case first tries
many different methods, and follows that
alone which proves possible or the most
easy; but to act in this manner and to try
different methods makes a near approach to
intelligence.

Near the end of the Chapter, he concludes:

To sum up, as chance does not determine
the manner in which objects are drawn into
the burrows, and as the existence of
specialized instincts for each particular case
cannot be admitted, the first and most
natural supposition is that worms try all
methods until they at last succeed; but many
appearances are opposed to such a
supposition. One alternative alone is left,
namely, that *worms, although standing low
in the scale of organization, possess some
degree of intelligence.*

When my curiosity about earthworms was piqued by the
erection of the arbor/arch in our vegetable garden, about
the last thing I expected to learn was that these little
creatures have brains and, as Darwin said, they exhibit
intelligence – they have the capacity to think and to solve
problems.

So, do earthworms have an inner life? We have to
answer they surely do, although their inner life is different
from Jack's, not as complex or developed. Worms have the

ability to process sensory input, light and darkness, vibrations, tastes, smells and touches, and with the sensory input they are able to experience the world their senses have revealed to them. They know their own burrow and they can identify and utilize leaves and other materials to plug the entrance to their burrow. They are able to identify other members of their species – they visualize (in the broadest sense) them and sometimes travel together. So, yes indeed, much to my surprise, earthworms have an inner life. I have a whole new respect for the earthworms in our garden and I experience them very differently now than I did for most of my life.

* * * * * * *

It seems sometimes like the universe delivers exactly what you need, or so the saying goes. Or perhaps it's just that a receptive mind is primed for helpful surprises. Shortly after I wrote the first part of this Chapter, I happened upon an article about plant intelligence. That led me to another and another and another. Eventually, I was awash in theories about whether plants are conscious or not – whether they have an inner life. One group of scholars says no. Plants do not have nervous systems or anything even remotely resembling a brain and therefore can't possibly have an inner life. Another group sees it differently. They start with the established fact that plants can react to stimuli in very specific ways and alter their behavior in response to the stimuli. Consider that certain plants can sense when ants are approaching to collect nectar and they react defensively by closing up to foil the attempted pilferage. Other plants can sense hornworms nibbling on their nether regions and warn surrounding plants by exuding a particular scent that the nearby plants react to by releasing chemicals that drive the hornworms away. In other words, the plants are communicating information from one to another. Plants also can be described as expressing preferences in favor of beneficial conditions by turning their leaves toward the sun or directing their roots toward water.

Suzanne Simard is Professor of forest ecology at the University of British Columbia. She has spent years researching whether and how trees communicate with one another in the forest. Her findings are startling. She's shown that trees are connected to one another by an underground network of mycelium, threadlike fibers. It is through this network that trees are able to "talk" to one another, communicating things like the status of nutrients, which a tree with a surplus will then send to a tree experiencing a deficit. The trees also show preferences for their offspring over other members of the forest community they're connected with. They send nutrients more readily to their "children" than they do to trees they are related to only more distantly. Conventional wisdom had been that trees compete with one another for resources in the forest. The discoveries of Dr. Simard and others have upended that thinking. While there is certainly some competition, it now seems that the citizens of the forest cooperate with one another as well – and to a remarkable degree.

In a 2017 study, researchers from the Center for Bioscience Research and Education at the University of Bonn, Germany, investigated whether anesthetics had any effect on plants. Their findings were pretty remarkable. The same anesthetics used to render humans and other animals unconscious were administered to particular plants, including Venus flytraps and peas. While subject to the effects of the anesthetics, the plants became inactive. Once the anesthetics wore off, the plants returned to their normal activities. Some of this was captured in time-lapse videos. Particularly interesting to me were the pea plant videos. Normally, pea plant seedlings have tendrils that very slowly sway back and forth, searching for something to attach to. After application of the anesthetic, the seedling tendrils stopped moving at all. It almost looked like they'd gone to sleep. When anesthetic was applied to the Venus Flytrap, which normally snaps an articulated leaf shut to trap and digest an insect, the plant became entirely unresponsive for about an hour until the anesthetic wore off. It then resumed its normal behavior of trapping flies. The New York Times published a story about this study and suggested that for plants to be rendered unconscious by anesthetics, they had to be conscious in the first place. That drew quite a backlash, with some people accusing the Times of anthropomorphizing plants. Perhaps.

Researchers have also found that plants have memory — that they are able to store, recall and apply information about past experiences. For example, one study showed that when a plant was dropped a short distance, it's leaves would close up. But after a few repetitions, the plant *realized* it wasn't being harmed by the drop and it abandoned the defensive leaf-closing reaction.

So, are plants intelligent like Darwin's Worms? I don't know the answer to that. But we shouldn't completely foreclose the possibility that plants have an inner life. It's certainly not like yours or mine or Jack's or even Darwin's Worms, but we may in time come to a fuller understanding and conclude that they do.

Let's pivot now and allow our story to venture closer to home — to the human brain — or at least the brain our experience seems to tell us we have. So far, we've explored the inner life of Jack and earthworms and plants and Pet Rocks based on inferences from their behaviors. While we have confidence these inferences are correct, our view has been only objective — we have viewed these inner experiences from the outside because we can't experience what they're experiencing in the way they're experiencing it. We have instead looked at results — actions or reactions — and deduced what precipitated those results. But there is an inner life we are more intimately familiar with because we experience it directly. It's our own inner life. Uniquely, we have the subjective experience of our own inner life. We don't need to deduce what's going on inside our own brains because we know it intimately. We know it first-hand. Or so it seems. Let's see what we can learn and, in the process, try to understand whether human cognition is different somehow from other animals (and perhaps plants) and, if so, in what ways.

Chapter 7

Cogito Ergo Sum

Before the days of the photocopier, the Mimeograph machine reigned supreme. Mimeo, as it was colloquially referred to, became ubiquitous in offices and schools in the 1940s and 1950s. The way Mimeo worked was you'd create a stencil by typing onto a sheet of special stenciling paper. The typing cut the letters out on the paper. When the stencil was complete, it was attached to a round drum and a copy was produced when ink was forced through the stencil onto a second sheet of paper as the drum turned. Mimeo ink had a distinctive purple hue and a very distinctive smell, a little like wet glue. The handouts you got in school, including tests, were always produced by Mimeo. Sometimes they were still wet and left a purple stain on your fingers.

On my first day of High School I received a mimeo sheet listing in that distinctive purplish ink the requirements I would have to satisfy to get out of the place four years later. Beneath the mandatory science, math and humanities courses I would need to take, lurked this unexpected entry: "Foreign Language – two years." Other kids noticed it too and we all chatted about the options. I learned that French was the preferred choice. All the cool kids, particularly the cute girls, took French, a course of study from which they emerged with what they doubtless imagined were darling little French accents. But I didn't have any real interest in learning French. Spanish was another option. But I'd never been to Mexico and didn't really anticipate going there (little did I know I'd end up traipsing around Mexico, Central America and South America dozens of times for work and pleasure over the ensuing half-century and Spanish would therefore have been an exceedingly wise choice).

The only "foreign" language choice left to me, the only other one offered, was Latin. I don't know why I chose it, other than by default, but that's what I did. Maybe it was a childish act of rebellion. Or maybe, since my Grandfather who had died five years before spoke Latin fluently, it was my unconscious effort to emulate him. I didn't know much about it. I was aware it was ancient and referred to as a "dead language." I also knew that some books I'd read already were originally written in Latin, stories like the Aeneid, a poem composed by Virgil in ancient Rome.

Don't even ask why I was reading the Aeneid at such a young age. The truth is I happened upon it on a bookshelf at home. Dad and his brother and sister divided Grandpa's things when he died and each one took some of Grandpa's collection of books. All the books were old, published mostly in the latter part of the 1800s or the early 1900s. They were musty and bore the patina of age. I'd like to say I was interested in books like the Aeneid because I was intellectually curious, but that would ascribe motives to my young self that are far too virtuous. The unvarnished truth is I thought it would make me *seem* smart and be impressive to family and friends, particularly my father, for me to have read these volumes. And that was the motive force that led me to pluck the little thin green volume of Virgil's Aeneid from the bookshelf at the tender age of eleven. In spite of those dubious motivations, I actually enjoyed the story of Aeneas. It wasn't quite up to the literary heft of the Hardy Boys, which I was also consuming at the time. But the story was interesting nonetheless – a tale filled with Greek Gods and the many tragic tribulations of Aeneas as he left his homeland in Troy and eventually founded the new city of Rome.

Although the foreign language requirement in High School was just two years, I ended up taking Latin for all four years of my enrollment at Cherry Creek High. The teacher in all years but one was Mrs. Wilson, who looked, spoke and acted in all respects exactly as you'd imagine a High School Latin teacher in the mid-1960s. She was a bit portly, seemed always to wear flower-print dresses, had wavy salt and pepper hair that was clipped short, and she of course was fitted with rimless glasses. We didn't start out reading ancient texts in the first year. We started with vocabulary and moved on to grammar. We learned immensely useful things, like conjugating the verb love: *Amo, amas, amat, amamus, amatis, amant* (I love, you love, he/she/it loves, we love, you love, they love). By my junior and senior years, we were actually reading and, hard to imagine, speaking to one another in Latin. We read little snippets of text at first, simple things, phrases, then sentences and then paragraphs. Eventually, we were reading some of the classics in their original Latin form. The one still committed to my memory to this day is Julius Caesar's Commentaries on the Gallic Wars. It began: *Gallia est omnis divisa in partes tres*, which meant: *Gaul is divided into three parts*. Caesar had conquered ancient Gaul and the victor was thus recording the history of his conquest. We eventually read the Aeneid in Latin, along with other ancient texts, which were about as far afield from suburban Denver in mid-century as one could possibly imagine.

You would have guessed that four years of Latin was more than enough, but that was not to be. As a college undergraduate I was confronted with yet another foreign language requirement and having already invested four years in Latin, my eighteen-year-old self reasoned why bother with Spanish or French or the broader offerings available by the time I was in college, Russian, Chinese, and Japanese, to name just a few. No, instead, I continued with my Latin studies. And not just for two years, mind you, which would have satisfied the collegiate foreign language requirement. No, I took Latin for all four years in college. In the end, I devoted eight precious and irreplaceable years to the study of Latin. Happily, it turned out that my eight years of study has served some purpose.

Cogito ergo sum is, conveniently, a Latin phrase and my more than passing acquaintance with the language allows me to recognize *cogito* as the verb "think." We find it as the root of English words like cognition, cognitive and cognate. *Ergo* is commonly translated into English as "therefore." It connotes one thing occurring after and as a result or consequence of another. *Sum* in Latin means to be, to exist, and *sum* is the present case of the verb. Put it all together and you get:

"I think, therefore I am."

We have Rene Descartes, whom we have briefly encountered before in this book, along with his fluency in Latin, to blame or praise for this phrase. Although, to be perfectly accurate, Descartes originally recorded the thought in French, not Latin, in *Discourse on the Method* in 1637. It wasn't until seven years later that he published *Principles of Philosophy*, which *was* written in Latin, and it is there we finally find the famous words: *cogito ergo sum*. In these writings Descartes was, as many had before him, trying to make sense of the world and his place in it. He was employing logic in an effort to distinguish between what was true and what wasn't and he, like other philosophers, was trying to set an anchor – to find some principle or concept he could count on as true and then build an understanding on the foundation of that truth. To get to that foundation, he first concludes there is no certainty to what we think of as Reality. We know that sometimes our perceptions are deceptive or at least can't be fully counted on, as we saw with the visual illustrations at the end of Chapter 3. We may think we see, hear, feel, touch or taste something that turns out not to be the case. Since our perceptions are extremely fallible, we cannot count what our senses tell us about the world as undeniably true. So too, our reasoning – our ability to arrive at a correct conclusion from particular premises – is sometimes flawed as common experience demonstrates to us time and time again and as we saw with Dr. Duncan MacDougall at the beginning of Chapter 1.

Descartes notes, as an example, that when we're dreaming we think we are experiencing something real, but the dream is just an illusion and we are (at least some of the time) ignorant of that fact while we're dreaming. So, what we think we experience of the real world could be like a dream – just an illusion. Rejecting sensations and reasoning as the foundation of truth, Descartes settles on what he calls his first principle of philosophy, the fact that "I" am thinking these thoughts and having these doubts about what is real proves unequivocally that the Self exists. Because I think, I must be. Descartes concludes that the very existence of doubt about our existence necessarily establishes the existence of the Self, the one that is doing the doubting. For Descartes, that is the certain, firm and comforting foundation upon which further explorations can begin and further understanding of the world can be built.

Descartes continued his philosophizing in *Meditations on First Philosophy*, first published in 1641, after *Discourse on the Method* and before *Principles of Philosophy*. In *Mediations,* Descartes builds on his first principle that the Self exists and he examines the nature of that Self. Ultimately, he "proves," using his logical method, that what he dubs the mind – the "I" that is doing the thinking – has to be separate from the corporeal body, even though the two are conjoined for a time while the body (assuming the body actually exists) is alive. The cleavage of the incorporeal mind from the physical body is generally called dualism or Cartesian dualism and it fundamentally altered the path of Western thought.

Having separated the mind from the body, Descartes reasons that the Soul must be located outside of the body, in the mind. Perhaps not surprisingly, he also concludes that the Soul doesn't have an expiration date – it isn't perishable but persists and continues after the death of the body. It is immortal. Although Cartesian logic was criticized by many thinkers, both during Descartes' lifetime and since, dualism became and remains deeply embedded in, if not a hallmark of, Western thought and culture. The thinking that there is a body, which includes the brain, and something separate from the body – some magical essence – is so much a part of our collective story that it's exceedingly difficult to view the world through any other lens. And once the magical essence of mind comes onto the scene, the course is set and all thinking leads invariably to the immortal Soul and the Divine, that which gave rise to the Soul. It may be that we end up in the same place Descartes did as we explore these topics in this book. But for now, let's continue to steer clear of the notion that there is a mind separate from the body so we don't get trapped into the pre-determined outcome of an immortal Soul. Instead, let's begin with what we know – or at least what we seem to know.

I seem to experience an inner life. Scientific inquiry about the source of that inner life has progressed quite far, although we still don't fully understand the physical mechanisms and processes that result in our subjective experience of an inner life. Those processes are where nearly all the scientific research has been concentrated. There are thousands of studies that have examined the human (or animal) brain to see precisely what portions of the brain become activated under various conditions. Researchers have extensively mapped the brain, finding the areas giving rise to feelings of love or hate, attraction or repulsion, excitation, hunger, warmth, cold, tasting, touching, hearing, smelling and seeing, dreaming, and on and on and on. There have been numerous studies of the brain while meditating, thinking and visualizing. Scientists have investigated and isolated the physical and chemical processes that result in emotions, memory and thinking and have studied and mapped the brain in excruciating detail. But all this science is directed toward answering "how" questions – questions about the mechanisms employed by the brain in processing, storing and interpreting information. The reason for that focus is because those are the questions that can be answered by the scientific method, by experimental techniques. But these experiments and the discoveries they have revealed are all about mechanics, not substance. What we are exploring in this book is a very different and, in many ways, a much more mysterious and deeper question: what is my inner life? We can't answer that question by examining brain processes. Instead, we need to understand how we are experiencing those processes – we need to understand our inner life. To do that, we need to examine the nature of the subjective experience the brain is having, something not easily capable of or well suited to scientific inquiry.

In our Reality the brain is a physical organ in the body of many animals, both vertebrates and invertebrates, including you and me. The brain itself is isolated from the world outside of the body. Essentially, it exists in a dark and silent void inside the brainpan. On its own, the brain can't sense anything. It can't see or hear, smell, taste or touch. It doesn't have the ability to experience anything at all. On its own, isolated and alone in the skull, the brain doesn't know anything about time, space or matter. The brain in this unconnected state has no conception of the world around it or the body within which it is entombed.

We know from long study that the brain has a number of distinct functions. One of those functions is to receive and process sensory data into information that is useful to our body. We normally recognize five senses – sight, sound, smell, touch and taste – and the body has sensors capable of receiving sensory data corresponding to the five sensations and relaying that data to the brain for processing. It is from this data that the brain is able to experience the world and it is from those experiences that the brain constructs the world – constructs its Reality.

The brain's ability to "see" is a consequence of sensory input from the human eye, a sensor capable of recognizing light, electromagnetic radiation, within the range of about 390 to 700 nanometers. The raw data received by the two eyes is transferred via the optic nerve, which connects the eyes to the brain. There is a specific region of the brain, the visual cortex, adapted to processing the raw visual data. The visual cortex resides in the cerebral cortex at the back of the brain. The cerebral cortex exists in both the left and right sides of the brain and the visual cortex on the left side processes data from the left eye, while the visual cortex on the right-side processes data from the sensor we call the right eye. These eye and brain processes combine to give us the experience of sight.

The brain's ability to "hear" arises from sensory input received by the ears. The ears are surprisingly complex sensors, beautifully adapted to the task of receiving vibrations from the external world and transmitting data about those vibrations to the brain. The ears consist of an outer flap of skin and cartilage that focuses and directs sound into the ear canal, where it interacts with the tympanic membrane (appropriately called the "ear drum"), a thin piece of tissue at the end of each ear canal. When sounds, which are just vibrations, come in contact with the tympanic membrane, they set it to vibrating and the vibrations cause little bones in the middle ear to move. The little bones generate neural impulses in more than 10,000 sensory cells that make up the cochlear nerve. Eventually, the impulses make their way to the brain where they create the sensation, the inner experience, of sound outside of the body.

The senses of taste, touch and smell have their own miraculous structures and receptors in the body that receive and transmit data to the brain over pathways dedicated to each particular sensor. Collectively, these specialized sensors in our body connect the brain to the outside world and it is because of this vast array of sensory input that we are able to perceive the world. We use those perceptions to construct our story of the world around us. But what is this inner life we experience as a result of all of this sensory input? Let's explore that next.

Chapter 8

The Narrative

When we pay close attention to our inner life, we see that it has different aspects or qualities. In its most basic aspect, our experience of the world is like a movie, a deeply engrossing, totally consuming movie that includes not just sights and sounds, but tastes and smells and touches as well. We constantly experience the world around us as filtered by and through our senses and interpreted by our brain. I call this ongoing story the Narrative.

Most of the time the Narrative is so absorbing of our attention that we're not even aware we're immersed in it. Some years ago, I had to fly from Denver to Washington D.C. I didn't have anything to read and stopped in the airport bookstore to pick up a book to occupy my time on the flight. My eyes were drawn to *A Walk in the Woods*, a book by Bill Bryson that I hadn't read. I was familiar with and had read some of Bryson's other books and always enjoyed his dry British wit and his breezy writing style. That was exactly what I wanted for this plane ride. Once onboard, I settled into my seat, opened the book and started to read. I vaguely remember the plane taking off and the next thing I knew the Captain was announcing our descent into Washington. Although I know I was on the plane for about three and a half hours, I remember almost nothing that occurred during the flight. I was so absorbed in the often hilarious story of Bryson's middle-aged effort to traverse the Appalachian Trail, that I was unaware of the events that doubtless occurred around me while I was reading – the drink and meal service (which I apparently declined), people getting up from their seats and walking past me in my aisle seat, and even the passage of time all occurred without my conscious awareness.

For some people, watching sports can be absorbing in the same way as reading the book was for me. You become so involved in the action of the football, basketball, hockey or soccer game that you're not aware of anything else going on around you. Or maybe you've experienced something like this while participating in some other activity. Maybe it was a long hike or a walk or a drive through the countryside. Maybe the activity had an element of danger or maybe it was quite mundane. Whatever the specific circumstance, I think we've all had this kind of deeply absorbing experience where we are focused solely on one thing and even the perception of time feels altered – either flying by unnoticed or slowing to a crawl. These types of experiences involve an all-absorbing concentration – the kind of deep concentration that blocks out everything else.

The unfolding Narrative of your world in real time is just that kind of experience. You are so absorbed in what's occurring before you that you lose track of yourself, you forget that you are a person, a brain encased in a skull, receiving sensory input, distilling it all down into what you perceive as the unfolding events of your experience. You forget that the brain is operating the body, causing it to breathe and circulate blood, releasing chemicals that cause muscles to contract or release, digesting food, processing waste and the hundreds of other little tasks that keep us animate.

One of my favorite movies of all time is *Raiders of the Lost Ark*, which I am sure I've seen fifty times. *Raiders* opens with the central character, Dr. Henry Walton "Indiana" Jones, Jr., and a few native porters tromping through a foggy South American jungle with tropical birds tweeting in the background. It's obviously an expedition of some kind. A porter hacks at the underbrush with a machete, revealing a large carved stone, suggesting they're on the right track for whatever they're looking for. Eventually, the party comes to a waterfall cascading into a pond. Scrambling up a small hill, Indiana locates the stone entrance to a temple and enters, encountering an overgrowth of vines and of course, spider webs. Continuing into the temple, he finds the sacred golden idol of a fertility goddess resting on an ancient round stone pedestal. He deftly swaps the golden idol for a similarly weighted bag of sand and walks away, smugly satisfied that his dexterity and cleverness have allowed him to avoid the many deadly bobby traps laid in the temple to which he might have succumbed. That of course was not to be. Instead, after a few seconds the temple begins to collapse around him and Jones is forced to flee for his life. To escape, he has to outrun an enormous stone ball rolling after him and threatening to either crush him or block his exit. Miraculously, he succeeds, catapulting his body out of the temple entrance just in the nick of time and landing back in the jungle. It's heart-pounding cinema at its best.

Indiana Jones is just a character in a movie. The character has no awareness that he is being played by the actor, Harrison Ford, or that the scenes taking place in the movie are occurring on constructed sets. Indiana isn't aware that there are lights and cameras and microphones and wires galore, strewn about the set. He doesn't know he's just reciting words from a script that a team of writers penned and he's speaking the lines that were assigned to him. To Indy, his love interest, Marion, is the daughter of his mentor, not the actress Karen Allen, who is just playing a role. If you can imagine it, to the character Indiana Jones the full extent of his Reality is whatever occurs in the film and that alone. That is Indy's Narrative, the story within which he exists. All that came together to allow the film to be made, the writers, the producers, the director, the other actors, the post-production team, the composer of the soundtrack and the scores of others, are not within Indiana's realm of experience. They are not part of his Narrative. But looked at from the perspective of the director of the movie, Steven Spielberg, the Narrative – his Narrative – would be quite different. Spielberg experienced the planning of the film, the selection of the actors, directing the performances of Harrison Ford, Karen Allen and the rest, and then guiding the combination of all the separate elements into a coherent film in the editing room. So, Spielberg had a Narrative, a set of experiences relating to Raiders of the Lost Ark, but his Narrative was very different from what Indy would have experienced. Neither Indy's Narrative nor Steven Spielberg's are right or wrong. They are just different.

The Narrative is our story. It is, in a very real way, our life. It includes everything that happens during the day that our sensory apparatus is capable of perceiving. The Narrative begins as each new day dawns and we shake off the slumber of the preceding night. It continues as we dress and begin our daily activities and abides as we enjoy dinner and then prepare to wind down for the day. The Narrative comes to a temporary end as we slide into bed at night, pull the covers over our shoulders and close our eyes to find sleep. It then begins anew the next day in the same way.

Star Trek: The Next Generation ran for seven seasons beginning in 1987. *TNG*, as it was known to the cognoscenti, had some wonderful technology and my favorite of all the devices was the Holodeck. The Holodeck was a room on the Starship Enterprise that projected holographic images in a way that simulated whatever place and objects that had been programed into the Holodeck computer. The Holodeck allowed you to return to the earth and picnic at a favorite lakeside spot, climb mountains or experience historic events. Anything that could be programmed into the computer could be recreated with perfect realism on the Holodeck. You got to experience sights and sounds, of course; but also tastes, smells and even the way things felt were perfectly simulated and seemed "real." The Holodeck was so advanced that it could even generate images of people, holographic people that seemed realistic in every detail.

The third episode of season two was titled *Elementary, Dear Data*. The Holodeck had been programmed with a Sherlock Holmes mystery and Chief Engineer Geordi LaForge and the android, Commander Data, played the parts of Dr. Watson and Sherlock Holmes in the Holodeck-generated adventure. The game was to solve the Holmesian mystery and catch the evil-doer. But Data always spoiled the game because he knew all of the Sherlock Holmes stories and figured out who done it very shortly after each session started, to the chagrin of his shipmates who were playing other parts in the little game. Geordi was frustrated and tried to explain to Data that he was ruining the fun, which was trying to solve a mystery that had an unknown outcome. After discussion of the dilemma with other crew members, Geordi came up with the cure: he instructed the computer to create a unique Sherlock Holmes mystery with an adversary that could outwit Data.

Once the new story starts playing on the Holodeck, we learn that a crew member has been kidnaped by the evil genius Dr. Moriarty. Data tracks Moriarty to his lair, where he and Geordi confront him. They're pretty shocked when Moriarty makes it clear he's aware that they are role-playing in a Holodeck simulation and that he knows he is a character in that simulation. By interacting with the Enterprise computer, which the Holodeck character shouldn't have had any knowledge of, Moriarty has also learned about the Enterprise and that the Holodeck is housed on the starship. At this point, Geordi realizes his error. He instructed the computer to create an adversary that could defeat Data – not Holmes – and the computer complied by giving the Holodeck character Moriarty self-awareness, as well as access to knowledge of the Reality of the wider world beyond the Holodeck. Oops! Careful what you ask for, Geordi.

Eventually, Captain Picard joins the others on the Holodeck and Moriarty asks Picard to let him leave the Holodeck and join them in the "real" world. Picard demurs, explaining that even though Moriarty has acquired self-awareness, he can still exist only within the four walls of the Holodeck. Picard promises to work on a solution to the problem and to free Moriarty when a solution is found. Picard tells the computer to conclude the Holodeck program and everything within the Holodeck, including the Moriarty character, disappears, apparently stored in the computer's memory.

You can see the parallels between what we've been exploring and the ideas treated in this Star Trek episode. The Holodeck is analogous to the Narrative. It is the unfolding story that the characters on the Holodeck are experiencing in real time. The characters generated by the Holodeck computer are normally just acting their roles in whatever scene might be unfolding at the moment. They are at the most basic stage of the Self. They are awake and aware, but they are not self-aware. Although they experience the Reality they inhabit on the Holodeck, they are not aware of their awareness. They are just acting in a play, but they don't know that's what they're doing. They also don't ask existential questions. They don't ask who they are or where they came from. It doesn't occur to them that there is anything outside of or beyond the experiences they're having on the Holodeck. Unlike the other computer-generated characters in the Holodeck simulation, the computer created a different kind of Moriarty, a Holodeck being that had the capacity of self-awareness. That self-awareness allowed Moriarty to question the nature of his existence and to realize that his Narrative was wider than the Narrative the other Holodeck characters experienced.

The Reality theme was played with a bit more in a later Star Trek episode called *Ship in a Bottle,* where Professor Moriarty is reprised and brought back to life on the Holodeck. Moriarty confronts Captain Picard with his promise to find a way for Moriarty to escape the confines of the Holodeck world and join other self-aware beings in the "real" world. Picard claims they've been trying but haven't yet been successful. Moriarty then stuns everyone as he walks to the door that connects the Holodeck with the corridor on the Enterprise and steps out of the Holodeck and into a hallway, a feat that was supposed to be impossible. When questioned about how he was able to perform this magic, Moriarty coyly exclaims "I think, therefore I am," referring of course to our friend Descartes. Eventually, the Enterprise gang figures out that Professor Moriarty never left the Holodeck, he just reprogramed the simulation so other parts of the Enterprise became part of the Holodeck program. So, everyone had been unknowingly prancing around on the Holodeck, thinking they were on other parts of the ship. Pretty clever Moriarty. Picard then uses Moriarty's ruse against him, pretending to beam him out of the Holodeck and onto a shuttlecraft so he can explore the universe. The shuttlecraft, though, was also part of the Holodeck simulation. Picard ends the Holodeck program and steps out of the Holodeck to the real Enterprise. The episode concludes with Picard mentioning to a crew member who's been aware of everything going on, that perhaps the crews' entire reality is just a simulation generated by someone else's version of a Holodeck. The crew member appears concerned at the prospect and tests whether it's true by saying "end program," the command given to terminate a Holodeck session. Nothing happens and the crew member appears relieved, convinced that his reality is real and not a Holodeck simulation.

The Star Trek episodes illustrate something we already know – the Narrative can be a confusing thing. We're not very good at judging Reality and distinguishing that which is real from that which isn't. For Moriarty, Reality was limited to the Holodeck simulation, even when it seemed like he had stepped beyond that world. There was simply no way for him to perceive any Beyond. Beyond for him, didn't and couldn't exist. But for "real" people, the Enterprise crew, their Reality was different. They experienced a Narrative that was based on their own perceptions and cognitive abilities, which were different from Moriarty's, and they therefore experienced a different Reality.

Narratives are not limited to humans. All creatures experience a Narrative. Of course, the nature of the Narrative varies from one species to another. Each creature is aware of its surroundings and perceives them in a fashion dictated in part by the nature of its senses, but also determined by how its brain processes the sensory input. Most bats have a sensory ability that humans don't possess. Although first studied in the 18th century, it wasn't until the 1930s that we understood the mechanism that allowed bats to navigate with great precision in total darkness. Donald Griffen studied this question at Harvard and discovered that bats send out high pitched sounds, usually beyond the 20,000 hertz upper limit of human hearing, which bounce back to them and they use to construct a map of their world. This ability, which Griffen dubbed echolocation, allows bats to perceive their world without the illumination humans would need in the same environment. Through echolocation, bats can identify prey and predators and a host of other critical features of their world. They can, in effect, "see" with sound. The nature and quality of the bat's Narrative is different from ours and is shaped by the way they perceive their world. Of course, it isn't just bats and humans that experience a Narrative. All animals do, including Jack and Darwin's worms. Each experiences a Narrative that is uniquely theirs, cobbled together with data generated by their sensory apparatus and organized by their brains.

We have so far been considering our experience of the Narrative in real time or at least with very little lag between what's going on "out there" and our perception or experience of those events. You can think of it like watching a live play, sporting event or concert, where the events are occurring at about the same time as you are experiencing the events. However, there's another way we can and often do experience the Narrative. Our human brains, along with those of many other animals, have the ability to store the experiences of the Narrative and replay those stored experiences more or less on demand. We have a name for this stored Narrative – these stored experiences – we call them memories. Psychologists have a more specific descriptive phrase for these stored experiences. They call them Declarative Memory and they subdivide that into two categories, episodic memory and semantic memory. Episodic memory consists of autobiographical events, past personal experiences. The episodic memory usually extends to more than just the sights and sounds of the event but also includes the emotional content of the event – how you felt at the time – whether you were happy, sad, afraid, surprised or the like. Semantic memory consists of facts, concepts and other things you've learned, like the fact that $1 + 1 = 2$ or the fact that Montpelier Vermont, with less than 8,000 residents, is by far the least populous of the State capitals. While episodic and semantic memory are different, they are intimately related because semantic memories, the facts we know, are usually acquired in an episodic context. For example, my command of the Latin language, my semantic memory about Latin, arose in the context of Mrs. Wilson's classes in High School and later in college. So, I have some episodic memories of Latin classes and I also have a semantic memory of the facts I learned in those classes.

Episodic memory is what we're talking about in the context of the stored Narrative. It is a record of some experience that occurred in your past. To a greater or lesser degree, all the Narrative that passes before the screen of our perception is stored in the brain for future use. There are lots of fascinating questions about the precise mechanism the brain uses to store experiences, as well as the accuracy and reliability of the memories, the Narrative, when retrieved. For example, it's thought that the details of a particular experience are stored separately in different parts of the brain. Sights are stored in one place, sounds in another, smells in another and feelings associated with the experience are stored somewhere else. The brain associates all these separate pieces with one another and when the memory is recalled, the disparate sense impressions are brought back together and combined. So, the Narrative is not stored in the brain like a movie is stored on film. The process is more like the way computers work, associating bits of data, in this case, sense impressions, with one another, storing them in different places on a hard drive, and stamping them with time-sequencing information so it all can be retrieved and brought together to be replayed about as it originally occurred.

It's also important to recognize that the brain perceives the retrieved Narrative as different from the original experience. The brain experiences the replayed Narrative as a re-watching. In other words, the brain knows that experiencing a once stored and now retrieved Narrative is different from the original experience. That has to the case because we otherwise wouldn't be able to distinguish between the memory of an event and the original experience. To say it another way, we are automatically and inherently able to notice the difference between having an original experience and reliving the experience at a later time as a stored memory. In fact, the ability to tell one from the other is so significant that mental health professionals regard a circumstance where the brain is unable to distinguish between a current experience and a recalled one as a neurological or psychological malfunction. They have a name for the condition. It's called a hallucination, which psychologists define as an apparent perception that arises without external stimuli.

How much of what we experience are we able to recall? It's a question for which researchers don't have a good answer. What we recall depends on a variety of different factors, like how long ago the original experience occurred, how many times we've replayed that piece of the Narrative before, the emotional context of the original experience (how emotionally intense it was), whether the emotions were happy or sad or mundane or unusual, how the snippet of Narrative connects to other snippets of Narrative, and a host of other factors. Sometimes our recollection of pieces of the stored Narrative seems crystal clear and certain. Other times, it's fuzzy and we're not sure whether our recollection is right or not. The most eminent experts in the field of memory science tell us a number of pretty startling things. Among the most interesting: memory is very unreliable and the details of an experience are often not remembered, but are filled in on recall with what we think "probably" occurred; sometimes we have gotten information about an event from a source other than our first-person experience of the event and we don't recognize the difference; and sometimes what we think we remember never happened at all – a so-called false memory.

Even accepting all the uncertainty about memory, we know that the Narrative is stored in the brain to some level of accuracy and that scenes of the Narrative are subject to recall at a later time. As we begin to explore that aspect of our inner life that is the stored Narrative in greater detail, we can identify a number of really interesting features. First, the stored Narrative that records your life experiences doesn't begin at birth, but sometime after, and it continues until the present moment, where it coalesces with the current Narrative. I have no recollection whatever of the event of my birth, which is odd when you think about it. I had led a comfortable existence in my mother's womb for nine months, floating in fluid the same temperature as my body, breathing by absorbing oxygen through the umbilical cord and taking in nourishment the same way. Suddenly, I was thrust into an alien, inhospitable environment. The fluid drained from my lungs and I took my first breath. The cool air of the hospital room was a shock to my system and I was swaddled in a blue blanket to keep me warm. I experienced my mother for the first time, at least from the outside. This experience certainly must be one of the most momentous of my life, far more momentous than when I broke my leg while skiing or nearly severed the second finger on my left hand with a carpet knife, both experiences I remember in perfect detail. But I don't remember my birth at all. I simply have no recollection whatsoever of the event.

I also don't remember driving home from the hospital with my parents after I was born, arriving at the gala homecoming in the apartment as a newborn, eating, drinking, playing with the dog, learning to roll over or sit up, learning to walk, my first birthday, my second birthday or much of anything else that must have occurred in the early years of my life. In fact, my Narrative is largely blank until about the age of three. It's as though nothing happened during those formative years. But I know that couldn't be the case. I've seen yellowed Polaroid pictures of family and friends gathered around the table for my early birthday parties, of Bobby the Irish Setter and of me in a cowboy outfit with toy six-guns strapped to my side. I've seen the ancient 8 milimeter home movies taken when I was little that attest to my existence and agency. But I am unable to summon up any Narrative of those early years.

What seems to have happened is either my brain didn't process the Narrative into a coherent story or for some reason, it didn't store the Narrative of those formative years for later retrieval. My lack of an early childhood Narrative is hardly unique. Indeed, it is so common that Psychologists have labeled the condition infantile or childhood amnesia. There are a raft of theories about its cause. Freud once proposed that it was a reaction to childhood trauma, a theory he later abandoned. Others argue that the brain doesn't develop sufficiently to store autobiographical memories until about the age of four. Still others argue that memories don't arise until the brain develops sufficiently to create a sense of Self. Regardless of the mechanism or the cause, the point is that my Narrative (and that of most everyone else) begins long after birth and not with the first sensations that made it to my brain as a newly born human being.

A second feature of the stored Narrative is that it seems more or less continuous. To be sure, there are gaps in the Narrative, days, weeks, months or years where you don't remember at all what happened or the details of things you believe may have occurred. I'm not suggesting the Narrative is perfect or that it's complete, just that the Narrative begins at some point during your life and has continued until this moment. The richness of the detail in my Narrative varies from time to time. Some days, weeks, months, years and even decades are a blur. Others I recall in rich and full detail. Some experiences I remember well. Others I know happened, but I don't remember the details of them at all.

A third aspect of the stored Narrative is that it, like the current Narrative, exists only in the first-person. The Narrative is always experienced from my personal subjective perspective. In 1985, my youngest son Henry was a baby, just one year old. I had to fly to Parkersburg, West

Virginia, for a business meeting. The route to Parkersburg was circuitous, requiring a couple of stops and plane changes. It was winter, cold and rainy, when I landed after dark at the little airport in Parkersburg following a brief stop in Charlotte. I was surprised to be met by a uniformed gate agent as I deplaned. She asked if I was Mr. Appel, to which I replied that I was, and she handed me a letter-sized piece of white paper that had been folded in half. On the front was written "Mr. Garry Appel" in red ink. I unfolded the paper and read: "Phone your wife immediately" and then it gave a phone number I didn't recognize with a Denver area code.

I remember my breath coming in quick gasps and feeling my heart pounding in my chest as I asked the agent, who was still standing there, if I could borrow a phone. She escorted me about twenty feet to the gate desk. I remember punching the phone number on the black desk phone, but the call didn't go through. The gate agent, still standing with me, told me to first dial "8" to get an outside line. I punched in the 8 and then the long-distance number I didn't recognize that was written on the white piece of paper. My wife answered. Not making any effort to disguise my concern, I asked: "what's going on?" She started to cry and I could hear her straining to breathe. I asked again, "Honey, what's the matter?" Eventually, she said, "you need to get back here right-away." "Why," I pleaded, "what's the matter?" "Henry's in the hospital. We're at Children's. The doctors don't think he'll make it to the morning," she said.

I could barely breathe. The blood drained from my head. I gasped for air. "I'm in West Virginia. I don't know if I can even get out of here tonight. I'll see you as soon as I can." I hung up the phone and all manner of thoughts, helpful and stupid, flooded my brain at once. What was the matter with Henry (I hadn't asked)? Should I try to get home (of course I should) and miss my meeting in the morning? Or wait until morning and then leave if necessary (of course not)? How to get home? Any flights out of this little airport this late? Or rent a car and drive to Charlotte? Would there be flights out of Charlotte so late? How far is it to a bigger airport, like Pittsburg? I said to the gate agent, who was still by my side, "It's an emergency, I need to get back to Denver tonight." She looked at me caringly and said: "there aren't any flights out of here until the morning." After what seemed an eternity, she helped arrange a rental car back to Charlotte and a red-eye flight from Charlotte to Chicago to Denver that arrived in Denver about 6:30 in the morning. Worried out of my mind on the return trip, I retrieved my car from the parking lot at Stapleton, the name of the Denver airport at the time, and drove the twenty minutes to Children's Hospital. I found my wife in the NIC-U, the Neonatal Intensive Care Unit, and was greeted with these words: "He made it through the night and the doctors think he'll make it." We hugged each other for dear life and both began to cry.

I remember these scenes – this portion of the stored Narrative – in exquisite detail, like the events took place yesterday. I remember the emotions I felt. Even thinking about it now, so many years later, recalls those emotions and brings tears to my eyes. I remember what I saw. I remember the sounds and the smells. I remember how I felt, the fear, the anger, the helplessness. I remember all my thoughts, both crazy and sane. But what is truly interesting and remarkable about these scenes within the Narrative of my life is that I don't *know* what any of the other characters in this drama saw or felt or sensed or thought. I can *assume* the gate agent was caring, concerned and sympathetic about my situation, but I don't know the story from her side. I don't know what she was experiencing. What I know of her experience of her encounter with me on that winter night was only because of *my* experience of her cues – what she said to me, her facial expressions and the like. The same is true of my wife. Although I knew her intimately, I did not experience the events from her side. All I knew of her experience of the events was from my experience of her experience.

These scenes were experienced solely from my vantage point and that's how they were recorded in the Narrative. The Narrative is always this way. It is always told only in the first-person, from my point of view. There is no instance in the Narrative where the story is told from the viewpoint or perspective of another person. It is very distinctly and solely *my* story.

A fourth feature of the stored Narrative, which also is true of the current Narrative, is that I am the central character. It is the story of me, my actions and inactions, my joys and sorrows, the events which I experienced in one way or another. On November 22, 1963, President Kennedy was assassinated in Dallas Texas. My Dad had been the Chairman of the Denver Democratic Party a couple of years before and he attended the funeral for the President in Washington D.C. I remember hearing the President had been shot. I was playing marbles in the sand at Slavens Elementary at the time and after recess our teacher made an announcement to our sixth-grade class. I had a special affinity for Kennedy. I'd met him briefly three years before when he made a campaign stop in Denver while Dad was the party Chairman. He shook my hand. Even though the President is a character in my Narrative, I did not experience the campaign stop in Denver through his eyes. Instead, I saw his campaign stop only through my eyes. I was the character, the central character, experiencing the events only from my perspective. My Narrative does not, because it could not, record how the then-candidate Kennedy felt while campaigning in Denver, and I could not experience what he thought or felt or sensed as he was felled by the assassin's bullets in Dallas on that November day in 1963. After Dad returned from the funeral, he told me about it, what he saw and the feelings he had, but my Narrative contains only my experience of what Dad told me. I do not and could not know the events as my father saw or felt them. Those formed a part of his Narrative, not mine.

Finally, a fifth important feature of the stored Narrative, a feature shared with the current Narrative, is that it exists only when the central character, Me, is conscious (in the sense of being awake). When the Me character falls asleep in the Narrative, there is no story to extract. As a result, the current Narrative is not active and there is no stored Narrative, no record, no memory, unless I am there to experience the events. Just like falling asleep, on the few occasions in my life when I have lost consciousness, there is a gap in the Narrative that begins when the loss of consciousness arises and ends when I return to wakefulness.

I remember seeing the movie The Reivers in 1969 at the grand old Denver Theater. The movie house had sat on 16th Street since the Great Depression and was eventually demolished in 1980. I was there on a weekday, during the summer, with two friends, whose names I will withhold to protect what remains of their reputations. The primary purpose of our outing was not to see the movie, but to get drunk, that day on peppermint schnapps. I remember little of the movie, but remember in detail swigging the clear, sickly sweet liqueur from the clear bottle while the movie was playing. Not too long into the film, I predictably became sick to my stomach and staggered and stumbled to the men's room, where I spent the remainder of the film in a stall, bent over a white porcelain toilet with a carved wooden seat. After a time, I passed out or at least fell into slumber and the next recollection I have was one of my friends rousing me after the movie ended and helping me out of the bathroom, out of the Denver Theater and onto 16th street. This scene is indelibly part of my Narrative. I can recall and replay it at will. But I have no recollection at all of the time when I was passed out on the floor of the bathroom. The Narrative there is blank.

Many years later I had a minor surgery to repair an inguinal hernia. I arrived at the outpatient surgery center around 6:00 a.m. I remember having to fill out some paperwork and eventually being led to a pre-op room, where other patients were as well. A curtain was drawn around my little space and I undressed, donned a hospital gown and lay down on the hospital gurney. It was cool in the room and I remember getting under the covers and pulling the blanket up to keep warm. After a while, a nurse arrived to insert a line in the vein on the back of my wrist. The big round clock on the wall pointed to 7:00. Eventually, the whole bed, with me aboard, was wheeled off to the operating room. I recall the anesthesiologist asking me to count backward from 100 and I remember saying "100," then "99" and "98" before the Narrative paused as I slipped into unconsciousness. Then follows a gap in the Narrative of unknown length until I awakened in the recovery room. I looked at the large round clock hanging on the wall. It said 8:00. After a while, I dressed, was wheeled to the car and my wife chauffeured me home for bed rest the remainder of the day. It's interesting to notice that I am aware of the gap in the Narrative but have only external clues about the length of that gap. Were it not for the external clues, like my awareness of images of the clock at 7:00 and 8:00, I would have no idea at all of how long the cessation in the Narrative lasted. This is always true of the gaps in Narrative, whether occasioned by sleep or another cause of unconsciousness. We are aware that the gaps exist, but we only know how long they've lasted when we are able to reference external cues. In the case of my anesthetic experience, I assumed I'd been unconscious for an hour. It could have just as well been a week. I wouldn't have any way to know.

The Narrative is the experience we are having at the moment or the recalled memory of what we experienced in the past. But who is this main character in the Narrative? What is its nature? What can we learn about the Self? That is where we head next in our exploration.

Chapter 9

The Selfs

It is of course the Self who is the star of the Narrative, Me, the central character, the one whose Narrative it is. But what is this Self? What is its nature and what are its features and characteristics? To this point in our journey we have observed the Self in several different aspects, although we haven't examined those different aspects in any detail. It's time now to do that. Let's get to know the Self more deeply.

One Self we've become familiar with is the Self that it is having the experiences generated by the senses and interpreted by the brain. This is the Indiana Jones Self, the Holodeck characters (other than Moriarty), the Me that received the urgent note to call home at the Parkersburg airport. This is the Self that is merely a character in the Narrative. It has no awareness of anything other than what is occurring in the moment in the Narrative. The perspective, the point of view, of this Self is always in the first-person. It knows nothing else and is not capable of a broader view of Reality. About four-hundred-twenty years ago, in the play *As You Like It*, William Shakespeare placed these words into the mouth of his character Jaques: "All the world's a stage, and all the men and women merely players." This is a perfect summation of the first Self we've discovered. Let us call this Self the Actor.

While some creatures may be limited to the first-person perspective of the Actor Self, humans are not. The human brain has developed and evolved and become complex enough that it can perform an amazing trick – it can divide the Self into two distinct parts, the Self that is the character in the Narrative, the Actor, and a second Self that is observing the Narrative. This second Self, which we can call the Observer, experiences the Narrative from a different perspective – the third person. This shift in perspective creates a schism, a real division of the Self into two separate aspects and the perspective of the Observer Self, the Narrative it experiences, is different from the Narrative of the Actor Self because the Observer sees the Actor in the Narrative. The opposite, of course, is not true. The Actor Self does not see the Observer and it does not experience the Narrative from the third-person perspective. The Narrative of the Actor Self is therefore more limited because it doesn't include the Observer. These two separate aspects of the Self, the Actor and the Observer, quite literally experience things differently from one another. They experience two different Realities. They live in two different Castles.

Now here's the really fascinating part: the Observer Self that is observing the Actor Self as a separate "thing" in the world doesn't recognize that the apparent separateness between it and the Actor is just an illusion – a trick played by the brain – and that the Actor it is watching is the same as the Observer that is doing the watching. To the Observer, the illusion of separateness is so strong, so compelling, that the Self has effectively split into two separate entities, each having distinct characteristics and a distinct perspective.

The simultaneous first and third-person perspectives abiding within the same brain isn't limited to humans. Animals other than humans experience this schism too. As we saw in Chapter 5, Jack is capable of cognitive mapping – creating a mental model of his world in which things are located, including Jack and his red ball. Without the third-person perspective of the Observer, the cognitive map wouldn't make any sense to Jack and he couldn't utilize it to plot a course to the red ball. It is only the shift in perspective from the first-person to the third-person, and the division of Self into two parts that is a consequence of the shift in perspective, that makes the cognitive map possible. And Jack and his kin aren't the only animals in this club. It's a broad and inclusive group that can count many members of the animal kingdom within its orbit. All these creatures have the same ability and partake of the third-person perspective.

Our brains did not stop their physical and functional evolution with the emergence of the Observer and the separation of the Observer from the Actor. As our brains continued to grow, expand and become more complex as a species, developing more capabilities, something truly remarkable arose – the capacity for language. The origin and development of language in humans is a topic about which experts – linguists, anthropologists and archaeologists – diverge quite significantly. They haven't been able to reach any consensus about how language arose or even when it began. Some argue passionately that the capacity for language evolved over time. Others argue it happened all at once in a great evolutionary leap. Some argue there was one proto-language, a mother tongue, and that all other languages evolved from that common ancestral language. Others argue that many different languages evolved independently and there was no common historical language. Because of the multiplicity of largely inconsistent views, what follows is not offered as a summary of current scholarly thought, because there is no consensus view. In this field it seems like everyone has their own theory and the theories are literally all over the map.

Instead, I here present my opinions, based on what I know, what I've read and what I've experienced.

Language is miraculous. It gives us the ability to communicate with one another, which has huge social and cultural implications. But on an even more basic level, language is miraculous because it gives us the ability to name things in our world and along with the naming, the ability to think symbolically begins to emerge. Nouns arise first in the development of language. This is the *earth* and that is the *sky*. There is the *water*. We live in a *cave* or a *hut* or a mud *home*. I am *me* and you are *you*. That *person* is my *mate* and these are my *children*. They are all part of my *tribe*. By assigning a noun to an object, a thing in our experiential environment, we construct our world – our Castle – bit by bit, brick by brick.

An important consequence of the naming process is that it necessarily creates separation among each of the nouns, making each thing a distinct object and dividing each one from all others. A *table* of course can't be a *chair* and a *fire* can't be a *chicken*. For each noun to fulfil its function, it must be assigned to something definable, something distinct and separate. By naming things in this way, we divide our world into little pieces of this and that. I became acutely aware of this phenomenon a few years ago in South Africa. My wife and I were out observing animals in the bush, in South Africa they call it the veldt, with the help of a guide. We were seated in a Toyota Landcruiser. It had no roof or doors. The guide spotted two lions, a male and female, who had killed a wildebeest and were engaged in the lengthy process of consuming their prey. The lions' dinner table was about a hundred yards from a little pond and as one of the pair needed a drink of water, it would slowly trundle down the road to the pond, it's belly full with about sixty pounds of partially digested Wildebeest, leaving the other to guard what remained of the kill. We were parked in the Landcruiser on the side of the road, watching this scene unfold, as the male lion, much larger in real life than I'd imagined, began walking toward our open and very exposed vehicle. Thinking it would be a wonderful time to drive off, I glanced at the guide with a look that undoubtedly betrayed my terror at the impending close-encounter. The guide said in a low whisper: "stay still and he'll pass on by." I followed the instructions dutifully, not moving a muscle, not even breathing as the lion walked toward us and then passed by so closely I could easily have reached out and touched him with my right hand. I was amazed that the lion didn't so much as look up at us as he passed by on his way to the pond.

After the lion passed and I was able to breathe again, I asked the guide why the lion didn't seem to notice us. His reply taught me something important. He said the lion didn't see us as we did, three humans sitting in seats in an open Toyota. In the lion's world, all he perceived was a big boxy, largely inanimate thing in the environment that posed no threat. As long as we didn't stand up, he saw us as a unit, as one thing. He didn't experience us as separate things that could be divided from the vehicle. The lion's Narrative, his Reality, was different from mine and I had made the mistake of thinking that his Narrative and mine were the same. Lesson learned.

There is another important consequence that comes from the naming of things. In addition to separating every thing from every other thing, we are creating something new with our nouns – we are literally building our Reality. I find it easiest to conceive of this process like building an igloo-shaped structure. Each new name creates a new separate thing, an object, and as we name more and more things, we stack brick upon brick until we have eventually constructed a windowless, doorless fortress. The Self is encased in this fortress, trapped inside the Reality its newly emergent capacity for language has created. We quite literally construct this Reality and when we're done, we are imprisoned within it – imprisoned by the world we have created. But, because we define our existence in terms of this Reality, we're unaware that the prison even exists. Our experience of Reality is the way we define the milieu within which the Self resides. It becomes the Narrative. There is no breaking out of it because there is nothing beyond. There is nowhere to go that we can think or talk about. There is no other world, no Reality, in which the Reality within the igloo resides. If we think we have found a crack in the prison walls and release the Self into a place "outside" of the Narrative, it's just a delusion. All we've done is construct a new Reality. It's like the Star Trek episode we visited in the last Chapter. Like our Self, Professor Moriarty could exist only within the Holodeck. Although he seemed at one point to step out of the Holodeck and into the "real" world, it was a trick. He'd just reprogramed the simulation so it appeared he was "outside." He wasn't. It was just an illusion. The same is true of the Self's relationship to Reality.

Once the things within our perception have been named, separated from one another and we have thus constructed our Reality, there is a second step that comes into play in the creation of language. Although all the nouns are separate from one another, they interact with one another in various ways. We need a way to describe these interactions with our language and we do that by assigning words to represent the interactions. Thus, John *runs* after Mary and Tom *sits* in a chair. Lisa *goes hunting* and *kills* a deer that she *brings back* to camp so the whole group can *eat*. Bill *harvests* grain from the garden that he *planted* and *watered*. Tina *mills* the grain and *mixes* it with water to form a dough, which she *bakes* in the oven to become a loaf of bread. The loaf is *broken* into pieces, which are *passed to* the family to *consume* with the deer. These actions, all of which are merely descriptive of the way things are interacting with one another, are the verbs of our language.

When you think of language, the first thing that probably comes to mind is stringing together nouns and verbs so that one person can communicate with another. That reaction is perfectly understandable because we're familiar with language of that sort. We use it every day. However, there is another sphere where language plays a pivotal role – inner language – which we might call thought. Thinking is symbolic. When I think of "food," I have a definite image or group of images in mind. Those images are not the food but are symbolic representations of food. Intentionality, the ability to form a goal, form a pathway to achieve the goal and then initiate action to propel you along the pathway, arises only where there is thought. Without thought, without intentionality, we can act only instinctually. Anthropologically, inner speech probably arose before and was the precursor to external language – verbal communication between people. Although scientific research is sparse, it's probably true that internal language may be verbal or non-verbal. I'm inclined to think that non-verbal internal language arises first and paves the way for the later emergence of words.

It can be difficult to imagine language without words because we are so habituated to talking. Perhaps it is easier to conceive of this if we call the process communication instead of language. If you think about it, you can probably remember lots of instances when you have communicated with someone or something in a non-verbal way. Can't you sometimes tell that your boss or your friend is angry with you before they say a word? That's non-verbal communication – language without words. If you're still having a hard time, I have a little practice that will let you experience wordless internal language. It goes by different names, but I learned it as Deep Looking Mediation.

Find a partner, preferably someone you know well. Sit on the floor with legs crossed or in chairs opposite one another, as close together as you can, but without touching. Begin by gazing into each other's eyes. Let your gaze soften and defocus. You can blink if you need to. It's not a staring contest. Imagine you're looking into the other person, past their eyes, into their deeper essence. Try not to think about what you're experiencing. Just accept the experience for whatever it is. Keep this up for a while, perhaps five or ten minutes. This practice can be very profound and will most likely result in a deep sensation of intimacy.

Notice there were no words that passed between you and the other person. In fact, when you reflect on your experience of the other person during the practice, you'll probably see that you didn't need to speak any words internally. You were able to participate in the experience and perhaps have profound feelings as a result of it, but that all occurred on sub-verbal or non-verbal level. Maybe you sensed sadness in the other or joy or fear or perhaps something else. But you had that feeling without needing to say to yourself: "I feel sadness in this person." Instead, the feelings that arose were experienced without words. You were sensing and feeling, but without the necessity of expressing those sensations and feelings verbally to yourself. Because this practice is wordless – non-verbal – it can feel extremely intimate. Like you shared something very deep with the other, both giving and receiving in a way that you could not have done had you tried to put it into words. This is the way deep non-verbal communication feels.

If I place myself back at an early stage of humankind, before verbal language arose, I can imagine sitting around a campfire with the rest of my tribe. I have a tribe-mate, Bob and my internal expression for Bob is a mental image, a picture, a symbolic representation of Bob, just like Jack's mental image of the red ball. In my brain, Bob has people permanence. I know he continues to exist even when I can't experience him with my senses. I would also have separate mental images for other things, like *water, stream* and *bucket*. If I saw Bob leaving our camp, my brain would receive sensory input telling it that the Bob object had risen from his seat, picked up the bucket object and that he'd begun walking in the direction of the stream object. With this internal symbolic language, I am able to "think" – to draw the conclusion that Bob is fetching water and to predict that soon there will be fresh water in our camp. My personal language allows this thinking to occur. Without the internal language, there can simply be no thought and although I could observe what was occurring in the Narrative, I would have no way to predict future events. In this scene I didn't need to communicate with Bob. I was just observing what he was doing and how he was interacting with other objects in our shared environment. Bob's actions and interactions with other objects in the environment were part of my Narrative, part of my story of what was occurring in front of me. Tomorrow, I would be able to recall the little snippet from my Narrative of the day before and remember the scene of Bob heading off to fetch water from the stream. My internal language is indispensable to my thought process.

As human development progresses, the symbolic images of things in the environment may give way to or be combined with different kind of symbols, what we would call words. It really doesn't matter which we chose because both my internal image of Bob, my visualization of him, and the word "Bob" are symbols. Neither the picture nor the word is actually Bob. Both just stand in place of the actual Bob thing.

While my internal language allows me to talk to myself, to comment on the events occurring in the Narrative, I can't communicate effectively with others because we don't use the same symbols. Even when we evolve or develop to the point that we both use vocalizations as the symbols for things in the world, we can't communicate with one another – we don't have a shared language – because the nouns and verbs of our separate internal language are not the same. I might say to my brother Jacob: "Is Bob fetching water?" But suppose in Jacob's personal internal language, "Bob" means "bird," "fetch" means "building" and "water" means "nest." So, Jacob would hear the question: "Is the bird building a nest?" Obviously, there's no way Jacob and I can communicate effectively if we rely only on our respective internal languages. What we need is a common language.

External communication is the sharing of an internal dialogue with others. When creatures agree on the meaning of these externalized sounds (or some other technique, like gestures) and begin to recognize shared symbols, a shared language arises. Vervet monkeys are an interesting example of shared language. They give off alarm calls, as many other animals do. However, the Vervet has different calls for different predators. The alarm for the presence of a snake or a leopard or an eagle are all different sounds. When another Vervet hears an alarm, it behaves appropriately to the specific predator warning. If a snake is near, the Vervet climbs a tree for safety. If the alarm warns of an eagle, the Vervet hides on the ground. This is a form of external language.

Human language is more complex than the warning calls of the Vervet. To arrive at human language, we need to share the same meanings for the same words, both nouns and verbs, and we need to agree on a common syntax – the way we connect the words in our shared language. Once we forge agreement on a common language, we can communicate with one another about the things in our mutual world and how those things relate to and interact with one another. In fact, by agreeing on nouns and verbs we create a mutual Reality, one that we share – at least to the extent of our shared vocabulary.

Because I have the capability of language, my inner life includes the ability to use words to comment on the Narrative, a capacity I seem to utilize with regularity. A highway near my house has what traffic engineers call "metered entrances." To me, they're just red and green lights that make you stop for a while and then signal that you can move onto the entrance ramp to the highway. I find them annoying because they impede my driving and my pet peeve is when they control my driving behavior needlessly, like when the highway is nearly empty. Last week I found myself in just that place. The highway had very low traffic volume at 8:00 a.m. on Sunday morning, yet the signal forced me to stop at the beginning of the entrance ramp. As I sat motionless in my car, I became aware I was talking to myself – I was narrating the scene unfolding before me. I heard myself say:

> "This is so stupid.
> If they're going to have these signals, they could at least program them correctly.
> Who does the programming anyway?
> Why am I waiting?
> I should just ignore the red light.
> There aren't any cops around.
> I'd see them if there were."

And then the signal changed to green, I pressed the gas pedal and barreled down the ramp to enter the highway, leaving my inner dialogue behind.

I teach about a dozen yoga classes each week. I also practice yoga every day, occasionally taking a class taught by another teacher. When I am practicing yoga, it is easy to tune into my inner dialogue, particularly when I'm in a class. Because of my awareness of my inner dialogue, I assume that students who take my yoga classes have their own inner dialogue when they are practicing yoga. I took a class earlier this week from a teacher I quite like. She brought the class into a pose that for me that day felt challenging – it was hard to stay in the pose. I was aware of the Narrative throughout the class, that is, I was present and aware that I was present and I was aware of the sights, sounds and other physical sensations of the unfolding events. As the teacher cued the challenging pose, I was aware my body was moving into the shape required of the pose, I was aware that both legs were straight, I was aware my weight was distributed evenly on both feet, I was aware my spine was flat and parallel to the floor, that my right arm was straight and reaching toward the floor and my left arm was straight and reaching toward the sky. As one breath turned into two and then three and four, I noticed my inner dialogue:

"How much longer is she going to keep us in this pose?"

"I'm tiring and starting to strain. I hope it isn't much longer."

"I could just come out of the pose, but a lot of my students are here and do I want them to think I can't hold this pose?"

"On the other hand, it would be good to let them see me coming out of a pose when I need to and accept that as ok."

"Really, this is a long hold for this pose. It can't be much longer."

This kind of commentary occurs often during our waking life, as we are experiencing the live Narrative and often as we replay portions of the stored Narrative. The commentary, the self-talk, is always coming from me or at least an aspect of me. I am always the one doing the talking. The narration is always mine. Even when I'm imagining what someone else may be thinking about a situation or circumstance, it is me expressing what I imagine they are thinking. There hasn't been a lot of research done on this inner commentary. Lev Vygotsky was a Russian psychologist in the 1920s. From his study of children, he noticed that when children acquire the ability to talk to others, they also develop an internal speech – the ability to talk to themselves. Sometimes the internal speech is a monologue and sometimes it's a dialogue. Some people do more of it than others. Some of the internal speech is negative and some is positive. Sometimes the "inner" speech is actually spoken aloud. Sometimes it seems to be silent. Research has shown that Inner speech often moves at a fast clip, usually much faster than external speech, up to 4,000 words a minute – ten times faster than external speech. Although researchers aren't sure why, there's evidence that our internal speech is more condensed and doesn't use full sentences. There's also a theory that our external speech is constrained by how fast we can vocalize, including muscular movements of the lips, tongue and vocal cords. If we could only move those muscles faster, according to the theory, we could increase the speed of our external speech.

Who is talking to whom with the internal commentary on the Narrative? It's not the Actor Self that is talking, because it is just carrying on its role of acting in the Narrative in the first-person. In the case of the metered entrance to the highway, which I mentioned above, my Actor Self was sitting in the car waiting for the light to change. It was playing a part in the Narrative, just acting out the scene. We get a clue to the source of this internal commentary when we notice that the perspective it reflects is in the third-person. So it couldn't be the Actor Self commenting because it is confined to a first-person perspective and the Narrative is in the third-person.

Wherever the commentary is coming from, it arises because I am observing myself sitting in the car at the signal and reflecting on myself as if the me doing the thinking was separate from the me driving the car. The Observer, the second aspect of Self we identified in Chapter 9, operates from a third-person perspective and so it's possible the Observer is the one doing the narrating. But the Observer emerged before the brain acquired the capacity of language and language must therefore not be necessary to be an Observer. We know that's true because we've seen that

Jack and other animals utilize the Observer, the third-person perspective, and they don't necessarily have the capacity for language, at least not the kind of language we have noticed in the commentary on the Narrative. The emergence of language seems therefore to have given birth to a new Self, the Self that both witnesses the Narrative in the third-person *and* offers the third-person commentary. We can call this newly-emerged third Self the Narrator.

As we begin to pay attention to the monologue and dialogue of the Narrator, we see at the most basic level that the Narrator is commenting on physical objects. For example, my Narrator may say, as I drive south on University Boulevard, "up there on the right is Bonnie Brae Ice Cream." This is just a simple commentary about a thing in my Reality – the ice cream shop. The Narrator might also comment about the relationship between things. "Bonnie Brae Ice Cream is up there on the right, the next building after the wine shop." Or I might utter this internal dialogue in response to unfolding events: "that driver ran the red light and almost hit the two kids crossing the street with their ice cream cones." At a deeper level, the Narrator begins to comment about more abstract concepts. When I was at the metered on-ramp, my Narrator veered into self-reflection: "Why am I waiting here anyway?" And in the yoga class, my Narrative was about how others in the class might react to my coming out of a pose early, what their response would be to my actions. At this point, the Narrator is thinking in a way we understand to be human. The Narrator is aware of and considering feelings and emotions and states of mind.

When Descartes proclaimed *Cogito Ergo Sum*, I think therefore I am, he meant in an ironic twist that his ability to think – to conceive – of his non-existence confirmed that he existed. We have arrived at a somewhat different place, drawing more subtle and far-ranging conclusions. Our ability to conceive of our non-existence demonstrates that we have a brain capable of generating a third-person view of our Reality, including the Self within that Reality. It doesn't prove, as Descartes argued, that the Self experiencing the third-person view is necessarily separate from or outside of the brain or anything other than a biological phenomenon.

We have also determined that having an inner life is not unique and that all beings have one, although the nature of each creature's inner life is not the same. The inner life of each creature exists on a spectrum, ranging from the least complex to the most. On one end are creatures who are capable of experiencing only the first-person perspective of the Actor Self and they experience the Narrative only from that point of view. In the middle are creatures in which the Observer has emerged. The Observer sees the Actor from a third-person perspective and becomes aware that it is separately experiencing the Actor. Finally, on the other end of the spectrum, when the biological complexity of the brain increases sufficiently, language emerges and with language a new Self arises, the Narrator, which uses its new-found language to narrate, to comment on, the Narrative. It is only at this point that self-awareness has emerged – the Narrator has become aware of its awareness of the Narrative.

All of these Selfs are amazing and capable of miraculous feats. However, unlike Descartes' conception of the mind, none of the Selfs we've encountered thus far require for their emergence or existence any magical properties. All are just a product of the biology of the brain, part of the physical body. But maybe there is magic to be found. To move on, we need to dig a little deeper and gain a greater understanding of these Selfs. One way to do that would be observe how they evolved over time, from species to species, and I find myself wishing I had a time-machine so we could directly observe that evolutionary process as it unfolded over the eons. Then I realize, we do have a time-machine of sorts. As we watch a child grow and develop from birth to adulthood, we are privileged to witness their movement through the very same stages we've just uncovered. From this vantage we can observe cognitive development and the emergence of the Selfs as the child grows and matures. Let's turn there now to shine more light on how our own inner life comes to be.

Chapter 10

It's a Boy!

It was dry and cold in the first few days of December in 1984. The temperature hadn't poked its head above freezing for a few weeks and at night the mercury dipped as low as 20 degrees. The path of Denver's winter sun had shifted far to the south, but the warming rays were still sufficient to melt the couple of inches of snow that had fallen around Thanksgiving. The baby's birthday, December 5, had been pre-ordained by the obstetrician, who had scheduled the C-section weeks in advance of the blessed event. And so it was at 7:30 a.m., just as the sun rose on this Wednesday, that my wife was being wheeled into the operatory at St. Lukes Hospital.

I wore a pale blue surgical gown and off-white surgical gloves as I stood at her side, watching the scalpel slice through her flesh from side to side a few inches below her navel. I was trying not to faint. After the cut, the skin and subcutaneous layers to a depth of a little less than an inch were retracted, revealing the brick-red abdominal muscles, which remained intact as the doctor pushed them out of the way, exposing the uterus. After a little slice through the uterine wall, the Obstetrician thrust his two big hands, gloved in off-white just like mine, into the gash and then in no more than a second withdrew them, extracting a wrinkly little red creature from my wife's belly. The helpless little being was handed to a nurse. Waiting for a first breath and feeling queasy and lost in time, I finally heard a soft gasp. A cry soon followed before the tiny one was cleaned, dried, swaddled and returned to mom's arms. We had decided to name him Henry and so the birth certificate attested. Delivered into the world at 8:18 was our new little baby boy.

At birth Henry was helpless and he would remain that way for much of his early life. Unlike his older brother, Jon, who was nine, Henry couldn't fix his own meals. He couldn't even order take out. He couldn't wipe his face when he drooled mother's milk down his chin. He couldn't pee into the toilet. He couldn't make simple conversation about the events of the day. He couldn't ambulate from place to place. He couldn't even roll over from his back to his belly. He couldn't tell if an object was near or far or whether a sound was to the left or right. He couldn't even hold his head up. What he could do was cry when he was hungry or wet, suckle when offered a breast or a bottle, sleep about twenty hours a day (at least when we were lucky) and evacuate his bladder and bowel, often at the most inopportune times. These characteristics were not unique to our son. They are the common lot of all little humans.

What we could not see, at least not directly, was the stunningly explosive growth Henry's brain was undergoing. When we brought him home from the hospital in early December his brain weighed about three-quarters of a pound. By the beginning of March it would double in size. Sixty percent of his metabolic energy was being devoted to growing that little brain. Even at this early stage of his life, he had about as many neurons in his brain as he would have as an adult and the neurons were making connections to one another at an astonishing pace. Imagine what it would be like if every single thing you saw, heard, smelled, tasted or felt, was brand new. That was the way it was for Henry. Every face, every sensation, every experience was brand new and his brain was working overtime making connections. In just thirty-six months, his tiny little brain would grow to eighty percent of its adult size.

When he was born, like all babies, Henry couldn't see very well. His vision was blurry, about like mine is now without glasses, 20/200. He couldn't experience many colors, red being the chief exception. He had no depth perception and could focus only on objects about a foot from his face. It still isn't well understood exactly how visual development takes place in a baby's brain. But we do know that the brain sets about wiring itself for vision very early in the life of a newborn and the process happens very quickly. Vision seems to be pretty complicated. Part of Henry's brain responded instinctively to particular visual stimuli. Other brain regions were getting wired for the distinct purpose of detecting *what* an object was. Still other areas would help him determine *where* something was. At this early stage of development, Henry didn't recognize objects as being separate from one another. The mobile of different shaped and colored animals that hung over his crib was just one thing and he didn't even recognize the mobile as separate from the rest of his visual environment. His brain would need to learn that objects are separate from one another. The newborn needs to be taught to create their Castle by naming and separating things one from the other. Interestingly, their native or default visual perception is that everything is one.

Henry's hearing developed before he was born and was fully functional in utero, probably in the early fall, about six months after he was conceived. By the time he was born he was already accustomed to hearing. While he was in the womb he regularly heard the whooshing sounds of blood flowing through the vessels surrounding his mom's uterus, the gurgling of her digestive system, her ever-present and comforting heartbeat and he had even become familiar with her voice. When he was born he seemed to hear pretty well. He could distinguish between the different voices of family members. We had a Dalmatian puppy named Luisa when we brought Henry home and she was prone to loud barking. Whenever she was within earshot and let out a loud bark, Henry's little body would jerk involuntarily, startled by the loud and unexpected sound. Within a couple of months, he would listen intently to familiar sounds, like our voices.

As an infant, Henry loved to be touched. His newborn body incorporated a surprisingly complex array of touch sensors, all of which were in the various layers of his skin. His sense of touch consisted of three discrete sensations, temperature, pain and pressure, and his little body was covered with different types of touch sensors that received data and transferred it for processing to the somatosensory cortex of his brain. Like all humans, Henry even had specialized receptors wrapped around his diminutive hair follicles that were sensitive to the pressure produced when one of his hairs was bent. When his little hands gripped something, like my forefinger (which happened a lot), the pressure receptors in his hands and fingers received pressure data and relayed it to his brain so he'd know, among other things, how hard to grip. The temperature sensors in his skin didn't register anything at all when his surroundings were at about 89 degrees, the temperature of his skin. It was only when the ambient temperature exceeded or fell below that stasis point that his brain would register warmth or coolness. Although we tried our best to insulate Henry from any pain, it sometimes happened that he bumped his head, got an ear ache or a diaper rash. He could feel two different types of pain. One was sharp, pricking pain and the other was dull aches and burning sensations. He had a separate set of sensors for each type of pain.

Like hearing and touch, Henry's sense of smell developed even before he was born. In fact, his sense of smell was probably the first sense to develop in the womb. Research has shown that scents in the mother's environment migrate into the amniotic fluid and the fetus is exposed to those scents at a very early stage of development. When Henry emerged into this world, he was already able to smell quite well and to distinguish among different scents. By the time he was a few days old, he could easily identify the smell of breast milk and studies have shown that infants can smell the difference between their mother's breast milk and that produced by someone else. Henry was able to detect scents by inhaling air, which passed by scent receptors in his nasal passages. Odor molecules in the air chemically bonded with his scent receptors, which relayed information about those molecules to his brain. Specific combinations of odor molecules triggered particular neural impulses that Henry's brain interpreted as, for example, mother's milk, and he'd be attracted to the milk. Other odor molecules might be interpreted as, for example, acrid or unpleasant and he'd instinctively try to distance himself from those kinds of smells.

When he was born, Henry's taste buds, all 10,000 of them in his mouth and throat, were fully formed. Like all newborns, he showed a clear preference for sweet flavors (which includes breast milk). Henry's taste buds were super-sensitive and sour or bitter flavors always elicited an overwhelmingly negative reaction. What was happening in his little body was that molecules in what he put into his mouth chemically bonded with his taste buds, which sent information about those particular chemical bonds to his brain. His brain interpreted that information as "tasting" in a particular way – sweet, sour, bitter or salty. Many studies have shown that the sense of taste shows up very early in fetal development and that babies often show a preference for foods their mothers consumed while pregnant. I can definitely confirm that anecdotally. For many months while she was pregnant with Henry, my wife's diet consisted mostly of sushi and Mexican food. As soon as he started eating solid food, Henry seemed irrepressibly drawn to the taste of both cuisines and, even to this day – more than thirty years later – they are still two of his favorite foods.

As miraculous a being as Henry was at birth, his actual capabilities at that stage of existence were fairly limited. He could react to light and sound and touch and smell and taste. But he couldn't plan. He couldn't really think. He couldn't create a cognitive map. He couldn't talk, either to himself or to others. He couldn't picture all the great things he would one day be able to do. He couldn't ask where he came from, where he was going or what was his purpose in life. The true miracle of Henry's existence resided in his potential – that which he would become. I was privileged, as each parent is, to observe that becoming as he grew and developed over the years from an infant into an adult. I saw his body grow in strength, stature and coordination and I knew his brain was connecting billions of synapses with one another based on the data and experiences he was collecting on his journey. I saw his cognitive abilities blossom like a million flowers exploding in a riot of color in a summer garden as he transformed from a state of dependence and incapability to a being of agency with mental capabilities that allowed him to ask: "how did I come to be" and "what is my purpose here" and to search for answers to those questions. As I watched Henry over the space of a little more than a decade, until about the age of ten, I saw him following the evolutionary development of the human species over tens of millions of years because, in the short span of his early childhood, Henry retraced those evolutionary steps – but on a vastly accelerated scale.

In 1936 Jean Piaget, whom we first encountered in Chapter 5 in connection with Jack's capacity for object permanence, published his groundbreaking theory of how the brain developed from infancy to adulthood. Piaget, a Swiss psychologist, developed his theory, so the story goes, by observing the cognitive development of his nieces and nephews and later, his own children. He proposed four stages of development, beginning with the sort of deep dependence and limited cognition in infancy that we've already seen Henry demonstrate. In this stage, Henry's inner life and his knowledge of the world around him arose solely from the physical interactions he had with the world, like touching and grasping my fingers and beard, seeing and hearing the faces and voices of his mom and brother, Aunts, Uncles and cousins, and tasting whatever was at hand to thrust into his mouth. When he was about seven months old, Henry developed object permanence, the understanding that objects which he could not directly perceive didn't cease to exist when they were out of sight. At that stage, he recognized our dog, Luisa, as she continually bounded into and out of his perceptual sphere. He knew Luisa persisted as a thing in the world, even when he couldn't see or hear her.

As Henry's intellectual abilities developed, aided in large measure by the mobility his continuing physical development permitted, his world expanded. Toward the end of this first of Piaget's phases, Henry began to understand some basic words like "no," "bottle," "Mom" and "Dad." These words were symbolic, like Jack's red ball. They were sounds that stood for an object that wasn't directly perceptible, sounds that acted as placeholders for a thing not within his perception. At about the same time, he devised little experiments to test how his world worked and increase his understanding of that world. We used to cut up pasta for him and put it in his little blue plastic bowl. The first time he grabbed a handful of spaghetti and flung it to the floor I thought he was just making a mess. But I soon realized it was a test, an experiment. He wanted to see what the outcome would be. And having done it once, he repeated the experiment over and over again to see whether the response was consistent or whether it varied. He was testing his world. Figuring out how it worked. Determining the rules.

As Henry developed from an infant into a toddler he began to use symbols, language, and he acquired the capacity to store and retrieve experiences, memory. He started experiencing the Narrative, which was stored in his brain and could be recalled, to a greater or lesser degree, when needed. For example, when presented with a little bowl of green chili, he remembered the look, the smell and the taste and knew it was something he wanted to consume. When he wanted a toy that he couldn't see, he could imagine it in his developing brain and, as he got older, the toys had names and he could direct us to fetch the toy simply by uttering its name and making a grasping gesture in the air with his hand. In this second of Piaget's stages, everything was of course still about Henry. As far as Henry's brain was concerned, the whole world revolved around him and existed solely to do his bidding. The world was there to find the right food or bring him juice to drink, to bring him a plaything (or another one), to put him to bed or release him from his nap, to change his diaper or, later, to help him to the little plastic training potty. At this stage, his inner life was centered on and firmly anchored to his wants, needs and actions. He was oblivious to the needs, wants and emotions of others and of the effect he had on the others around him.

Self-awareness emerged in Henry during this second of Piaget's stages, at about eighteen months. When he was an infant and he'd see his reflection in the big full-length mirror we had in our bedroom, he didn't recognize himself. He just experienced the image in the mirror as something in his environment. Sometimes he was amused by the image and he'd point to it so we'd look at it too. By about a year and a half, there was a significant shift in the way his brain worked. At that point he recognized the image in the mirror was "him." It was *his* reflection. This phenomenon has been studied at length. A common way to get at this issue experimentally is to surreptitiously make an obvious mark on the child's face and then let the child look into the mirror. Before the shift occurs, the child doesn't seem to take much notice of the mark. But after the shift occurs, the child seeing the mark will lift their hand up and touch it on their face. Researchers are in agreement that this shows the child recognizes the mark is on *his* face and that the image in the mirror is *him*.

Many experts in the child development field have observed that self-awareness seems to arise in children at about the same time language emerges and the two seem to be intertwined. This isn't surprising because, as we saw in the last Chapter, it is language that permits commentary on the Narrative. That is, you can't very well talk to yourself until you have some capacity for communication – a language. Once you are able to talk to yourself, the division of Self into different aspects occurs and self-awareness arises.

By about age four, Henry had entered the third of Piaget's developmental stages. He interacted with other children and was able to play games. He understood goals and processes to achieve goals and was aware that following certain patterns of behavior would lead to particular outcomes. He was, of course, still very self-centered. But he understood cause and effect – if you do this, then that will be the result. He also was good at testing those operational rules, sometimes in an abstract way. For example, he learned to lie. One day, after a coloring session on the floor, I asked him to please put the crayons away in the box before we went into the kitchen for dinner. When he joined me in the kitchen shortly after, I asked whether he'd put the crayons away and he said he had. A few minutes later I noticed the crayons in the same place they'd been before and invited him back to the living room, where the following conversation ensued. "Henry, didn't you tell me you put the crayons away?" "Yes," he said. "Why are they still all over the floor," I asked. His sincerely delivered reply was: "I don't know. I put them away." It was a blatant lie. Probably another experiment.

By the time he started Middle School, it was clear Henry's inner life was coming much closer to that of an adult, although not completely there. He was able to comprehend abstract concepts, like morality. I saw the Observer Self fully emerge as he had a clear third-party perspective on issues that confronted him in his daily existence. When he took a test at school and wasn't satisfied with the grade, "he" judged "himself." That is, he adopted the view of a third person to evaluate his performance. And the Narrator Self had emerged in his inner life as well. As he judged his own actions or contemplated what course of action to take, he spoke to himself (and often out loud), debating one course of action and weighing its consequences against other options. "I don't know whether to ask Paige or Leslie to the school dance. Paige and I are already good friends and it would be easy to go with her. But I'd like to get to know Leslie better. But what if Leslie says no? Or what if Paige really wants to go with someone else and just goes with me because we're friends?" Ah, the dilemmas of the adolescent.

As I observed the progression of Henry's cognitive development from infant to adult, from a stage of instinctual existence to the full flowering of the human intellect, I watched in microcosm the evolutionary development of the inner life that eventually became what we experience today – the Narrator Self who can ask abstract questions. Our pre-human ancestors were animated at first solely by instinct – desire, motivation and action without thought. It was just that kind of instinct that caused Henry to cry when he was hungry, uncomfortable or in pain. At birth (and for some time after), Henry didn't have the cognitive equipment – the brainpower – to act in any other way. His cry was an instinctual response to a particular stimulus. It wasn't thought out. It wasn't planned. Henry didn't think to himself, "I'm hungry. If I cry out loud, I'll get some food. So, let's cry." Instead, his hunger produced an unplanned and involuntary response by his little body – a cry. When he soiled his diaper, he cried because of the discomfort, not because he knew crying would bring relief following a diaper change. These actions were all instinctual.

As the brain of our ancestors evolved, the Observer Self arose and, just like in the young Henry, the mute Observer of our distant ancestors was able to perceive the Narrative from a third-person perspective. That Self enabled more complicated behaviors, like the squirrel that is able to keep track of its cache of nuts stored for the winter or Jack's ability to find his red ball.

Finally, our remote ancestors, thousands of generations back in time, evolved what we would recognize as a brain with the capabilities of a modern adult like Henry. They were capable, like Henry is today, of adopting a third-person perspective of the Narrative and of language, both internal and external.

All creatures, past and present, have an inner life. We need a vocabulary to be able to talk sensibly about that inner life and to understand the differences from one type of cognition to another. Consciousness, sentience, intelligence, awareness, knowledge, perception, cognizance, mindfulness, and self-awareness. The words we use to talk about aspects of our inner life can be very confusing. Sometimes the same word is used to describe different characteristics and experiences and sometimes we use different words to describe the same inner phenomena. A well-known dictionary defines "consciousness" as "the state of being awake and aware of one's surroundings" and as "the perception of something by a person," and as "the fact of awareness by the mind of itself and the world." This is troublesome because "consciousness," at least according to these definitions, encompasses essentially all of the different aspects of our inner life. We need a way to describe different qualities or aspects of our inner life and to get there we'll need to adopt some clear definitions. For the remainder of this book I'm going to use as our main guideposts, *sentience, consciousness and awareness.*

Sentience is the ability and capacity to feel or to experience a sensation. It derives from the Latin word *sentire*, which means to feel. Although not always used with that meaning today, it was a common usage in the eighteenth century, particularly as a way of distinguishing the ability to think or reason from the ability to feel. Darwin's worms are able to experience the world around them to at least some extent. They feel and we know they feel because they react to adverse stimuli in a way that tries to abate not just the stimuli but the harm that will come from the stimuli. If a worm perceives vibrations it interprets as a predator coming its way, it will react by retreating to the safety of its burrow. If it feels sunlight on its skin, it seeks shelter because the sun will dry its skin and prevent it from breathing. If it feels the touch of my hand or breath, it moves away to avoid the harm that would come from my touch. These are the reactions of sentience. The pain Darwin's worms experience may not be the same as the pain you or I or Jack experience; but the difference is one of degree, not of quality. When you cut a worm in half, it clearly reacts to what's occurred. That reaction shows there is feeling and sensation and is the hallmark of sentience.

The word *conscious* has been used and defined in so many different ways that it almost makes me want to not use the word at all. It is sometimes used in its original Latin sense as the joint knowing by two people ("con" meaning with and "scio" meaning knowledge). In a spiritual sense, consciousness has been used to connote a connection between a being and God or another spiritual truth. Medically, conscious just means awake and capable of perception. At night when you're asleep, you are not conscious. When you wake up from your night sleep, consciousness returns. If you're knocked out by anesthesia, you are not conscious. One of the things that becomes apparent with these examples is that a being is conscious when it is capable of experiencing the Narrative and (absent some cognitive deficiency) capable of storing it in memory. So let's use *conscious* or *consciousness* in that most basic and fundamental sense to mean being awake and capable of experiencing the Narrative.

Yesterday I left my house with Jack on his leash. I told him we were taking a "walk" and he knew that meant a stroll in the neighborhood as opposed to a drive to Wash Park. As we left the house by the front door, we went down the driveway to the sidewalk and began to walk toward a little park about five blocks from the house. While on the walk, I saw the spring flowers and noticed the trees just beginning to leaf out. I saw and heard the cars passing by on the street adjacent to the sidewalk and felt a gentle warm breeze. During the walk, I had the capacity to experience the Narrative as it unfolded and I was doing so in real time as the events occurred. I was, as we say, in the moment. I was both sentient and conscious.

In addition to experiencing the events of the Narrative as they occurred, my brain was simultaneously accessing stored Narratives of this same walk and mapping my environment, predicting my path, triangulating the direction of my forward motion, judging potential dangers along the way, and other similar predictive tasks. Jack was probably doing something very similar. He was, as always, disappointed that we were going on a "walk" instead of going to the "park" and he made his disappointment known by resisting the leash a bit, making me drag him along for the first few paces. Sometimes I bring a tennis ball on the walk so we can play fetch when we get to the park and I had surreptitiously tucked a tennis ball into my pocket before we left the house. To provide encouragement to Jack, I retrieved the tennis ball from my pocket while we were walking and bounced it on the sidewalk a few times to show him that something he enjoyed was coming up when we arrived at the park. This gave him a goal. He knew, because we'd done it many times before, that when we got to the park the leash would come off and there would be a rousing game of fetch for as long as I could stand it. Given the goal, Jack knew where we were going and the route to get there. He knew from prior experiences, his stored Narrative, which direction we were heading, where we would turn and how far each phase of the journey would be. He was projecting, predicting, our joint future movements toward the goal of getting to the park to play fetch with the tennis ball.

As we walked, other things diverted his attention along the way, like the scent of another dog on the fencepost we passed. Smelling that, Jack stopped to investigate, sniffing deeply. I don't know what he was experiencing. I don't know if he recognized the scent and it triggered a memory or if the scent was just a feature of the landscape that he was attracted to. When he lifted his leg on the same fencepost, I didn't really know whether he was covering up the other dog's scent, claiming the territory as his own, or just adding his scent to the others. When he's done investigating, he remembers the overall goal and returns to calibrating, predicting, the path to the park, using the dimensional model his brain has constructed based on his stored memories and his current perceptions.

Both Jack and I are conscious. We are awake and aware of our environment and have the capacity to experience it. We are both using our senses, sight, hearing, touch, taste and smell, and the input those senses send to our brains to help us know where we are. In other words, we are both experiencing or own Narrative. In addition, both of our brains are utilizing to some degree, the current Narrative and our respective stored Narratives to create a real-time model of the environment in which we're immersed. And our brains are, among other activities, determining where we are in relation to our goal and predicting how to move from our current location to where we want to end up. This is the state of consciousness.

Awareness is different from consciousness and awareness is where things start to get really interesting. In this book I use awareness to mean being aware of our own consciousness − having the experience of experiencing consciousness. As I walked down the sidewalk with Jack, there were times when I was "in the moment" − when I was so totally absorbed in the current Narrative that I lost track of time and even of my own presence. But there were other times on our little walk when I was not lost in the current Narrative. At one point I stopped, knelt down and smelled a newly emerging spring flower which I hadn't seen before. I was conscious of the flower. I saw its shape and its pale purple color and smelled its subtle fragrance. Although I was experiencing all those sensations, I was at the same time aware that I was kneeling down and smelling the unknown flower. That is awareness − the experience of knowing that I was viewing the Narrative, the awareness that there is a Me character walking toward the park, smelling the smells, hearing the sounds and feeling the sun and the gentle warm breeze on his skin. I am, in other words, experiencing my Self as I experience the current Narrative. This is the meaning of *awareness*.

Is Jack aware or is that state beyond his abilities? Is awareness limited to humans? It's a matter of degree. Awareness is not necessarily all or nothing, but it exists on a spectrum. For Jack to navigate from point A to point B on the dimensional model that his brain constructs, he must see the object Jack as a separate thing operating within the model. To that extent, he adopts a third-person perspective about his Self and generates what we've called the Observer aspect of Self. That is surely a form of awareness because he is experiencing Jack in the third-person. His inner life is not limited to experiencing the Narrative in the first-person. But the depth of his third-person experience is restricted. He can experience his Actor Self for the purpose of cognitive mapping. But his experience of Self doesn't go much farther than that. He doesn't experience his entire consciousness in the third-person. He isn't aware of his inner life. My awareness, on the other end of the spectrum, is deeper and more nuanced. I fully experience my consciousness. I can experience my feelings, emotions, physical sensations and thoughts in the third-person. I can fully detach from my first-person consciousness and experience the entire breadth of my experience from afar — in the third-person. There is thus a significant degree of difference between Jack's awareness and mine.

The capabilities that give rise to an inner life are just that. Just because we have a particular capability doesn't mean we employ that capability all the time. Sometimes we rest just in sentience. Sometimes we become conscious. And sometimes we experience awareness. These stages describe what is possible in human cognition. They aren't meant to describe a constant state. It's like saying a car's top speed is 100 mph. That doesn't mean the car always travels at that speed. Our inner life works the same way.

If we return to Darwin, not because of his worms, but because of his theory of evolutionary development, it's easy to see that the capacity for a deeper inner life can be followed from one species to the next as an evolutionary process. Some species are endowed with the most basic brain functions and their inner life is limited by the functions their brain is capable of performing. As we see the complexity of the brain evolve from one species to the next, the inner life of the brains of the members of those species acquire a deeper and more complex inner life that essentially tracks the physical development of the brain. As far as we know, the most complex and developmentally evolved brain is found in *homo sapiens* and so it's hardly a surprise that the most developed and evolved inner life is also found in humans.

None of this means we are better than other creatures and it doesn't give humans the right to treat other species with less developed brains and less developed inner lives as somehow inferior, less than or to be dominated. To the contrary, once we recognize that the differences between all species are really just a matter of degree, then we discover a kinship with other beings that should bring us closer together, not farther apart. If we ignore the sentience of Darwin's worms or the consciousness of Jack, we betray the deep kind of awareness that is a legacy of our big brains. It is only by honoring all other beings that we give full expression to the great gifts evolution has bestowed upon us.

It also seems that our understanding of the cognitive abilities, the inner lives, of other animals is constantly evolving and we often underestimate or misjudge the abilities of our planet-mates. Originally, we thought that only humans were aware and the supposed difference between humankind and other species was used to support or justify all kinds of ugliness and maltreatment, the range of which is truly breathtaking. Even to this day, we cage other beings so we can gawk at them, we use them as experimental subjects in ways that are harmful, and we kill them with impunity. Our cruelty has not been limited to other species. We've done the same thing to our brothers and sisters and we're not talking about the distant past. We are guilty of dividing humankind, the unitary species *homo sapiens,* into groups based on characteristics like skin pigmentation or country of origin and then ranking those groups based on supposed (but completely false) cognitive differences.

We have now learned through deeper investigation that other animals – certain apes, elephants, dolphins, orcas and certain crows – exhibit the awareness of Self. The gold standard for testing self-awareness is the mirror test, which I described earlier in this Chapter in connection with Henry's development. It seems that members of these other species recognize a mark on their body when looking in the mirror, just like Henry did when his brain developed sufficiently. Recently, Japanese researchers concluded that the Bluestreak Cleaner Wrasse, a small coral reef fish, exhibits self-awareness. The researchers injected a colored gel just beneath the surface of the skin of the little fish in locations where the mark could be seen only in a mirror. When they viewed themselves in a mirror, the fish noticed the mark and tried to rub it off by scraping their bodies against surfaces in the test tanks. The colored gel was injected in different places on the fish, with the same result. To verify the test, the researchers injected clear gel and the fish didn't try to scrape it off. They also injected colored gel but removed the mirror and the wrasses didn't engage in the scraping behavior. Their conclusion: the Cleaner Wrasse recognizes the reflection in the mirror as its own body – it has a sense of Self. It is aware. Perhaps other studies will show that many animals have an abstract sense of Self not unlike humans. Recognizing our demonstrated fallibility in judging the cognitive abilities, the inner life, of other creatures, we need to do a much better job of honoring our cognitive gifts and become much more circumspect about the harm our actions visit upon others.

* * * * * * * *

Based on our present knowledge, humans are unique in their ability to ask abstract questions, questions that are primary, questions about the origin of things like you and me and the Reality that seems to contain us. These are questions that arise because we are aware of our awareness of the Narrative.

When we examine how humankind has answered these fundamental questions, at least two things stand out. First, it turns out there is not just one answer, but many answers to the same question and sometimes the answers seem inconsistent with one another. Second, the disparate answers attract adherents who coalesce together and form institutions that seem to have a vested interest in "their" answer and work to perpetuate it by suggesting (and sometimes forcing) others to adopt it. In the following Chapter we'll examine the teachings of the world's largest religions about Reality, the Self and the Soul. We'll explore what they say about the origin of things, including the Self, and the Self's role in the world – it's relationship to Reality.

As we survey this terrain, bear in mind the extent to which our life experiences already provide us with answers to these questions and whether the teachings from the different religions are consistent with or different from our perceptions.

Chapter 11

In the Beginning

My grandfather – the same one you met in Chapter 4 – was an early member of Temple Emanuel in the first decade of the 1900s. Half a century later, when my father had married and started a family. Dad had issues with Emanuel. Mostly, he thought they were too dogmatic. As an act of rebellion, Dad and some of his friends broke off and formed a new congregation, which they named Temple Micah. In the beginning, they held services in the basements of their homes. As the congregation grew, they raised the money to build a building on Monaco Street that housed a good-sized sanctuary, as well as offices for the rabbi, an administrator and several classrooms. Temple Micah was what was called reformed, which meant liberal. While most Jewish kids had a bar or bat mitzvah, we didn't have that particular ceremony. Instead, we were confirmed. Other Jewish kids got their religious training on Saturday. We went to classes on Sunday. Our teachers were, by and large, adult members of the congregation.

Dad taught Sunday school for as long as I can remember. A class he championed and taught was called "Understanding Other Religions." As you'd expect, this involved reading selections from the foundational texts of other religious traditions, including the Christian Bible (the New Testament), the Quran and the Bhagavad Gita, among others. In class on Sunday morning we'd hear about what these other religions taught and how their teachings differed from Judaism and the teachings of what we called the Old Testament. Heady stuff for a nine -year old. But Dad wasn't satisfied with a detached intellectual study of other religions. We supplemented our readings and lectures with attendance at the religious services held by these other faiths, presumably so we could experience their religious beliefs within the context of their ceremonial offerings. Sunday mornings often found a little troupe of ten or eleven Jewish boys and girls seated in the pews of a local house of worship. The ones I remember were all Christian denominations, Catholic, Russian Orthodox, Anglican and Baptist to name a few.

One bright and chilly winter morning our little crew was ushered into a pew in the middle of the vast Cathedral of the Immaculate Conception on Logan and 15th Streets. From our pew, the building seemed enormous. It was a soaring and luminous space with seventy-five colorful stained-glass windows arrayed on all sides of the building well above eye-level, so that you had to look up to see them. The choir of twenty-five or thirty members wearing robes was ensconced in the balcony at the rear of the church, just below the brass-colored pipes that played notes, high and low, from the organ. As the mass began, I noticed everyone getting up from their seats and starting to kneel on the upholstered bumpers that hung at the back of each pew. Although we'd been told we were just observers and wouldn't be expected to actively participate in the mass, we hadn't been instructed about whether to stand when others did and nobody told us anything about kneeling. So it was that I and each of my classmates remained seated as everyone else began to kneel. At just that moment I felt a stingingly sharp pain on the top of my head. Fearing something had fallen from the high ceiling, I turned my head and started to look up and noticed in my peripheral vision a figure hovering behind me. I turned around and beheld a dour lady holding a five-inch-long metal crucifix in her right hand which she had apparently just beaned me with. As I began to protest, she said – and not as quietly as she might have – "KNEEL," which I dutifully did with the immediacy of chastened dog. The rest of my classmates, observing the encounter, immediately followed suit and got down on their little knees as fast as they could. And none of us needed any more lesson than that when on each subsequent occasion that kneeling was called for, we each made straight for the floor. This smack on the head was my first direct experience of Catholicism and the lesson my young brain understood with staggering immediacy was the same lesson peoples the world over learn from their usually more extended religious training – to accept the teachings and honor them by following the ceremonies.

This was more or less my introduction to world religions, a study which I surprisingly have continued for most of life. In college I branched out to eastern religious traditions and after a hiatus in my studies that lasted many years, I became a practicing Buddhist. During my lifetime of study I have always marveled at the variety of religious beliefs. But what strikes me now more than anything else is the ubiquity of religious affiliation. Of the roughly 7.6 billion people on this planet, the vast majority identify as a member of an organized religion. Although the numbers are subject to some dispute owing to the difficulties involved in counting across many nations, about 2.4 billion are members of one of the many Christian denominations. About 1.3 billion of those are Roman Catholics and 900 million are Protestants. About 1.8 billion adhere to the Islamic faith. Of those, 90% are Sunni and most of the rest are Shia. A little over a billion people are Hindus (most of which reside in India, where 80% of the population is Hindu) and about 500 million people are Buddhists (half of which reside in China).

Somewhere in the range of 400 million people are claimed by various indigenous religious groups. When we tote up all the devotees, we find that nearly eighty percent of the world population is affiliated with one formal religious group or another.

The remainder, what's left over of the planetary population, consists of about a billion people who are non-religious, claiming no affiliation with any religion. A good portion of those belong to one of the many cultural groups that don't align with a particular religious tradition and all of those cultural groups have their own creation mythology – stories passed down through the ages that explain the origin of all things – even though they aren't religions *per se*. For example, think about the origin stories of the indigenous American tribes, the First Nations peoples of Canada or the aboriginal peoples of Australia.

When we consider the people who claim a formal religious affiliation and those who do not, but are members of cultures that have their own creation myths, we have to conclude that nearly everyone on the planet is affiliated with one group or another that has developed an origin story and incorporated that story into the teachings it imparts and preaches to its adherents.

My childhood acquaintance with religious practice and affiliation, both that of my family and that which I studied, gave me some insight into what it meant to be a member of a religious group. But back then I wasn't looking at religion analytically, I was just experiencing being a person with a religious identity. As I tasted more of life, I gained a deeper understanding of the experience of religious life and I credit my Buddhist and Yogic practice for providing a much deeper understanding of why people gravitate to religion and what they receive in the bargain.

I gained an even more fulsome understanding of this phenomenon after I'd been teaching yoga full time for a few years. As a yoga teacher, I wanted to better understand the role I played in leading a yoga class and the teacher's role in the wider yoga community. Here, I'm not talking about yoga as exercise; I'm talking about devotional yoga – yoga with its ancient Hindu roots – yoga as a lifestyle, which, speaking plainly, means a religion. It took a while for me to understand and appreciate the difference. On one level, yoga in the West is just a form of exercise and efforts have been made to strip it of its Hindu roots. There are sporadic reports of evangelical Christian groups protesting the teaching of yoga in schools because they claim it's an effort by Hindus to surreptitiously convert children to the Hindu religion. While I don't agree with that conspiracy theory, the argument isn't completely without merit. Devoted yogis in the West, a community I've been a part of for some years, regularly decry the exercise-centric aspect of yoga and most would admit yoga encompasses far more than exercise and the poses we flow through in a typical class.

Yoga, in the wider sense, includes eight different aspects, called limbs. The first two are the dos and don'ts (in Sanskrit, the *yamas* and *niyamas*), like not lying, stealing or killing and embracing cleanliness, contentment and discipline. Sound a little like the Ten Commandments? The other limbs or practices of Yoga involve breathing techniques (*Pranayama*), turning the senses inward (*Pratyahara*), concentration (*Dharana*) and meditative absorption (*Dhyana*). Ultimately, the aim of these practices is enlightenment, a merging with the divine (*Samadhi*). This is starting to sound a lot like a religion.

As I taught more and more yoga classes, tried to make sense of my role as a yoga teacher and thought more deeply about yoga as a whole, I started to make of list of what I saw. The list looked this:

- Yoga is a community of practitioners who gather together to share a common experience.
- The gatherings are occasioned by various ceremonies, including chants, song, special costume, and language.
- The gatherings take place in a special place (often called sacred by teachers and studio owners) set aside for the activity at specified times. These gatherings are promoted by teachers and yoga studies and viewed by those who take the classes as a refuge from everyday life.
- The gatherings are led by persons with special training, insight and personal knowledge of the path of yoga. These leaders are often revered.
- There is a sense of mystery surrounding yoga.
- Yoga has a distinct belief system consisting of ancient sacred knowledge, much of which is contained in venerated texts and passed down orally from teacher to student.

Once I compiled this list and sat down to look at it I said to myself: "this is a religion and you're a priest." It shouldn't have been news. I had had previews of this before. There were examples every day of students telling me how yoga brought them peace or understanding or a feeling of connection with the world. In fact, one student who came to one of my Sunday classes every week told me very explicitly: "I was brought up a Baptist in the South. I went to church every week. I haven't been to church in years, but your yoga class gives me the same exact feelings." I brushed his statements off at the time, but I should have taken them more at face value. He was telling me that his experience of yoga class was just like the church services he had left behind.

Regardless of religious affiliation, Christian, Muslim, Hindu, Buddhist, some other spirituality or whether the affiliation is membership in a non-religious cultural group, what purpose does an individual's association with these groups serve? Why do such a great percentage of humans belong to these groups? What draws them in? What keeps them there? What needs does it satisfy? Why does it feel good? We can identify three broad and general functions that each if these groups perform and that the members of the group benefit from: fostering social cohesion through rituals and shared beliefs; facilitating control by means of shared values, norms of behavior and thought; and providing access to answers to existential questions. Let's explore each of these functions in greater detail.

Religions and non-religious cultures are based on specific beliefs and to be a member of the group you need to adopt those beliefs. This doesn't mean there is no leeway for dissent among members and no tolerance for some outliers that disagree with some beliefs but stay with the group anyway. But it does mean that by and large, the members of the group share the same beliefs. For example, all Christians believe there is one God, that Jesus Christ is the son of God and that Christ was the Messiah. The core beliefs of the group are reinforced through rituals, like communal worship services, prayers before meals, and birth, death and marriage ceremonies, to name just a few. The common beliefs and communal activities foster social cohesion among the members of the group – they let each member feel a part of something, a belonging. They also tend to isolate those who are not adherents, as my story about kneeling at a Catholic mass illustrates. By not kneeling when the ritual required everyone to kneel, I unknowingly displayed a rejection of an important ritual, one which the lady behind me wielding the big crucifix evidently felt a pressing need to emphatically invite me to conform to. The shared beliefs and rituals allow the group members to feel kinship for one another, a likeness between me and you. This sense of "you are like me and I am like you" is a glue that binds one to another, creating social cohesion.

The shared beliefs and the rituals that reinforce those beliefs foster the adoption of common values, thoughts and behaviors. Think for example about the Ten Commandments. There is a shared belief among Christians that God revealed these rules of conduct to Moses on Mount Sinai. The first five commandments deal with the relationship between adherents and their God. God reinforces "I am the Lord thy God," that there can't be any other gods, that graven images are taboo, that the name of God shall not be spoken in vain and that the Sabbath day is to be kept holy. The remaining five covenants deal with the behavior of one person toward another. Children must honor their parents. Killing, adultery, stealing, lying and covetousness are prohibited. These rules are intended to ensure a harmonious and peaceful society, as well as instilling group-wide values. These commandments naturally give rise to similar values among Christians, like the relationship between an individual and God. Although there is certainly a wide range in the way these common values are applied in practice, the underlying value is still the same from person to person. For example, some

Christians honor the Sabbath by not working at all, while others may work all day long. But every Christian would agree that the value itself, honoring the Sabbath, is something they subscribe to.

Finally, all religions answer existential questions, those relating to fundamental issues of human existence. This aspect of religiosity is what I'm most interested in exploring now. Even though the core tenets of the various religious systems vary considerably from group to group, it's intensely interesting that all religions offer their adherents a belief system that supplies answers to questions about Reality, Self and Soul and that shape their adherents' views and beliefs about those concepts.

In a moment we'll begin to examine the teachings of each of the major religions so we can understand their particular views about Reality, Self and Soul. What we'll see is that the teachings vary – in some respects quite significantly – from one group to the other. But it will also become clear that even though the details of the teachings vary, there is an unmistakable commonality among each philosophy. That commonality is found in three elements. First, each system identifies an Otherness, something "out there," something Beyond, something supra-human and supra-natural, as the source of the Reality we experience. The contours of the Otherness vary, but the fact that there is some Otherness and its role in relation to Reality – the phenomenal world – is common to all systems. Second, each belief system links the Self and the Soul to the Otherness. Finally, all the disparate teachings link Reality, Self and Soul with one another. Let's look at the specifics.

* * * * * *

The source of the Indus River, the place where it begins its journey, is the cold, snowy high mountains of the Himalaya, at an altitude of 18,000 feet, in a region we today call Tibet. At that height its waters are frigid and flow swiftly, contained by steep, barren, rocky slopes. Following the downhill grade to the north and west, the Indus reaches the region of Kashmir at an altitude of about 15,000 feet, where its waters are replenished by glacial melt from the Karakoram Range. From there the Indus passes north of present-day Islamabad in northern Pakistan, eventually descending to an elevation of about 1,400 feet where, unleashed from the steep rocky valleys of the mountains, it spills onto the Punjab Plain. There it's joined by the five rivers of the Punjab and the waters of the Indus slow and spread out to more than a mile during the regular seasonal floods. At an altitude measured in hundreds of feet instead of thousands, the Indus then begins to meander and snake its way south toward the Arabian Sea. Along the way, it irrigates a vast fertile delta where farmers have for generations cultivated rice, wheat, sugarcane, barley, cotton, coconut, mango and fig.

More than four thousand years ago and perhaps as many as eight, the Indus and its tributaries sustained the lives of the people who settled in its broad valley. Over time, small groups coalesced into larger and larger settlements and, eventually, into a society – a culture. The so-called Harappan or Indus Valley Civilization is, at least according to some scholars, the birthplace of Hinduism, which eventually spread throughout the length and breadth of the Indian subcontinent. In fact, the name of the place, India, was taken from the Indus River. What we know of the early history of this region, until about 1,500 BCE, suggests a religion among its peoples with iconography not unlike that which later developed into the Hindu gods. Hinduism proper seems to be a combination of influences that trickled into northern India from the west and the north. Beginning in about 1,500 BCE, nearly a thousand years before the Hebrew Bible and 2,200 years before the Quran, the first of the great Hindu texts, the Vedas, were composed. In fact, the Vedas were compiled five hundred years before Moses of the Hebrew Bible was likely to have walked the earth. The four Vedas, compilations of hymns and verses, are the oldest of the many Hindu sacred writings and are regarded as revealed, as opposed to created by man. Other sacred Hindu writings, the Upanishads, the Bhagavad Gita, and the Puranas, were composed after the Vedas. There isn't any agreement among scholars about the dates of these texts. However, the Upanishads were probably created in the range of 800 – 500 BCE. The Gita was composed next, but still prior to the dawn of the Christian era. And the Puranas have the broadest range, from about 300 CE and into the 17th century.

Unlike the other major religions, Hinduism doesn't have a specific founder. Indeed, Hinduism is widely regarded not as a single religion, but a collection of numerous different traditions that have varying philosophical underpinnings. There is no Hindu governing body, no organized clerical order, no supreme religious authority and no particular holy text. Hindus can be theists or atheists and can believe in one god or many. Because of this unique diversity, many people, including many Hindus, regard it more as a way of life than a religion. Nonetheless, we can draw some generalizations about Hindu beliefs. Dharma is an overarching concept of righteous or ethical living. While the specifics of dharma vary, the notion that dharma should govern one's life is commonly held. Karma is another commonly held belief. Karma is usually defined as the cosmic law of cause and effect. It is believed that actions, whether good or bad, have consequences and those consequences aren't limited to the present life. So, a person's present circumstances are the result or consequence of all of their prior actions, both in this life and in prior lives. Similarly, actions in this life are the cause of future effects, both in this life and in future ones. The cycle of birth, life, death and rebirth is called *samsara*. To most Hindus, the goal of life is to find freedom from the endless cycles of samsara. That freedom is called *moksha*, which results in liberation from *samsara* and (often) union with the divine.

Hindus believe all living creatures have a Soul called *atman*, which is eternal. Atman is one of the basic principles of all Hindu traditions. According to Hindu teachings, Atman is the unchanging core of being, while everything else changes around it. Atman is the Self, the very essence of a person. If you were to erase the body and all thoughts and emotions, what remains is Atman, the Soul. All Souls are on a journey of spiritual discovery leading eventually to the divine. In some Hindu traditions, physical things interfere with the Soul's journey. In others, it is the experiences of Reality that lead to liberation. For Hindus, the Soul, the divine presence, isn't reserved to humans or even just to living beings. Instead, the divine can be found in everything that manifests in the material world, animals, plants, mountains, the sky and the water flowing in a river. Most Hindus worship Brahman as the supreme god and also other gods and goddesses, such as Brahma, Vishnu, Shiva, Devi and Krishna. However, these seemingly separate deities are usually regarded as not really separate but instead as merely different aspects of the same God.

Creation stories are the way religions explain Reality – what it is, how it came to be, how it's shaped and how it unfolds. It's not surprising that there are lots of different Hindu creation stories and beliefs. This reflects the diversity we find in Hinduism and its lack of a central sacred text and consistent beliefs. Some of the creation stories are narrative, told through characters, and others are philosophical, based on concepts. The ancient texts provide many different answers to the questions where did we come from and why is the world the way it is.

The Hindu view of creation is affected by the Hindu view of time. In general, Hindus believe time is cyclical and they believe there is not one Reality, but many that arise one after the other in a serial unfolding. Each world comes into being and is then eventually destroyed, giving rise to a new Reality. The Rig Veda is the oldest of the four Vedas and it contains a variety of different creation stories describing how the world was created from non-existence. The following story from the Rig Veda is told through characters. Brahmanaspati was the father of all gods and Aditi was their mother:

> 1. Let us with melodious skill proclaim these generations of Gods,
> That one may see them when these hymns are chanted in a future age.

> 2. Brahmanaspati produced them with blast and smelting, like a Smith,
> Existence, in an earlier age of Gods, from Non-existence sprang.

3. Existence, in the earliest age of Gods, from Non-existence sprang.

Thereafter were the regions born. This sprang from the Productive Power.

4. Earth sprang from the Productive Power the regions from the earth were born.

Daksa was born of Aditi, and Aditi was Daksa's Child.

5. For Aditi, O Daksa, she who is thy Daughter, was brought forth.

After her were the blessed Gods born sharers of immortal life.

6. When ye, O Gods, in yonder deep close clasping one another stood,

Thence, as of dancers, from your feet a thickening cloud of dust arose.

7. When, O ye Gods, like Yatis, ye caused all existing things to grow,

Then ye brought Surya forward who was lying hidden in the sea.

8. Eight are the Sons of Aditi who from her body sprang to life.

With seven she went to meet the Gods she cast Martanda far away.

9. So with her Seven Sons Aditi went forth to meet the earlier age.

She brought Martanda thitherward to spring to life and die again.

Another story from the Rig Veda is called the Purusha Sukta. It describes how Purusha, the Cosmic Being or sort of primeval god, manifested all beings from different parts of his body, along with the Sun, the moon, the sky and the earth.

Thousand-headed is Purusa, thousand-eyed, thousand-footed. Having covered the earth on all sides, he stood above it the width of ten fingers.

Only Purusa is all this, that which has been and that which is to be. He is the lord of the immortals, who grow by means of [ritual] food.

Such is his greatness, yet more than this is Purusa. One-quarter of him is all beings; three- quarters of him is the immortal in heaven.

Three-quarters of Purusa went upward, one-quarter of him remained here. From this [one-quarter] he spread in all directions into what eats and what does not eat.

From him the shining one was born, from the shining one was born Purusa. When born he extended beyond the earth, behind as well as in front.

When the gods performed a sacrifice with the offering Purusa, spring was its clarified butter, summer the kindling, autumn the oblation.

It was Purusa, born in the beginning, which they sprinkled on the sacred grass as a sacrifice. With him the gods sacrificed, the demi-gods, and the seers.

From that sacrifice completely offered, the clotted butter was brought together. It made the beasts of the air, the forest and the village.

From that sacrifice completely offered, the mantras [Rig Veda] and the songs [Samaveda] were born. The meters were born from it. The sacrificial formulae [Yajurveda] were born from it.

From it the horses were born and all that have cutting teeth in both jaws. The cows were born from it, also. From it were born goats and sheep.

When they divided Purusa, how many ways did they apportion him? What was his mouth? What were his arms? What were his thighs, his feet declared to be?

His mouth was the Brahman [caste], his arms were the Rajanaya [Kshatriya caste], his thighs the Vaishya [caste]; from his feet the Shudra [caste] was born.

The moon was born from his mind; from his eye the sun was born; from his mouth both Indra and Agni [fire]; from his breath Vayu [wind] was born.

From his navel arose the air; from his head the heaven evolved; from his feet the earth; the [four] directions from his ear. Thus, they fashioned the worlds.

Seven were his altar sticks, three times seven were the kindling bundles, when the gods, performing the sacrifice, bound the beast Purusa.

The gods sacrificed with the sacrifice to the sacrifice. These were the first rites. These powers reached the firmament, where the ancient demi-gods and the gods are. [Translation by Michael Myers]

Also from the Rig Veda, but much later in time, comes the wonderfully compact Hymn of Creation, the Nasadiya Sukta:

The non-existent was not; the existent was not at that time. The atmosphere was not nor the heavens which are beyond. What was concealed? Where? In whose protection? Was it water? An unfathomable abyss?

There was neither death nor immortality then. There was not distinction of day or night. That alone breathed windless by its own power. Other than that there was not anything else.

Darkness was hidden by darkness in the beginning. All this was an indistinguishable sea. That which becomes, that which was enveloped by the void, that alone was born through the power of heat.

Upon that desire arose in the beginning. This was the first discharge of thought.

Sages discovered this link of the existent to the nonexistent, having searched in the heart with wisdom.

Their line [of vision] was extended across; what was below, what was above?

There were impregnators, there were powers: inherent power below, impulses above.

Who knows truly? Who here will declare whence it arose, whence this creation?
The gods are subsequent to the creation of this. Who, then, knows whence it has come into being?

> *Whence this creation has come into being; whether it was made or not; he in the highest heaven is its surveyor. Surely he knows, or perhaps he knows not.*
> *[Michael Myers translation]*

This story, probably written between the ninth and tenth centuries before Christ, is enigmatic, to say the least. It seems to pose questions more than it's concerned with answering them. It suggests the world came into being but struggles with the idea of something arising from nothing. It suggests that only the creator knows whether the world was created or already existed – then teases that even the creator doesn't know. It proposes that there was nothingness and then suggests the paradox that the creator existed in the nothingness. This story is obviously much more esoteric than the others we've seen, seeming to encourage contemplation about the source of Reality, Self and Soul more than offering definite and concrete answers.

And finally, here's my favorite of the Hindu creation stories. I love the imagery.

> *Before time began there was no heaven, no earth and no space between. A vast dark ocean washed upon the shores of nothingness and licked the edges of night. A giant cobra, Shesha, floated on the waters. Asleep within its endless coils lay the Lord Vishnu. He was watched over by the mighty serpent. Everything was so peaceful and silent that Vishnu slept undisturbed by dreams or motion.*

From the depths a humming sound began to tremble, Om. It grew and spread, filling the emptiness and throbbing with energy. The night had ended. Vishnu awoke. As the dawn began to break, from Vishnu's navel grew a magnificent lotus flower. In the middle of the blossom sat Vishnu's servant, Brahma. He awaited the Lord's command.

Vishnu spoke to his servant: 'It is time to begin.' Brahma bowed. Vishnu commanded: 'Create the world.' A wind swept up the waters. Vishnu and the serpent vanished. Brahma remained in the lotus flower, floating and tossing on the sea. He lifted up his arms and calmed the wind and the ocean. Then Brahma split the lotus flower into three. He stretched one part into the heavens. He made another part into the earth. With the third part of the flower he created the skies.

The earth was bare. Brahma set to work. He created grass, flowers, trees and plants of all kinds. To these he gave feeling. Next he created the animals and the insects to live on the land. He made birds to fly in the air and many fish to swim in the sea. To all these creatures, he gave the senses of touch and smell. He gave them power to see, hear and move.

The world was soon bristling with life and the air was filled with the sounds of Brahma's creation. However, a wicked demon appeared and stole the world. He threw it far out into the cosmic ocean. Vishnu quickly killed the demon and changed into animal form to rescue the world. Brahma was delighted at the world's safe return from the depths, for he was then able to finish his task of forming the land and all living things.

But one day, this Universe, like all others before it, will be wiped out when Lord Shiva, the destroyer, grows angry with the world's evil. At this time, he will dance his ferocious dance of destruction and once again there will be a time when nothing exists but Brahman.

Hindu cosmology is more complex in some ways than the Abrahamic religions because it doesn't necessarily provide clear answers to questions like how did I get here and what is the source of all this. In part, this is because, as we noted before, Hindus reject the notion of a beginning and an end and instead believe in a continuous cycle of life, death and reincarnation – *samsara*. The *Bhagavad Gita* explains: "As a man abandons worn-out clothes and acquires new ones, so when the body is worn out a new one is acquired by the Self, who lives within." Even the world we know, although it came into being and will have an end, is only one of an infinite number of manifestations of the universe. With that world-view, origin questions have less importance. As we saw earlier in this section, the Hindu answer to the purpose question – what is the purpose of my life – is much clearer. Despite the diversity of beliefs in Hinduism, most are united by the belief that the purpose of life is liberation – liberation from the endless cycles of birth and death, liberation from *samsara*.

* * * * * * *

By the middle of the first millennium BCE, the Indian subcontinent was awash in different cultural and religious traditions. Hinduism had gotten a start and various Yogic traditions had proliferated. Into this cultural stew a royal prince was born to Queen Mayadevi in about 500 BCE. His name was Siddhartha Gautama and he later became known as the Buddha. His birthplace was called Lumbini and it lies on the southern boundary of present-day Nepal, barely eight hundred miles from the Indus River Valley. Unlike the rugged and heavily-uplifted mountainous regions of Nepal, Lumbini is low flatland at not quite 500 feet above sea level.

Siddhartha was raised in great luxury, but at the age of twenty-nine he gave it all up in search of ultimate truth. He became a mendicant, an ascetic begging for alms, traveling throughout what is now India. Siddhartha studied and practiced in various traditions on his journey but found the paths they offered him insufficient to achieve the truth, the enlightenment, he was searching for. After about six years, as the story is usually told, he found himself in the village of Bodh Gaya in the Bihar Province of northeastern India, where he seated himself beneath a Bodhi tree, resolving not to arise until enlightenment came. Remaining motionless in seated meditation for seven weeks, enlightenment finally dawned. One of the gifts enlightenment bestowed was what are referred to as the Four Noble Truths, the foundation of Buddhism: suffering exists in the world; suffering has causes, including craving and ignorance; suffering can be brought to an end; and there is a process, The Noble Eightfold Path, that will bring an end to suffering. The Noble Eightfold Path consists of eight practices, tools to be used on the path to enlightenment: right understanding, right thought, right speech, right conduct or action, right livelihood, right effort, right mindfulness, and right concentration. These tools are guidelines in Buddhist practice, not dogma.

Like Hinduism, there are numerous ancient Buddhist texts. The Buddha taught for about fifty years and his teachings were delivered orally to his students. The Buddha's lessons were memorized by the students and ritually chanted at gatherings of followers, a tradition that continues to this day. At the dawn of the Christian era, about 25 BCE, the Buddha's original teachings were recorded on strips of dried leaves that were then bound together into bundles. This work is called the Pali Canon or Tipitaka, which means three baskets, since the work is divided into three parts. The first part, the Vinaya Pitaka, consists of rules of conduct to be followed by monks and nuns. The second part, the Sutta Pitaka, includes the main teachings (called Dhamma or Dharma) of the Buddha. The third part, the Abhidama Pitaka, is divided into seven sections that are thought to be the scholarly activity of monks who lived after the Buddha and were intended to organize the Buddha's direct teachings into a coherent system of philosophy.

In the four-hundred-year period between 200 BCE and 200 CE, more than 2000 new sutras were written in the growing Mahayana Buddhist tradition. Some of those sutras remain cornerstones of Buddhist practice today. A sutra is typically a short teaching that centers on a particular concept. For example, the Heart Sutra is a conversation between the Sage Avalokiteshvara and the student Sariputra. In this Sutra the Sage explains to the student the concept of emptiness, the belief that nothing is really separate from anything else.

Avalokiteshvara, while practicing deeply with the Insight that Brings Us to the Other Shore, suddenly discovered that all of the five Skandhas are equally empty, and with this realization he overcame all Ill-being.

"Listen Sariputra, this Body itself is Emptiness and Emptiness itself is this Body.

This Body is not other than Emptiness and Emptiness is not other than this Body. The same is true of Feelings, Perceptions, Mental Formations, and Consciousness.

"Listen Sariputra, all phenomena bear the mark of Emptiness; their true nature is the nature of no Birth no Death, no Being no Non-being, no Defilement no Purity, no Increasing no Decreasing.

"That is why in Emptiness, Body, Feelings, Perceptions, Mental Formations and Consciousness are not separate self entities.

The Eighteen Realms of Phenomena which are the six Sense Organs, the six Sense Objects, and the six Consciousnesses are also not separate self entities.

The Twelve Links of Interdependent Arising and their Extinction are also not separate self entities. Ill-being, the Causes of Ill-being, the End of Ill-being, the Path, insight and attainment, are also not separate self entities.

Whoever can see this no longer needs anything to attain.

Bodhisattvas who practice the Insight that Brings Us to the Other Shore see no more obstacles in their mind, and because there are no more obstacles in their mind, they can overcome all fear, destroy all wrong perceptions and realize Perfect Nirvana.

"All Buddhas in the past, present and future by practicing the Insight that Brings Us to the Other Shore are all capable of attaining Authentic and Perfect Enlightenment.

"Therefore Sariputra, it should be known that the Insight that Brings Us to the Other Shore is a Great Mantra, the most illuminating mantra, the highest mantra, a mantra beyond compare, the True Wisdom that has the power to put an end to all kinds of suffering. Therefore let us proclaim a mantra to praise the Insight that Brings Us to the Other Shore. [2014 translation by Thich Nhat Hahn]

The meaning of the Heart Sutra may seem somewhat impenetrable at first and, indeed, students of Buddhism may spend decades studying its subtleties. But the basic teaching is rather straightforward and is a cornerstone of Buddhism. Emptiness doesn't mean empty in the usual sense. It means lacking in separateness. The Sage is teaching that the body, the Self, is not a separate thing or object in Reality, but is composed of everything else, including all sensations, all thoughts and all feelings. The appearance or belief in separation is an illusion and once the illusion is penetrated, enlightenment ("the other shore") is attained. There is a lovely way of explaining this using the image of a piece of paper. It is taught that there is a left side of the paper and a right. Neither side can exist without the other. The left exists only because of the right and the right exists only because of the left. The same is true of everything in the universe. We can point to one attribute or another, but they are merely parts of a greater wholeness. Sutras like this one are lyrical, particularly in their native Pali or Sanskrit, and they are typically memorized and then chanted repeatedly, often to musical accompaniment. They are studied by devotees to reveal the depth of their teachings.

Buddhists do not believe in a god or gods that created the universe or that directs its activities. Unlike other religions, Buddhism does not have a creation story. In fact, it is said that the Buddha was asked many times by his followers to teach about the creation of the universe and he refused to answer, not because he didn't know, but because he believed the question was meaningless and inconsequential. The Buddha believed that asking the origin question merely led you into the weeds, as nothing turned on the answer. This is illustrated by the story of the poison arrow. The Buddha inquires of a student: if you are shot by a poison arrow, should you find out who shot the arrow, what kind of bow was used and what type of bird feathers were used as fletching? No, he answered, you should remove the arrow. The Buddha believed the creation question was like the poison arrow. The issue isn't where we came from, but where we're going and how to get there. Dwelling on the source of creation, in the Buddha's view, distracted from finding the path forward to true enlightenment. Buddha's focus was on living a life that moved toward liberation and the origin question simply had no relevance to that path. As the revered Buddhist monk and teacher, Thich Nhat Hanh, once expressed it, we ask "questions like, 'What is the cause of the universe, the cosmos,'" only because we "are still caught in these notions of beginning, ending, being and nonbeing." Once you experience the insight that nothing is separate from everything else, the insight of emptiness, you can find liberation.

Buddhists are alone among the major religions when it comes to teachings about Self and Soul. Buddhism teaches that there is no enduring, unchanging Self. What we view as the Self is an illusion that changes moment by moment, but we wrongly view as permanent and unchanging. We view this illusory Self as Me. So, Buddhism teaches that the Self exists, but that it continually changes and is never the same from one moment to the next. Imagine that you're standing hip-deep in a river. The water flowing past you in one instant is not the same water that flowed past a moment ago and will not be the same as the water flowing by in the next moment. The river you are experiencing moment by moment is ever changing and never the same. Yet, it is the same river you have been standing in the whole time. The

Buddhist conception of Self is the same as the river. We perceive the Self as a permanent, unchanging thing – Me. But the truth is it constantly changes and is never the same. Because there is no enduring Self in Buddhist thought, there is no need for a Soul that transmigrates from one Self to the next one over time.

It is commonly thought that Buddhists believe in reincarnation, the cycle of endless births and deaths. While that's partially true, it doesn't mean a permanent and enduring Self dies and is reborn as another Self. Instead, it means that when a body dies, the components that came together to create that body at that instant, dissipate and re-form and reconfigure into something else, or parts of many something elses, over time.

The Buddhist Reality can be thought of in an historical dimension, that which we perceive as the world, and an ultimate dimension, which is transcendent. In the historical dimension, we see things as separate from one another. A tree is not a cloud and the mother is not the daughter. However, what we think we perceive in the historical dimension is an illusion and our work and the practices that facilitate that work is to see beyond the illusion, past separateness, past birth and death, past being and non-being – to experience the universe as it really is.

The teachings of Buddhism are deep and varied among different traditions that have arisen and evolved since the time of the Buddha. Each tradition emphasizes different core teachings and some lineages have developed entirely new teachings that the Buddha never spoke of. What unites the different traditions is the common vision that all people, regardless of their circumstances, can find liberation from suffering by following the path laid out by the Buddha more than two and a half millennia ago. The human lifetime is the only opportunity to loose the bonds of suffering. The Buddha told the following parable to drive this point home. Imagine a small floating ring drifting on the ocean, being driven this way and that way by the currents and the winds. Also imagine a blind turtle in the ocean that surfaces only once in a hundred years. The chance of that turtle rising directly under the ring and poking its head through is exceedingly small. The chance of being reborn in human form is even less likely than the turtle rising under the ring. So, the Buddha taught, treat this human lifetime as an exceedingly precious opportunity to follow the path to enlightenment.

* * * * * * *

If we traveled west from the land of the Buddha, through present-day India, then through Pakistan and the entire width of Iran along the coast adjacent to the Gulf of Oman and the Persian Gulf, a formidable journey of about three thousand miles, and if we took our time, dallying for about five hundred years, we would arrive in Bethlehem just in time to witness the birth of a male child to Mary, wife of Joseph of Nazareth. Mary was reportedly a virgin and according to later Gospel accounts, the child was conceived by the Holy Spirit, information that was imparted to Mary and Joseph in separate dreams. The child, named Yeshua in Hebrew and rendered as Jesus in English, grew up in Galilee with his parents, brothers, James, Joseph, Judas and Simon, and unnamed sisters. The region was ruled by the Romans at the time and would remain under Roman control throughout the lifetime of Jesus.

The Hebrew Bible preceded the birth of Jesus and probably had been around in its then-current form for close to five hundred years. It consists of twenty-four books, including Genesis, Exodus, Leviticus, Numbers and Deuteronomy, which are referred to as The Five Books of Moses or the Pentateuch. The Hebrew Bible includes two other sections, Prophets and Writings. Messianic notions had been around for a while by the time Jesus was born and the Hebrew Bible prophesies a messiah. The Christian belief is that Jesus is the son of God and the Messiah of prophecy. The Christian Bible consists of two parts. The first part is the Hebrew Bible, which Christians call the Old Testament. The second part is called the New Testament and consists of numerous additional books, including the Gospels of Matthew, Mark Luke and John, which chronicle Jesus' life and teachings. The consensus view is that the four Gospels were written during the first century after Jesus' death. The Christian view of creation is contained in Genesis, the first book of the Hebrew Bible/Old Testament. Consequently, Christians and Jews share the same teachings about creation.

Genesis tells us that it was God who created all that is and there was nothingness prior to the act of creation. The first passages of Genesis provide us with a compact creation story. In fact, there are two creation stories in Genesis. Here's the first one:

> In the beginning when God created the heavens and the earth, the earth was a formless void and darkness covered the face of the deep, while a wind from God swept over the face of the waters. Then God said, 'Let there be light'; and there was light. And God saw that the light was good; and God

separated the light from the darkness. God called the light Day, and the darkness he called Night. And there was evening and there was morning, the first day.

And God said, 'Let there be a dome in the midst of the waters, and let it separate the waters from the waters.' So God made the dome and separated the waters that were under the dome from the waters that were above the dome. And it was so. God called the dome Sky. And there was evening and there was morning, the second day.

And God said, 'Let the waters under the sky be gathered together into one place, and let the dry land appear.' And it was so. God called the dry land Earth, and the waters that were gathered together he called Seas. And God saw that it was good. Then God said, 'Let the earth put forth vegetation: plants yielding seed, and fruit trees of every kind on earth that bear fruit with the seed in it.' And it was so. The earth brought forth vegetation: plants yielding seed of every kind, and trees of every kind bearing fruit with the seed in it. And God saw that it was good. And there was evening and there was morning, the third day.

And God said, 'Let there be lights in the dome of the sky to separate the day from the night; and let them be for signs and for seasons and for days and years, and let them be lights in the dome of the sky to give light upon the earth.' And it was so. God made the two great lights - the greater light to rule the day and the lesser light to rule the night - and the stars. God set them in the dome of the sky to give light upon the earth, to rule over the day and over the night, and to separate the light from the darkness. And God saw that it was good. And there was evening and there was morning, the fourth day.

And God said, 'Let the waters bring forth swarms of living creatures, and let birds fly above the earth across the dome of the sky.' So God created the great sea monsters and every living creature that moves, of every kind, with which the waters swarm, and every winged bird of every kind. And God saw that it was good. God blessed them, saying, "Be fruitful and multiply and fill the waters in the seas, and let birds multiply on the earth." And there was evening and there was morning, the fifth day.

And God said, 'Let the earth bring forth living creatures of every kind: cattle and creeping things and wild animals of the earth of every kind.' And it was so. God made the wild animals of the earth of every kind, and the cattle of every kind, and everything that creeps upon the ground of every kind. And God saw that it was good. Then God said, 'Let us make humankind in our image, according to our likeness; and let them have dominion over the fish of the sea, and over the birds of the air, and over the cattle, and over all the wild animals of the earth, and over every creeping thing that creeps upon the earth.' So God created humankind in his image, in the image of God he created them; male and female he created them. God blessed them, and God said to them, 'Be fruitful and multiply, and fill the earth and subdue it; and have dominion over the fish of the sea and over the birds of the air and over every living thing that moves upon the earth.' God said, 'See, I have given you every plant yielding seed that is upon the face of all the earth, and every tree with seed in its fruit; you shall have them for food. And to every beast of the earth, and to every bird of the air, and to everything that creeps on the earth, everything that has the breath of life, I have given every green plant for food.' And it was so. God saw everything that he had made, and indeed, it was very good. And there was evening and there was morning, the sixth day.

Most experts date those passages to the late seventh or early sixth century before Christ. In the second Genesis creation story, which probably dates to around 500 BCE, God fashions the first human, Adam, from the dust and sets him in the Garden of Eden. Adam is given dominion over the animals of the earth and Eve enters the picture:

This is the history of the heavens and the earth when they were created, in the day that the Lord God made the earth and the heavens, before any plant of the field was in the earth and before any herb of the field had grown. For the Lord God had not caused it to rain on the earth, and there was no man to till the ground; but a mist went up from the earth and watered the whole face of the ground.

And the Lord God formed man of the dust of the ground, and breathed into his nostrils the breath of life; and man became a living being.

The Lord God planted a garden eastward in Eden, and there He put the man whom He had formed. And out of the ground the Lord God made every tree grow that is pleasant to the sight and good for food. The tree of life was also in the midst of the garden, and the tree of the knowledge of good and evil.

* * * *

Then the Lord God took the man and put him in the garden of Eden to tend and keep it. And the Lord God commanded the man, saying, 'Of every tree of the garden you may freely eat; but of the tree of the knowledge of good and evil you shall not eat, for in the day that you eat of it you shall surely die.'

And the Lord God said, 'It is not good that man should be alone; I will make him a helper comparable to him.' Out of the ground the Lord God formed every beast of the field and every bird of the air, and brought them to Adam to see what he would call them. And whatever Adam called each *living creature, that was its name. So Adam gave names to all cattle, to the birds of the air, and to every beast of the field. But for Adam there was not found a helper comparable to him.*

And the Lord God caused a deep sleep to fall on Adam, and he slept; and He took one of his ribs, and closed up the flesh in its place. Then the rib which the Lord God had taken from man He made into a woman, and He brought her to the man.

And Adam said:

'This is now bone of my bones And flesh of my flesh; She shall be called Woman, Because she was taken out of Man.'

Therefore a man shall leave his father and mother and be joined to his wife, and they shall become one flesh.

And they were both naked, the man and his wife, and were not ashamed. (New King James Version)

The first Genesis creation story explains both how the world was created and how humans and everything else arose – the source of Reality and the Self. The second story, inconsistent in certain details with the first, deals more specifically with the relationship between God and humans, as well as between man and woman. Whether you read these passages literally or figuratively, they come to the same thing: all that is – the phenomenal world into which we are born and through which we navigate our way during our life – is a consequence of the actions of something separate and apart from that world, an Otherness Christians call by the name God. There is a cause, God, and an effect, the phenomenal world. That world did not exist before God created it and God existed independent of and prior to the act of creation. So, Reality – all that is – looks, sounds, smells, tastes and feels as it does because that is how it was created by the creator, the Otherness. The Christian creation stories thus teach, in a very clear and compact way, about the source of Reality and the reason it is the way it is.

The purpose of the Self, according the Christian teachings, is equally clear: to honor God by trusting in him and setting aside petty concerns about the material world. If you do that, Christians believe, you will receive the ultimate reward, immortality, in which you transcend the material world and eventually return to God.

To find the Christian view of the Soul we can begin by looking back at the second of the creation stories from Genesis. "And the Lord God formed man of the dust of the ground, and breathed into his nostrils the breath of life; and man became a living being." This foundational teaching instructs that God creates the body first and then breathes life into the body, imbuing it with a Soul. The body is material. It is made of stuff. The Soul is immaterial. Most Christians believe the Soul is eternal and, with God's grace, survives the death of the body. If you believe in God's grace, you will share eternal life with God in heaven. If not, separation from God and eternal damnation in hell will be your fate.

* * * * * * *

If we traveled south from Bethlehem, where Jesus was born, along the eastern shore of the Red Sea we would arrive at our next destination after a journey of only 750 miles. If we busied ourselves for about six hundred years, while the Roman Empire declined and fell and Christianity expanded and flourished, we would eventually encounter an illiterate fellow named Muhammad. Born in the City of Mecca in 570 CE, his father died before Muhammad was born and his mother died when Muhammad was six. He was then cared for by his paternal grandfather Abdul-Muttalib for a couple of years until his grandfather died. At about age eight Muhammad came to live with his Uncle, Abu Talib. In his mid-twenties, Muhammad married a forty-year-old widow, Khadija.

Although Muhammad lived in Mecca, he frequently trekked to the mountains where he retreated to the Cave of Hira for solitary meditation. It was on one of those retreats in 610 CE that God, Allah in Arabic, revealed the first chapters of the Quran to Muhammad, through the angel Jabril (Gabriel). The angel instructed Muhammad to spread the revelations to his community. At the time, the predominant religious beliefs in the area were polytheistic and the inhabitants of the region worshiped many different gods and goddesses. People were resistant to Muhammad's teachings, especially the teaching of a single God, but also his teaching of equality of all men. The powers that be in Mecca arrayed against Muhammad, his family and his followers, and the Meccan powers implemented a social and economic ban against dealing with Muhammad and his circle. The death of his wife and Uncle shortly after one another in 619 CE, known as the Year of Grief, lead to great sorrow. But shortly after, the Prophet, as he became known, had a transcendent experience where he and the Angel Jabril journeyed to Jerusalem and then ascended to Heaven. It wasn't long afterward that Muhammad received an offer of support from the inhabitants of a town named Yathrib, many of whom had already converted to Islam. Muslims began to move to Yathrib and the Prophet followed shortly after. After the Migration, as it became known, the first Islamic mosque was built in Yathrib, which later became known as Medina. The Prophet settled into life there, teaching and shaping the community of the faithful. The religion grew rapidly, spreading throughout the region. Sporadic battles took place between the Medinites and the Meccans. Eventually, faced with an impending attack by the Muslims, the Meccans surrendered and accepted Islam.

By the time the Prophet received his last revelation – in Medina in 632 CE – Islam had spread widely to the whole of the Arabian Peninsula. He died later that same year. In all, the Prophet received 114 revelations sporadically over twenty-three years. The Muslims, now united by a common faith, also came under common secular rule by a single leader, largely putting an end to the factious and often warring tribes that had inhabited the region. After Muhammad's death, he was succeeded by his father-in-law, Abu Bakr, who assumed the title of Caliph, *Successor of the Messenger of God*. Within a hundred years, Islam would spread explosively, being accepted by populations in Spain, the Northern part of Africa, the Indian sub-continent and eventually the rest of Africa and a good part of Asia.

During his lifetime, the Prophet and his followers knew the Quran mostly in oral form. After each portion was revealed to him, Muhammad repeated the text to his followers, who committed it to memory and repeated it to others. Some of the followers wrote down each revealed verse and by the time all the pieces had been revealed, just prior to the Prophet's death, the entire text had probably been recorded, at least in uncollated form. The first Caliph, Abu Bakr, directed that a complete copy of the Quran be made, arranged in the order that had been directed by the Prophet. As Islam spread geographically after the Prophet's death, small errors began to creep into the language of the text of the Quran. To preserve the accuracy of the text, a standardized version was compiled in the early 650s and it is that same version which has survived to this day.

The Quran is written mostly in the first-person form, with Allah as the speaker. For example, "Verily, I am Allah: there is no god but I: so serve thou Me (only), and establish regular prayer for celebrating My praise." Allah was speaking directly to Muhammad and through him to all people.

In an overall sense, the creation story of the Quran is similar to that of the Hebrew Bible and the Christian Bible. However, there are some significant differences in the details of creation. It's also interesting that the Quran doesn't begin, as the Judeo-Christian bibles do with a story answering the origin questions. In fact, there isn't a single place in the Quran where the creation story is relayed. Instead, bits and pieces of the creation story are found throughout the text, including how the world was created, how man came to be, and man's relationship to the world and to Allah. Scholars have explained the difference between the way the creation story is presented in the Quran and the Bible by observing that Islam is concerned more with social order and law than with religious myths. In addition, most of the populace was probably familiar

with the Judeo-Christian creation story, lessening the need
to repeat it.

The Quran describes Allah as *"the Creator of all things
and He is the Guardian over all things."* Allah's nature is
described in the following passage: *"Say, He is God, the One.
God, the Absolute. He begets not, nor was He begotten. And
there is none comparable to Him."* Allah created Reality:

> *It is He who created the heavens and the
> earth in six days. Your Lord is God; He who
> created the heavens and the earth in six
> days, then established Himself on the
> Throne. The night overtakes the day, as it
> pursues it persistently; and the sun, and the
> moon, and the stars are subservient by His
> command. His is the creation, and His is the
> command. Blessed is God, Lord of all beings.
> To Him belongs the kingdom of the heavens
> and the earth. He gives life and causes death,
> and He has power over all things.*
>
> *He knows what penetrates into the earth,
> and what comes out of it, and what descends
> from the sky, and what ascends to it. And He
> is with you wherever you may be. God is
> Seeing of everything you do.*
>
> *What is the matter with you, that you do
> not appreciate God's Greatness? Although
> He created you in stages. Do you not realize
> that God created seven heavens in layers?
> And He set the moon in their midst for light,
> and He made the sun a lamp. And God
> germinated you from the earth like plants.
> Then He will return you into it, and will bring*

you out again. And God made the earth a spread for you. That you may travel its diverse roads.

Do you reject the One who created the earth in two days? And the earth—We spread it out—How well We prepared it! So He completed them as seven universes in two days, and He assigned to each universe its laws. And We decorated the lower universe with lamps, and for protection. That is the design of the Almighty, the All-Knowing.

We created all things in pairs, so that you may reflect and ponder.

God created every living creature from water. Some of them crawl on their bellies, and some walk on two feet, and others walk on four. God creates whatever He wills. God is Capable of everything. He is the First and the Last, and the Outer and the Inner, and He has knowledge of all things.

Do the disbelievers not see that the heavens and the earth were one mass, and We tore them apart? And We made from water every living thing. Will they not believe? Then He turned to the sky, and it was smoke, and said to it and to the earth, 'Come, willingly or unwillingly.' They said, 'We come willingly.'

And We made the sky a protected ceiling.

It is He who created the night and the day, and the sun and the moon; each floating in an orbit.

And Allah created humans:

We created the human being from clay, from molded mud. He who perfected everything He created, and originated the creation of man from clay. Then made his reproduction from an extract of an insignificant fluid. Then He proportioned him, and breathed into him of His Spirit. Then He gave you the hearing, and the eyesight, and the brains—but rarely do you give thanks. It is He who created you from a single person, and made from it its mate, that he may find comfort with her. O people! We created you from a male and a female, and made you races and tribes, that you may know one another.

As with Christianity, Islam recognizes that the Soul exists. But Souls are not limited to human beings. Instead, Islam teaches that everything created by God has a Soul. The difference between man and the rest of creation is that man was given free will and one of the consequences of free will is the possibility of making bad choices. Souls were given to man, according to the Quran, by Allah, although man's knowledge of the nature of the Soul is limited. The Quran says: "And they ask you about the Spirit [the soul]. Say, "The Spirit belongs to the domain of my Lord; and you were given only little knowledge." After shaping man, Allah "breathed into him of His Spirit." The Soul, once brought into existence, exists for eternity. When the body dies in this world, the Angel of Death takes the Soul from the body, but the Soul is returned to the body when it's buried. There the person awaits the reckoning of the judgment day, where the body and Soul are recreated in their original form. After judgment, life continues, either in Paradise or in Hell, for eternity.

Although the details differ, Islam provides answers that are similar to Christianity on the topics of Reality, Self and Soul and the relation between them. The purpose of life for Muslims, as with Christians, is to glorify the Creator and there are specific ways to conduct your life to satisfy the glorification requirement. Allah, like the Christian God, is singular. Allah is an Otherness, separate from the Reality he brought into being. The Soul of man is persistent and, if the rules of life and glorification of the creator are properly adhered to, the Soul will be reunited with the Creator in the future.

* * * * * * *

Isn't it fascinating that the vast majority of people on this planet identify themselves as members of a religious group. Admittedly, some people adhere to the religious doctrines more zealously than other people do and some practice their religion's teachings with greater devotion than others do. Nonetheless, they still self-identify as members of the particular religious group. At the core of each religion is a world-view that includes a comprehensive belief system that answers fundamental existential questions, like where did I come from? Why is the world the way it is? And what is the purpose of life? These teachings define Reality, Self and Soul. The particular world-view and specific teachings define the religion and separate it and its adherents from other religions. Is it a coincidence that all religions provide answers to these same fundamental existential questions concerning Reality, Self and Soul or does it instead reveal a deep truth about human beings?

The sensible conclusion is there's a simple reason why each of the 7 billion + people on this planet yearn to know the answer to the exact same questions. And I think that reason can be found by looking deeply at our brains. And I don't mean looking at *how* brains do what they do. To answer our question we don't need to know what regions of the brain are activated by particular thoughts, feelings or sensations or what regions of the brain are connected together and how. We also don't need to unravel complex scientific questions about what processes take place within the brain to facilitate thought or sensation or feeling or what chemical or electrical actions or agents enable or facilitate those activities. The question we're asking here can't be answered by sticking your head in an fMRI machine, placing hundreds of sensors in or around the brain to monitor electrical activity or extracting chemicals from the brain. While those are interesting *how* questions that may provide answers needed to treat disease or correct apparent malfunctions of the brain, the answers to those *how* questions won't get us where we're going. Instead, we're going to dive more deeply into *what* the brain does, examining more deeply our inner life.

In service of that deeper understanding, we can employ a common analogy – the computer. I write these words by typing on the keyboard of my computer. There are two different classes of knowledge I might have about my computer. One sort of knowledge I could gather would be about how my computer does what it does. How is it that when I press a key on the keyboard a letter or number appears on my monitor? What hardware allows that miracle to occur? How was that hardware assembled, what are its separate components, where were the components manufactured and who assembled them? How do the computer's different components, the keyboard, the CPU, the monitor, the memory, the power supply, all work together? What software works with the hardware to do the work of the computer? Who developed it? What specific lines of code accomplish which processes? How does the word processing program work with the operating system and in what way? This would all be really interesting to know and understand and it might be necessary if my computer was malfunctioning and I wanted to figure out what had gone awry. But that type of knowledge isn't essential to gain an understanding of what the computer does. For that, all we really need to know is how to operate the computer. We need to know how to turn it on, how to start the word processing program, how to store our document, how to change it and how to send it someone else. That's what we want to understand now – *what* the computer does, not *how* it performs its magic. And so we turn now to a deeper exploration of our inner life, particularly how the Actor, the Observer and Narrator function and interact with one another, the deep nature of Self.

Chapter 12

Behold the Ego

Remember the arbor/arch in our vegetable garden from Chapter 6? Well, I was in the garden this summer looking at the squash plants as they vined their way up the side and then over the top and down the recently constructed arch, weaving in and out of the thin rusting wire that formed a grid of six-inch squares, encasing the timber structure. No fruit had emerged yet from the green and yellow summer squash plants or the winter kabochas and butternuts. But the profusion of big yellow blossoms was a promising sign and I expected to be picking plump squashes before the summer's heat gave way to the cooler days and nights of autumn.

As often happens in the garden, things grow in unanticipated ways and it becomes necessary to reposition this or that. Just such an occasion arose when I needed to relocate one of the three red flagstone steps I'd laid within the arch during the spring. That is why I found myself retrieving the shovel from the garage and thrusting it into the soil, eventually to make a level spot on which to reposition the stepping stone. As I withdrew the shovel from the ground with an ample load of dirt, I noticed movement at the bottom of the hole I'd just made. Watching for a moment, I recognized the movement as a wiggling by one of Darwin's worms, which I'd just unceremoniously exposed to the deadly, at least for him, rays of the sun. I was at least as startled as the poor worm, which caused me to exclaim "sorry, Buddy," and thus the little guy acquired the moniker Buddy. Hoping to undo the harm I'd mindlessly caused, I quickly refilled the hole with loose soil. At that moment I became hyper-aware of the Narrative I was experiencing. I became deeply immersed in that moment. My Actor Self then gave way to the Narrator Self and an internal dialogue began. I asked whether my rescue effort saved Buddy's life or accelerated the little guy's demise. I wondered what he had been doing at the moment my actions so disrupted his life. Then I started to wonder what Buddy's experience of what had just taken place looked like. What was the Narrative viewed from Buddy's side of our unexpected interaction?

As I pondered the latter question more deeply, I noticed how easy it was to anthropomorphize – to imagine Buddy experiencing the events as if he had human qualities and to project my thinking onto Buddy when trying to figure out his inner life. I found it considerably more difficult to imagine the experience from Buddy's perspective, free of my human thoughts, to imagine the experience as if I had the brain and senses of an Earthworm. Buddy certainly sensed that he had moved from the safety of darkness into the danger of light. He would also have sensed the atmosphere on his skin and probably felt the vibrations of the shovel as I plunged it into the garden soil before uncovering him. His instinctual reaction would have been to move away from the light and the vibrations and the drying air, but there wouldn't have been time for him to react fast enough to avoid being uncovered by my actions. When I realized what I'd done and covered him back up, the sensory triggers that would have fueled his instinct to move deeper underground would have abated and Buddy could resume his normal activities.

Was Buddy angry at me for uncovering him or grateful I quickly realized what I'd done and covered him back up? Probably not. His brain isn't sufficiently developed to form those thoughts or feelings. In the few moments while he was uncovered and vulnerable, did he think "why has this happened to me?" No, because Buddy doesn't have a sense of me-ness that is developed enough to make his Self an object in that way or to think abstractly.

If I had an analogous encounter with Jack, it would have been a different story. Jack's cognitive processes are considerably more developed than Buddy's. As we've already seen, Jack certainly knows what his body is and how it's oriented in space. As Jack sniffs his way through the neighborhood when we walk, he can distinguish *his* urine from the urine belonging to other dogs. He knows when I accidentally trim his nails too close to the quick that the pain is affecting *his* body. He has a sense of his physical Self. And what about his inner life? He has some experience of a Narrative, but does he experience his inner life only subjectively in the first-person or is there an objective quality to Jack's experiences – is he aware that he is experiencing? Does he experience awareness? Does Jack possess ego?

Ego is a belief or set of beliefs about the Self. The most prominent part of ego is the sense of individual importance, the feeling that *I* matter, the feeling that my existence and the things I do make a difference. Because the object of egoic beliefs is always the Self, the I, they cannot arise unless the brain can conceive of a separate Self. Until that threshold of cognitive development is reached, ego cannot inhabit a creature's inner life.

Egoic beliefs can be easy to confuse with self-centeredness, but the two concepts are distinct. Self-centeredness is the belief that everything revolves around and relates to me. As we saw in Chapter 10, babies exhibit self-centeredness. Their inner life consists of a world that caters to their needs and desires and nothing else. Babies don't recognize that others have needs too and that accommodating the needs of others is part of the human experience. Ego, on the other hand, can coexist with an awareness that there are others in the world and that their feelings matter. It is not necessarily the negation of the importance of others, but the existential belief that I am important that is the hallmark of the ego point of view. Ego tells us I matter. It doesn't necessarily need to diminish others to believe in the importance of Self.

Where does ego come from? We don't see it in the Actor Self, who's first-person point of view isn't sufficiently developed to permit reflection on the Self. With the Actor there is no separate Self that can be viewed as the object of the egoic beliefs. Even the Observer, although it adopts a third-person perspective, is not capable of self-reflection because it lacks a necessary ingredient – language. The Observer cannot think in the way we know to be human because it lacks the capacity for language that is a prerequisite to thought. It is only when we come to the Narrator that we find both the third-person perspective that creates an object out of the Self and the ability to talk about the Self's experience of Reality that the egoic view is able to emerge. The Narrator's unique self-awareness is where we find the emergence of the beliefs that we identify as ego. It is thus the capacity for the third-person perspective of the Self, coupled with the means of expressing that point of view, that furnishes the conditions needed for the emergence of ego.

But ego involves even more than the third-person point of view of Self coupled with the capacity to talk about that point of view. There is a third component, which we already know well – the distance that arises between the Narrator and the Actor Self – the cleavage of Self into a part that is seen and a part that does the seeing. All three of these conditions working together are responsible for the Narrator's sense of existential importance, the sense that the Self matters, the sense that the world would be different and less full without the Self. These are the circumstances and the conditions of the human brain that give rise to ego. Ego is not a new Self distinct from the Narrator. Instead, ego is a belief, doubtless a prominent and profound one, of the Narrator about the Self. Ego is the deepest level of the Narrator's Self-regard.

What does it mean to have an ego? I write this book because I think my thoughts are important and I want to share my important thoughts with others. That is ego. Years ago I bought a shiny black Mercedes convertible. That was ego. When you seek approval, praise and recognition from others, that is ego. When you give a gift to be recognized as a philanthropist, that is ego. While there are studies showing other species collect shiny things or the like to build their houses, they do it for instinctual reasons – usually to attract a mate. Humans, it seems, go beyond that. The egoic beliefs cause us to act as we do because the Narrator wants to feel that it matters or, to look at it from a different perspective, because it wants to avoid feeling like it doesn't matter. In fact, when you examine ego for long enough, you see that it is desperate to avoid feeling irrelevant and it will go to nearly any length to achieve that goal.

I taught law for twenty years and was a practicing lawyer for thirty-six. I gave it up for good in 2015. I didn't start out my life with the desire to be a lawyer. Far from it. It was the last thing in the world I ever thought I would do, let alone do it for three and a half decades. My Grandfather, the one I introduced to you in Chapter 4, was a lawyer. He started practicing law in Denver in 1902 and practiced with one of his classmates for nearly sixty years. My father was a lawyer too. I saw the work he did, at least from the perspective of a child watching his parent from some distance. I could tell he made a good living and he seemed to enjoy what he did. He was a very intelligent man and the law seemed to provide him with ample intellectual challenge and he seemed to meet interesting people and do interesting things. But I was rebellious when I was young. It was the seventies and the last thing I imagined doing was becoming a part of what we quaintly called "the establishment."

The path I chose instead, all those years ago, was art – photography to be precise. I had a darkroom in my apartment in Boulder and spent many many hours bathed in the red light of that little room, printing and processing images that I fully expected would one day to be hung in the homes of collectors. I was young and naïve. But soon I realized that the "art" didn't sell well enough to pay the rent and put granola on the table. Considering my options, I decided to segue into commercial photography, but just enough to support my "real" calling as an artist. And so it came to pass that a modest commercial photography business arose with the usual diet of the day, weddings, bar mitzvahs, birthdays and corporate headshots. It paid the bills – barely. But it was also mind-numbingly boring. After about a year I came to two startling realizations. The first was that after doing my photography job all day I had neither the time nor the energy for my art. The second realization was that the commercial photography business was only marginally profitable at best. My twenty-three-year-old brain then came to this conclusion: if I had to have a day job to support my real purpose – art – a career in law would be the best option. I applied for admission to Law School (the same one my Grandfather attended nearly seventy-five years before) and was accepted. I started working toward a law degree the very next semester.

Marriage and children followed and the time for doing my art diminished day by day and year by year. It eventually evaporated altogether. But the truth was I loved the law. I thrived in Law School and excelled academically. After graduating, I clerked for a year and the pay as a clerk to an appellate court judge (a plum job) was more than I could have made in three years as a commercial photographer. Moving into private practice after the clerkship, I fell into a specialty that I remained in for the duration – business restructuring and bankruptcy.

A new federal bankruptcy law had been enacted in 1978, just as I graduated from Law School, and few lawyers knew much about it. Employed in a large law firm at the time, a big break came my way. About six months after I started with the firm, one of the partners summoned me to his office. I walked down the hall to his spacious corner digs twenty-five floors from the ground and took a seat. He asked if I knew anything about the new bankruptcy law because he had a client that might need that kind of help. I said we had covered it in Law School and so I'd be happy to help out. That was mostly a lie. What we covered in Law School was that there was a new law. We didn't study it at all. But I went home that night with a copy of the brand-new law (a couple hundred pages in length, as I recall) and read it from beginning to end – twice. That was my preparation for the meeting the next morning with the client, a business that produced eggs and sold them to grocery store chains.

The owner, who let's call Tom Horner, had invented a new type of egg production house. It was circular and tall instead of long and all on one level. And it was completely automated. The hens were arrayed along a huge spiral that rose toward the top of the round building, ascending to about 100 feet. The food and water for the hens flowed on a conveyer belt in front of them as the hens remained stationary. When they laid an egg, it was transported by a different conveyor down to a ground-level collection spot for processing. The buildings, called hen-houses, were enormous. Each contained close to a million laying hens and the operation consisted of three of these houses. The circular hen-houses were incredibly efficient compared to the long, one-level laying houses that were typical at the time. The business, which we'll call Tom Horner Enterprises, was making money hand over fist and had lucrative contracts with all the major grocery stores in the Rocky Mountain region. It all worked brilliantly until one day in July.

It was hot in the summer on the plains where the three gigantic, metal clad hen-houses had been built and it was necessary to keep the buildings cool with huge air conditioning units. The air conditioning units consumed a lot of electricity, which was supplied by what was then called Public Service Company of Colorado. Public Service had a contract with Horner Enterprises to provide all the electricity needed to operate the business, including of course the air conditioning units, and promised to make enough available to satisfy all the business' needs.

It had been a hot summer and late June and early July had been particularly sweltering. The unseasonal heat eventually taxed the electric grid beyond the breaking point and it was on the 3rd of July that the electric current stopped flowing to the enormous hen-houses that stuck a hundred feet into the overheated air. By the time electricity was restored two days later, three million laying hens had died a gruesome death – literally melting as the temperature in the hen-houses rose above 150 degrees. When I visited the property, just after the July 4th holiday, the stench was so palpable inside that my lunch ended up being involuntarily contributed to the rotting pile of flesh that I had been invited to observe first-hand.

In this condition, egg production obviously ground to an abrupt halt and with it the ability of the business to pay its workers, its suppliers, and its substantial line of credit with United Bank. While the employees and most of the creditors were willing to work with the business so it could get the place cleaned up and start over, the Bank was not. It demanded payment in full, something the business was utterly unable to do. To make matters worse, the Bank had a lien on all the assets of the business, the buildings, the land they were built on, and all of the amounts owed to the business for eggs already delivered to the grocery stores. The value of those assets, even with the mess of three million melted hens, was considerably more than what was owed on the loan. But the Bank didn't care and it threatened to move in immediately, seize the assets and liquidate them to pay off the loan. This state of affairs is what I was presented with as a brand-new lawyer on that day in early July.

From my studies the night before, it seemed like the new law, called Chapter 11 of the Bankruptcy Code, could provide a way to hold the Bank at bay while rescuing the business from the catastrophic events it had no hand in causing. It was but a couple of days later that we commenced the bankruptcy case for Horner Enterprises, and it was completely fortuitous that this was the first such bankruptcy filing under the brand-new law. The case went well for reasons I need not belabor. Suffice it to say that the business was saved and later prospered, the employees kept their jobs, and the creditors got paid, helped in no small measure by a healthy settlement from the electric company that had created the problem in the first place. Oh, and the firm I worked for was paid a handsome fee for the work I did.

That is the serendipity that launched what became a wonderful career in the law. Despite my youth and inexperience, over the next few years I became recognized as an accomplished practitioner in this niche field of the law. That led to other cases in many different industries, oil and gas, real estate, retail, manufacturing, and airlines, to name just a few. To be effective at what I did I had to learn how each industry worked and that was a wonderful opportunity and an intellectual challenge. No two days were ever the same. The work was consistently challenging and enjoyable.

Interesting issues that arose in the legal cases I was retained to work on led to writing articles for legal publications about those issues. That was followed by invitations for me to speak at seminars around the country. And all that led to a teaching career at two Law Schools that spanned more than twenty years. I regularly worked twelve or fourteen hours a day, and often six and sometimes seven days a week. But the hard work felt good. It felt satisfying. It confirmed that I was important.

Working all the waking hours of the week left no time for art, which became an early casualty of my burgeoning career. The darkroom was disused and eventually dismantled and stored away and finally sold once I let loose of the illusion that I'd get back to it anytime soon. The camera gear collected dust on a closet shelf.

I believed the work I did mattered, that it improved people's lives. It saved jobs. It rescued businesses that didn't deserve the fate they'd been handed. Saving the businesses helped pay back creditors, many of whom were not big banks, but regular people who could ill afford to shoulder the loss. Well, it did all that — except when it didn't. Sometimes employees got laid off. Sometimes manufacturing plants had to be closed and sold off. Sometimes creditors weren't repaid. And eventually, I wasn't really helping anyone. I was just taking cases to keep the work flowing, to continue generating attorney fees. That's when I quit. One day, I just walked away from the law and never went back.

With the perspective that some years away brings, I can see that my working life was mostly about ego, being clever, being insightful, being skillful. It was about being important, being recognized, being praised. I mattered and what I thought and did made a difference. A life oriented like that both produces and stokes the fire of beliefs about the importance of Self. The danger of a life in that mold is that when the continual reinforcement of those beliefs is withdrawn, either because you walk away from the life that stimulates the beliefs or because the life walks away from you, nothing remains and the Self feels small and insignificant, irrelevant. I've witnessed friends and colleagues become extraordinarily miserable after a voluntary retirement or the loss of a job because their Narrator Self judges that it has become unimportant. It can be incredibly difficult to claw your way out of that hole. The deep belief that the Self matters, which is at the core of our being, has been shattered and there is nothing to take its place. It can be utterly debilitating. Happily, I somehow escaped that fate and have never once wondered if I did the right thing or longed to return to my former life. It was time to move on and that's what I did.

We all live ego-driven lives. It isn't really our fault. It's baked into our DNA. The set of beliefs we label ego is a consequence of the neurobiology our genes create, a consequence of the level of development and complexity of our brains. Even when we think we're acting selflessly, our actions are governed by our Narrator Self, the self-aware aspect, the ego. The ego even possesses the ironic capability of tricking us into believing our ego-driven and ego-satisfying actions are selfless. Most of what we do in this life is about ego and reinforcing the beliefs that the ego creates. I volunteered in a soup kitchen, preparing food during the day for a hot meal served to the homeless that night. It seemed pretty selfless. I didn't get paid for my labor. My intention seemed just to help others. But it was ego-driven nonetheless. It made me feel good to feel selfless. It made me feel like a better person. I have some friends who devote their lives to the service of others. They tend to the physical, emotional or spiritual needs of their fellow human beings. I have other friends who devote their annual vacations to building housing for the impoverished in Central America. Others I know built and sustain an orphanage for displaced children in the Middle East. Still other friends provide equipment to create potable water for the thirsty in Africa. It is the ego that motivates all of these actions and we are mistaken if we believe that ego operates only to gather material gain or wealth or happiness. Ego motivates it all, including that which benefits others.

I am not suggesting that it's wrong to be selfless or to want to help others. What I am suggesting is that ego doesn't discriminate about how it gets its satisfaction. Ego isn't good or bad. It isn't evil in its nature or the actions it motivates us to take. It just is what it is and we need to recognize that as self-aware beings, we are ruled by ego and that ego is about as sneaky as anything can be. It is always looking for self-affirmation, for feedback that the Self matters. And all of that is OK, as long as we see it for what it is and avoid the delusion of believing that some actions, the evil ones, are ego-driven and others, the selfless ones, are not. The truth is all actions are driven by ego and the ego is always looking for an angle that will give it what it craves – the existential sense of worth, of self-importance. Within the Castle, the ego rules.

* * * * * * *

As we traverse the spectrum from Pet Rocks to plants, to Darwin's Worms, to Jack and to Me, we see increasing brain complexity and cognitive ability. Along that same arc, the inner life spans the range from none to sentience, consciousness, and then finally to awareness. At least for the animate creatures on that spectrum, there aren't necessarily clean breaks from one species to another or from one cognitive state of development to another. They overlap. Buddy is sentient and has a modicum of consciousness but isn't self-aware. Jack is sentient and has a well-developed sense of consciousness and even some awareness. When we get to humans, their brains have gotten big enough, complex enough, developed enough, to allow us to experience the full blossoming of awareness.

Even in the simplest version of a brain there is an inner life. Buddy has senses and those senses produce sensations and those sensations lead to actions within his environment. At the most basic level, all creatures are endowed with a cognitive function we know as instinct. Instinct is desire, motivation and action without thought. This means that the creature responds to an external stimulus with a particular patterned behavior or physical reaction that isn't learned. Baby sea turtles crawl to the water automatically as soon as they hatch. Dogs shake their bodies in a cyclical flowing motion to dry their fur when wet. Human babies smile in response to pleasing physical, visual or auditory stimulation. When threatened, animals may move, retreat, attack, grow larger or smaller, curl into a ball, withdraw into a shell, become still or change color, among many other behaviors.

There are more than 200 species of chameleons. Chameleons have two layers of skin that are superimposed upon one another. The top layer is pigmented and the lower layer contains a lattice of small nanocrystals of the organic chemical compound guanine. Many chameleon species have the fascinating ability to alter the spacing between the nanocrystals, which changes the wavelength of the light that's absorbed and reflected by their skin. That changes their apparent skin color. The alteration of the guanine nanocrystal lattice happens in response to various stimuli, including changes in the temperature of the surrounding air and threats from predators. The change in skin color is instinctual. It occurs without thought or conscious direction. Staring at an oncoming predator, the chameleon doesn't think to itself: "I really need to change the color of my skin to green so I can blend into the background color of this tree and avoid being eaten" and then "time to activate my nanocrystal lattice to change my skin color." Instead, the stimulus, the threat from the predator, causes the physical change without conscious intervention. Instinct is thus response without intent. This instinctual aspect of brain activity is a consequence of what we have labeled *sentience*. It is the ability to experience and respond automatically to sensations. Neither consciousness nor awareness are necessary for instinctual behavior to occur.

Like all other creatures, humans have a whole range of instinctual responses that occur without our volitional intervention or control. Some of these behaviors, like laughing when we're tickled our blinking when an object moves quickly toward our face or moving when a snowball is hurled our way, are reflexive – simple physical responses to a specific stimulus. Other behaviors, like sexual desire or acquisitiveness, are complex behaviors that are a response to a multi-faceted matrix of stimuli. The characteristic these simple reflexes and complex behavioral responses share is that both occur without intentional control or thought.

For some creatures, all their responses are instinctual and their actions within their Reality are nothing more than responses to simple or complex stimuli. For other creatures, some behaviors are instinctual and others are not. Once we move beyond the realm of instinct, we find behaviors that are the consequence of choice. Choice is volition, intentionality. There are varying degrees of choice. For some creatures, the choices are relatively narrow and for others the choices, the different paths that might be taken, are vast. As we saw in Chapter 5, Jack makes choices. He is able to navigate through his world – his Reality – by constructing a cognitive map and utilizing the map to figure out how to get from here to there. He makes decisions. He makes choices. Buddy is not capable of making those kinds of decisions because he lacks the capacity of thought. Jack, on the other hand, has the capacity to decide. When he sets a goal like retrieving a toy to play fetch, he must choose which toy to retrieve to play the game, the red ball or the little blue ball. Thinking, mapping, he recognizes that the blue ball is closer to his current location and so choosing to retrieve the little blue ball would result in a quicker satisfaction of his goal to play fetch. But we already know he prefers to play the game with the red ball. So how does he choose which one to retrieve? There is clearly some process he engages in to arrive at the decision. It isn't random. That he employs a process, even if we don't necessarily know what it is, tells us there is thinking taking place and Jack's decision-making process is not frivolous or inconsequential. It is far more complex than we might at first have supposed.

But our human brains operate in an even more complex way than Jack's. Actual language, of a kind that Jack does not possess, with a syntax and a vocabulary, arises with humans. Faced with a choice of how to proceed, the Narrator Self begins to comment and to question and to second-guess. The Narrator verbalizes choices and options and ruminates about possible outcomes. We can see that the existence of choice has given rise to another quality – it has laid the foundation for anxiety. Anxiety, to a greater or lesser degree, is the inevitable result of having the ability to choose. The availability of multiple options and the awareness of the choice among options gives rise to the possibility of making an incorrect choice, one that does not produce the desired outcome. That potential outcome – the possibility of being wrong – gives rise to anxiety and the manifestation of that anxiety in our inner life is what we call worry. The Narrator is the Self that worries.

So far we've just been considering concrete questions, like how do I get to the red ball. But our human brains have achieved a level of cognitive development that gives rise to the Narrator Self and that Self is capable of asking and contemplating the answers to *abstract* questions. Faced with the choice of a driving route from my house to the grocery store, the Narrator part of me will evaluate the options just like Jack does when he cognitively maps. But I might also throw into the mix the fact that I always seem to take the same route to the grocery store and it's boring to always go the same way. Boredom is an abstract concept and thinking about boredom is an abstract thought. Or I might think: "It's such a nice day, maybe I'll walk to the store instead of driving." Again, this is abstract thought infiltrating the decision-making process. Jack doesn't think like that. It's not magic. His brain just doesn't have the horsepower.

Only at the stage where the brain has developed the capacity of abstract thought – the stage where the Narrator Self emerges – is there ego. Jack doesn't have ego. Buddy doesn't have ego. Egoic beliefs just aren't possible without the type of internal talk that consists of symbolic thought and the kind of thought that permits abstract thinking.

That same kind of abstract thought, using words that stand symbolically for ideas, states or conditions instead of just objects, is the predicate for another interesting development. It is at this point in the development of cognitive function that time and space get labeled and acquire meaning and get used to help us navigate through our daily lives. Time and space both get segmented, broken down into little pieces, each of which we name. Thus, there are years and days and hours and minutes and seconds to time. And there are places within space, each of which is bounded and the boundaries define each separate space. Thus, there is the universe, the Milky Way, our solar system, our planet, our country, our state, our city, our house and our room. This division of time and space is a natural consequence of the need to communicate goals and concepts. If we didn't segment time and space, we couldn't possibly communicate the concept, "meet me at the Starbucks in the University Hills Shopping Center at 10:00 a.m. on next Tuesday." Or "can you harvest the wheat in my upper field the second week of September?"

* * * * * * *

The Narrator Self has a broader perspective, a wider worldview, than the Observer and the Observer has a broader worldview than the Actor. The egoic characteristic, which is embedded within and arises because of the emergence of the Narrator, is needy and craves validation, seeking confirmation of self-importance. It is nervous. It worries. This is all a consequence of inner language and the self-awareness that co-arises with inner language. It is the Self's need to be important that leads it to the desire for an explanation of the new way of seeing the world that the Narrator Self experiences. The Narrator wants to explore the Reality it's become aware of, including the Self. That desire for an explanation is the product of the brain's natural inquisitiveness. That inquisitiveness is native to our species. We'll explore the roots and the consequences of that inquisitiveness in the next Chapter.

Chapter 13

Unmasking the Soul

Like many cities in America, Denver grew exponentially in the years following the end of World War II. Soldiers from the distant battlefields of Europe and the Pacific returned home, found jobs, married and settled down. Many of the newly-created families longed for a little patch of green grass to call their own, where the kids could play and the dogs could run. They longed too for a new house, in a safe place, surrounded by families that looked like they did. Most of the growth occurred just beyond the then existing homes and shops, which stood as sentinels, as tangible evidence of an earlier economic boom. The new housing developments were constructed on ground that had recently been prairie, alongside newly asphalted streets that were rolled out onto the mostly flat, treeless high dessert. The barely-cured asphalt baked in the dry summer heat and froze in the winter cold. No forests needed to be felled for the new neighborhoods. Only a few low grasses native to the climate at a mile high had to be plowed under to make way for the new homes. Trees would come later, tens of thousands of them, planted by the new suburban homesteaders.

Colorado had the foresight, written into State law, to set aside within each newly-platted residential development, ample land for schools to be built for the education of the young offspring of the residents who would populate the new homes. It was on one such reserved parcel that Slavens Elementary School was constructed in southernmost reaches of Denver in 1956. Named after Leon Earl Slavens, a local teacher and principal who'd retired after thirty years of service just a few years before, the one-story brick building was brand new when I showed up for kindergarten in the fall of 1957. By the fifth grade I had spent more of my years passing through the hallways of Slavens than not and the place felt very much like home. In those early years of my life, school offered revelations at every turn. There was so much to discover, so much information, so many new concepts, so many new ideas to munch on and consume. In the spring of my fifth-grade year, one such concept that captivated my imagination was the atomic structure of matter. In science class we learned that everything was composed of matter and that matter consisted of little particles called electrons that whirled around a central mass called a nucleus that was made of protons and neutrons. These atoms were almost unimaginably small and not unlike the solar system, the structure of which we'd become privy to earlier in the curriculum of that year. The atoms stuck together, we were taught, by some mysterious force and billions and billions of the little atoms combined to make the things we saw around us – chairs, tables, books, buildings, the earth, the sky and even our own bodies.

This newly revealed structure of everything fascinated me to no end. You might fairly say I became obsessed with the whole notion. As I puzzled through the implications, I realized in a ten-year-old sort of way, that if the elemental atomic particles mimicked the planets orbiting the sun, then there had to be a huge amount of empty space between the nucleus of an atom and its orbiting electrons. Not understanding how atomic forces worked, I surmised that if there was that much empty space in objects, it should be possible to squeeze one thing through another – if you did it just right. That insight is how I came to be laying on my back on my bed with the blue Roy Rogers bedspread, in my room, in my house in the suburbs in the spring of 1962. I realized that normally things seemed solid, but figured if I thought hard enough, I could force one thing through another. It was thought, willfulness, intentionality that I figured would motivate objects to pass one through the other. The two objects I chose for this experiment were: 1) the wall between my room and my closet and 2) my body.

I got up from my bed and walked to the selected wall, closed my eyes, concentrated as hard as I could, and gently pushed against the wall. I think I truly expected – in fact, I had no doubt – that at any moment I would find my body intact within the closet, having squeezed all my atoms through the sandwich of drywall and 2 x 4 pine studs that made up the wall. After a time, I opened my eyes and was dismayed to find I hadn't migrated anywhere at all. I was still in my room and not in the closet. My first experiment was a failure. I tried again, and again, and then again. Each time I assumed the failure lay in my inability to concentrate sufficiently to achieve the desired experimental result. Finally, after numerous attempts, I abandoned the effort.

In a broad sense, even though I wasn't able to squish my body through the wall and into the closet, my ill-fated physics experiment was not a failure at all because I learned something wonderful, something that would serve me well for the rest of my life. I learned at that very young age how to meditate – how to focus intently on a single thought or object and let go of everything else. It's a practice I continue to this day - every day.

When we become accomplished at meditation, we strive for nothing, we accomplish nothing. We don't go anywhere because there isn't anywhere to go. We let go of the Reality we have constructed and the Self that inhabits that Reality.

Meditation isn't something to do. It isn't an activity. It's the opposite, in fact. It's the absence of doing. Buddy and Jack do not lead lives driven by ego. No Narrator inhabits their inner lives or directs their actions. They do not have inner speech like you and I do. In some ways, ironically, Jack and Buddy lead inner lives of perfect meditation – quiet, peaceful and laser-focused on the present moment. When we learn to meditate, it is to quiet the inner talk, letting the Narrator take a brief vacation, and (sometimes) letting go of the Observer, releasing the entirety of the third-person perspective, returning to the single-pointed sentience and concentration of our earliest evolutionary days.

Meditation isn't the only circumstance where we can find this quiet place. We may experience the same sort of stillness and return to a less complicated inner life when we "lose ourself in the music," which really just means that we are reverting to the mental state, an inner life, where the Observer and Narrator temporarily vanish. It is a wonderful curiosity that development of the Narrator gives rise to anxiety and that meditation is an effective antidote for anxiety because it returns our inner life to the Actor Self.

Buddy and Jack lack the self-awareness the Narrator brings. Unlike you and me, they do not have a Self that knows it exists and whose awareness of its own existence gives rise to a sense of self-importance. Lacking a Narrator, the questioning part of the Self, and lacking the awareness of Self that the Narrator brings, they do not seek answers to existential questions – questions about where they came from, where they're going and how they relate to the world around them. The same awareness, the attribute that distinguishes the Narrator from other aspects of Self, gives rise to the ego and generates the need for a purpose, a reason for being. That hunger is what makes self-aware creatures, those with an ego, different from everything else. Other creatures (at least as far as we know) do not ask existential questions and those questions do not arise because the Narrator has not manifested in their brains. But humans do. "All men by nature desire to know," observed Aristotle nearly 2,500 years ago in his work, *Metaphysics*.

Like Jack and Buddy, babies do not have ego. The Narrator develops in each human over time as they grow and develop from newborn to toddler, to adolescent and to adult. We owe this knowledge mostly to Jean Piaget, whom we've encountered twice before in this book. Until Piaget, we thought that children's brains were just like adult brains, only smaller and stuffed with less information and experience. Piaget exploded that thinking in the 1920s, composing a theory of childhood cognitive development that we continue to build on today. Piaget observed that children acquire cognitive skills in stages over time, from birth through about the age of twelve. Although he didn't express it in the way I have in these pages, his observations can be seen to follow the same stages we've discussed, flowing from the sentient and conscious to awareness, from the Actor to the Observer and then to the Narrator.

If we could travel effortlessly through time, it would be fascinating to go back and observe the blossoming of sentience, consciousness, awareness as they emerged through evolutionary history from one species to the next, following the expanding sophistication of brains. But in a way, we can approximate the view we would get while traveling through time. Because human beings are born only half-baked, their brains take a while to develop *postpartum*. If we follow the path of human cognitive maturity from the earliest infanthood to adult, we will find that it is remarkably parallel in many ways to the historical evolutionary development of the brain. By observing the human child as it grows and matures, as we did with Henry in Chapter 10, we have the opportunity to watch a short synopsis, if you will, of a long evolutionary trail. We can see millions of years of evolutionary history replayed in just a little more than a decade. Among other implications, this means if we pay attention to the questions children ask as their Narrator Self emerges, we can get a good idea of the existential questions that arose in the very earliest days of our species, the days long before written records were made. We can also examine the records that are available to us, created over the relatively short period during which such records have been kept, looking to the ancient writings and the stories embedded in song, drawings and dance that expose those existential questions.

If you've raised kids or interacted with them as a teacher, caregiver or in most any other capacity, you remember their zest for exploration. From the very beginning, long before there is speech, infants seem absolutely driven to explore. They begin by exploring their bodies with touch and taste, seemingly fascinated with the shapes and contours of all the little parts of their body. Little fingers and toes find their way to the infant's mouth, where they unashamedly experience the tastes and smells of their newly minted physical Self. Then they explore their immediate environment – their cribs, their moms, their dads and the family dog. The infant expands its exploration of the world with the senses of sight and hearing as those faculties come more online, turning their head, endlessly curious to catch a glimpse of whatever is within their vision or to listen more intently to a sound. As the baby begins to crawl, it continues to explore, making its way here and there, investigating, touching, tasting and perceiving whatever is within its actual or metaphorical grasp.

The exploration continues and widens as the baby begins to toddle and eventually to walk, expanding ever more its range and its ability to experience the world around it. At this stage, the toddler travels its terrain ceaselessly, inspecting this and that. Everything is a source for further study. That is why we "baby-proof" our homes, locking cabinet doors to prevent inspection of dangerous chemicals or sharp objects and plugging electrical outlets to prevent fingers and moist tongues from encountering a shock. When they can climb, our little ones hoist themselves onto chairs and tables and kitchen counters in search of the unknown.

When vocalization begins, followed eventually by speech, they explore sounds endlessly, listening, repeating, playing with variations on themes. And so it goes for the early years of our lives, exploration at every turn. Eventually, the brain in that growing body approaches its full potential and with the mastery of speech comes abstract thought. Those newly developed thinking abilities exhibit the same inquisitive and exploratory tendencies as when the little person was newly born – the nearly insatiable desire to know. And with the ability to think abstractly emerges the thirst to know and understand the abstract, questions about Reality and Self: what is this world I perceive around me? Where did Reality come from? Where did I come from? Who am I? How did I come to be? These are usually the first existential questions that find expression in the young brain. The asking of these questions is wonderous, but not particularly mysterious. It is simply the logical extension of the native curiosity about Reality and Self that we humans display from the moment of our birth.

I regard it as hardly coincidental that the first answers religious and other philosophical systems supply respond to exactly those questions. It's deeply informative that the Bible, the source of belief for nearly a third of the people on the planet, begins not with an introduction or a forward or a description of God, but that it barrels headlong into an answer to a question that, at least in the Good Book, has no apparent asker – where did all that's before me, including my Self, come from? Front and center, Genesis supplies the answer to that unasked question as its first and presumably most important order of business. Put into a conversational paraphrase, the very first lines of the Bible say: "Listen up. I know you want to know how you got here and what here is. Here's the answer: God made it all, everything in your world, including you." It is immensely significant that the question is so profound, so primary, that it didn't even need to be asked and that the answer is the very first thing that appears in this religious text. The Bible is the clearest illustration of this point, but it certainly does not stand alone. Philosophers, from the ancient Greeks to those of the modern era, have ruminated for the entire span of our recorded history about this same question: the origin question – the question about the nature and source of Reality and of the Self.

Whether we observe the origin question as we see it emerge from the mouths of our maturing children or see the question as it rests at the foundation of religious and philosophical thought, we end up in the same place – the nature and source of Reality and Self is the most fundamental question for the Narrator.

Notice that the ability to ask the origin question arose only after the brain developed sufficiently for the Narrator to emerge and, as we have seen, emergence of the Narrator gives rise to the egoic nature. Also remember that at this stage in the cognitive development of a human being, there are three Selfs inhabiting the same brain, the Actor, the Observer and the Narrator. We therefore need to inquire which of these Selfs is asking the origin question? The answer seems clear that it must be the Narrator because it is the only Self that is capable of initiating this abstract existential inquiry.

The answer to the origin question is of course quite clear and the Narrator ought to be able to easily answer it from its memories and experience of the Narrative. The Narrator has seen many others be born and die, passing into and out of the Narrative. Thus, the Narrator is aware that it came from its parents and can reason based on observation that those parents came from their parents, who came from their parents, and so on, regressing back into the dim recesses of time. And the Narrator is also aware that those who are born surely die, having learned that lesson over and over again. But this poses a huge problem for our abstract-thinking Narrator – an enormous dilemma. On the one hand, the Narrator with its overwhelming ego characteristic, believes at its core that it is important, that it is significant. On the other hand, the Narrator knows from the Narrative, its experience of the world, that everyone dies. Thus the dilemma: How can the Self be important and significant if death brings an end to the Self? It is from this irreconcilable dissonance that the Narrator seeks to escape.

Springfield Massachusetts sits on the eastern bank of the Connecticut River, about half-way between Hartford,

Connecticut, to the south and Amherst, Massachusetts, to the north. Springfield has a proud history meandering all the way back to its founding by Puritans in 1636. Springfield was the birthplace in 1924, two years before my father's birth, of Ernest Becker, although he's not much celebrated there as a native son. Becker was an academic who taught and wrote extensively on cultural anthropology. He was a rebel. He clashed with every university administration where he taught, at Syracuse University in the early 1960s and later at Berkeley and at San Francisco State. He eventually headed north of the border and landed at Simon Fraser University in Vancouver, BC, where he found an acceptable, if not entirely peaceful, academic home.

In 1973 Becker published a book entitled *The Denial of Death*, which won a Pulitzer Prize in 1974. Tragically, and ironically, he died the same year. In the book, Becker argued that death was the great human motivator. His theory was that human character, both individually and collectively, is primarily motivated by the need to deny our own mortality – the fact that we will die. Although Becker championed this argument in the west, the fear of death as a great motivator of human conduct had long ago been identified in the east. In various traditions that arose in India more than two millennia ago, Abhinivesha, translated from Sanskrit as the will to live, was identified as one of the five mental states or Kleshas, that caused all human suffering. The will to live was seen as giving rise to the fear of death and it was the fear of death that caused us to suffer.

Over the last few decades, a theory emerged in social psychology known as *terror management theory*. Based heavily on the work of Becker, TMT proposes that man's instinct for self-preservation and the inevitability of death create a type of cognitive dissonance, an irreconcilable conflict. The psychological effect of this conflict is terror and the proponents of TMT have concluded, much like Becker did, that the terror arising from the conflict is ameliorated to some extent, managed and made tolerable, by cultural values like a belief in the afterlife. There have been a lot of research studies on TMT and it has a fair amount of academic support. But it's far from universally accepted and there's been substantial criticism of the theory on a variety of different grounds.

I mention terror management theory here because I think it's on the right track, but it doesn't go quite far enough. It's not just of fear of death that gives rise to beliefs inconsistent with the facts of the Narrative, although that's part of it. The fear is broader than that. It's the fear of insignificance that death would bring that we are desperate to avoid. The fear of not mattering. The eventual imminence of death is an aspect of the fear of insignificance, but it isn't the whole story. Death, un-being, is one possible instance of not mattering, but there are many others. Worry about how indispensable you are at work, whether your friends really care about you, whether you'll find a date for the prom, whether your music will find an audience, whether your art will sell, whether your husband still cares for you like he did when you were first married, whether you will make a lasting contribution to society; these are all examples of the fear of insignificance and many more could be found. Each example of the fear of insignificance involves rejection – a direct assault on the ego. And it is the ego aspect of the Narrator that responds to these attacks.

Faced with the existential terror of insignificance, the Narrator finds an ingenious way to harmonize its undeniable and unvarying experience of the Narrative with the drive to avoid insignificance. As we've already seen, the Narrator is aware of the Actor and sees that Self as a separate object in the world, distinct from the Narrator. That separation allows the Narrator to apply different rules to the Actor. So, the Narrator accepts that the Actor, the object in the Narrative, has a discrete beginning and a discrete end, which we call birth and death. But it does not apply those same rules to the separate Narrator. Instead, the schism between the two Self entities allows the Narrator to conclude that it is persistent, while the Actor is not. The cycle of life and death it has experienced unfailingly as a constant in its Reality applies only to the Actor Self. The Narrator doesn't die. This line of thinking by the collective Narrator Self of our ancient ancestors, the way out of the dilemma of insignificance, ultimately forms the basis of the religious dogma of all the religions of the world. It is the common thread that ties them all together.

When we return to the religious and cultural explanations that have arisen to explain death, we see that each is ingenious in different ways. Some, like the Buddhist, simply define the problem away by proposing that the apparent cycle of birth and death is just an illusion and so the perception of non-persistence is false. Others, like the Abrahamic religions, posit an unseen and unseeable world beyond that which we directly experience, created and ruled by untestable forces. Faith is demanded of adherents. Faith in this context means belief without direct experience, without proof. In these religions, faith becomes the price of admission to the club. The transaction is an easy one: avert unacceptable and intolerable cognitive dissonance by not

254 | The Great Journey

demanding proof of the dogma. The bargain made, peace and order are restored. All is right with the world again and the dissonance is no more.

What is common to all the explanations of the gargantuan disparity between what we experience and the beliefs we invite to govern our life is the proposition that there is something supra-natural, something beyond that which exists in the Narrative. The nature of the Beyond varies from religion to religion. But the fact of the Beyond is common to all. It is the Beyond that is the source of this persistent Self. It is the Beyond which gives the ego meaning because it allows the egoic aspect of the Narrator to reject its universal experience of finiteness and the consequent unimportance that would entail. Instead, the Narrator can now safely and comfortably rest in the belief that the Self lasts and that the Self is important.

We have a name for that which the Narrator falsely invents and concludes is persistent. We call it the Soul.

The Soul is not a thing. It is not an object. It is not matter or energy. It is not a part of us that persists and moves on to an unseen realm when our body dies. No, the Soul is none of that. Instead, the Soul is a notion, a figment, an idea. It is our plaintiff cry, the expression of the collective voice of all mankind, that the world must be different than that which we see, that we matter, that we continue, that we persist, that the end is not the end, but the beginning of supreme joy, the supreme joy in a world unseen and unheard, a world only dreamt by our collective brain that refuses to accept that we are what we are – and no more.

Let us speak the truth. The Soul is a product of the brain. The Soul is not magical, evanescent or ghostly. It is not supra-natural. It has arisen naturally as our brains have evolved and become more complex. The Soul is a biological by-product. It is a fiction. It is an invention. The Soul is our collective plea, sometimes whispered and sometimes shouted, in all cultures everywhere, that there be more than just this. It is our hope that the facts we observe from our earliest experiences until our last are not true. It is the shield we proudly hoist to insulate us from the stark reality of our existence. It is the way we are able to slog through from day to day. It is the way we accept injustice, inequality and that which is unfair. It is our excuse for living the way we do. It is our lust to be more than we think we are. The Soul is our invented importance.

Chapter 14

Imagine That

Well, that was a downer. I suppose we could just stop here on our journey and try to accept that the existence we hoped for, a Soul that persisted throughout time, was an illusion. Actually, not just an illusion, but a willful fabrication, an invention of the ego aspect of the Narrator to assuage our fear of unimportance. I could type "the end" and let you go off on your truthful, but not so merry, way.

Or perhaps there is more for us to discover.

My love of hiking was kindled when I was eight and had the privilege and good fortune of spending four weeks during the summer at Camp Cheley in Estes Park, Colorado. Cheley was founded in 1921 by Frank Cheley to provide a western outdoor experience to teen and pre-teen boys. By 1941 the camp opened its doors to girls, who to preserve decorum were housed in a different area of the vast camp property. Camp was my first experience being away from home for any extended length of time – actually, any length of time – and a four-week term seemed, at least before I arrived at camp, an unimaginably long stay. But the promise of daily horseback riding, fishing, hiking and crafts – basically a fairytale stay in the wild west – calmed my fears. In the weeks preceding the camp term, I enjoyed the attention of my parents as I was outfitted with real cowboy boots, a white cowboy hat, cowboy shirts with snap pockets (including a white one for Sunday Vespers service), leather hiking boots, a hiking pack and canteen, two thick wool blankets, a yellow slicker and various other accoutrement suitable for a young man heading off for a rather long stay in rustic mountain digs.

While I enjoyed all the camp activities, I loved hiking more than anything else. Many of our hikes were in the vast reaches of Rocky Mountain National Park, not far from the Cheley property. We'd pile into the "Vomit Comet," an aged Chevy Van, for the ride to the trailhead, trying to stifle the nausea induced by the tight quarters, lack of shock absorbers and bumpy dirt roads. This is the environment in which I learned to hike. In that first year, our hikes were mostly just half a day and usually just a few miles out and back. When I returned the next summer, some of the hikes lengthened to a full day and we even took a few overnight backpack trips. As the summers passed and I returned to Cheley year after year, the hikes got longer and more challenging. We eventually were climbing the tallest peaks in the Park. While there's just one fourteener, Longs Peak, there are many peaks above 13,000 feet.

I learned a lot of useful lessons climbing the peaks of Colorado. While some lessons seem like clichés, one stands out and is relevant to our journey together. There were plenty of peaks I climbed where you'd catch a glimpse of the summit from a few hundred feet below it. That little glimpse induced both relief and exhilaration and gave a little extra impetus to make the final push to the top. Then, as you climbed upward just a bit more and your perspective shifted, you'd see that what appeared to be the summit – the end of an arduous journey – wasn't and that there was a further distance to go. The awareness that what you at first thought was the top of the mountain was a "false summit" was dispiriting. It was a let-down. But what could you do but continue climbing and let go of your disappointment. After a while, you'd reach the actual summit, the very top, the end of the journey. There, elation would ensue, along with a celebration of some sort. Maybe a little sip of water. Maybe a picture or two. After the initial excitement of reaching the pinnacle settled, maybe you'd take some time to just experience the moment.

Our realization that the Soul is a phantom is a false summit. All that's happened is we've come to understand that what we thought was the top of the mountain wasn't. That doesn't mean there is no summit. It just means we aren't quite there yet and there's a little way more to go. And when we get to the top, just like all the mountains I've climbed, the view is going to be spectacular.

We've already seen that the Self we call the Actor has a more limited view than the Observer. The Actor perceives and is aware of a narrower world. It doesn't see as much as the Observer. Of course, it isn't aware of its limited point of view. It isn't upset or concerned about this state of affairs. In fact, it's cheerfully oblivious to the broader view of the Observer. In the same way, the Observer has a more limited view than the Narrator. The Observer has acquired a third-person perspective of the Narrative and it is aware of the more limited perspective of the Actor. But the Observer's world – its perspective of the Narrative – is narrower than the Narrator. The Observer doesn't have the capacity to speak, either to itself or to others, and it doesn't have the broader world-view that language ushers in. The Observer is conscious but isn't aware. It isn't aware of its consciousness like the Narrator is. And remember the development that allowed emergence of awareness and language also gave rise to ego, which we've considered an integral aspect of the Narrator's Self-image – the story it tells about its Self.

We've also seen that the Narrator has an ability unique among the Selfs. It can and seems driven to ask and seek answers to abstract questions, like what is the origin of me and all this, where do I go when I die and what is my purpose in this Narrative. We have a word in our language for this unique ability of the Narrator. We call it *imagination* – the ability to conceive of objects and connections between objects, nouns and verbs, things and ideas – that the Narrator has never experienced before. Imagination is a capacity, a power, a capability of the Narrator.

The ability to imagine can be confused with object permanence, Jack's ability to recognize that the red ball persists even when he can't see it. But the two cognitive capabilities are not the same. Object permanence utilizes memories, experiences that have occurred in the past, along with symbolic thought, to project present conditions. The red ball is both experienced and a symbol to Jack and when I throw it down the hall, he experiences it as long as he can see it. Once it moves beyond his sensory field, the symbolic representation takes over as he trots off down the hall toward the unseen symbol. Imagination isn't like that. Imagination is the ability to envision that which the Narrator has never experienced in the Narrative. It is that difference that makes Imagination so extraordinary and momentous and introduces a whole different level of cognition. Not confined or bound to the Reality of what is or what has been, imagination allows us to experience that which has never been, to conjure something completely new into existence. Even though the existence of an imagined experience is somewhat ephemeral and different from that which we experience with our senses, it is a type of existence nonetheless.

The ability to imagine gives rise to a completely new type of Narrative, distinct from the live Narrative and the stored Narrative we have previously explored. Imagination allows the Narrator to create a Narrative based on speculation about what might be or what might happen in the future. Although the future Narrative is grounded in the present, it extends the present Narrative into a possible future. We use the imaginative ability of the Narrator to plan future actions by trying out alternate future Narratives, to plan a course of action by choosing among different possible futures. When my wife and I decided to build the arbor/arch in the vegetable garden, we imagined a thing — the arbor/arch — that didn't exist. We had no sensory experience of the arbor/arch in our garden with vines growing up and over its sides. But we did have the ability to imagine what it might look like, what the end-product would be — how we might experience it in the future — and to optimize the design in a way we thought would best align with the projected object we imagined.

To do that we sketched one version of what it might look like, then another and another. We talked about what veggies we'd plant and how the plants would grow. Then we made choices among those possible future Narratives, the different versions that resided only in our imagination, and we chose a course of action to bring the thing into existence. Sometimes the actual Narrative comes to pass just as the future Narrative was imagined. Sometimes not. We seem to be a species of planners, using this remarkable ability of the Narrator to imagine a possible future and then crafting things and molding events to bring the imagined future Narrative into existence — to allow the imagined future to become the present.

An imagined Narrative can be extremely powerful and it can seem unquestionably "real." I experienced this recently in connection with a long-held belief. Born in Rome in 1901, Enrico Fermi, with whom I feel a special kinship owing to his fluency in Latin, became one of the most brilliant physicists of the mid-twentieth Century. Fermi emigrated from his native Italy to the U. S. in 1938 to escape repression from the fascist Mussolini regime. Fermi was recruited to work on the Manhattan Project during World War II and lead the team that created the first self-sustaining nuclear reactor. A couple of years later he moved to Los Alamos, New Mexico, and became the associate head of the team that developed the atomic bomb.

Fermi's interests were far-ranging. In 1950, while still working at the Los Alamos National Lab, he asked his assembled colleagues the now famous question, "where are they?" The issue which provoked this question had to do with extraterrestrial life: even if the chance of intelligent life developing in the universe was vanishingly small, there are so many stars out there, billions and billions of them, that many civilizations must have emerged. But we haven't seen any sign that those alien civilizations exist. Fermi's question became the cornerstone of what came to be known as the Fermi Paradox. In the years since Fermi voiced the question, many explanations of the paradox have been advanced. Some have argued other civilizations shield themselves from view. Others have argued that civilizations don't last long enough to become visible to their distant brethren. Still others have argued that intelligent extraterrestrial life lacks advanced technology or are too far apart to contact one another.

In 1961, an astronomer named Frank Drake lent the air of apparent mathematical certainty to the Fermi Paradox.

Drake created an equation to calculate the likelihood of intelligent life in the galaxy. Drake's equation arose at about the same time as the beginning of the systematic search for life in the galaxy. Although some of the variables in the equation could be estimated with relative certainty, like the number of stars or the number of stars that have planets, other variables could not. Variables like the number of planets where intelligent life would develop were really just guesses. Perhaps it wasn't surprising that the accepted result of the Drake Equation was that intelligent life was surely super-abundant. Most calculations resulted in the conclusion that there were millions of other civilizations in our galaxy and countless more in the observable universe. It was within this comforting scientific embrace that my own thinking about the prevalence of life in the universe was formed and for my whole life I've accepted and incorporated into my view of Reality that countless other beings exist in the universe.

Recently, a team at the Future of Humanity Institute at the University of Oxford in England offered a new solution to the Drake Equation that shook me to the core. They refined the calculation and concluded there was a 53% chance that we are alone in the Milky Way Galaxy and a 40% chance we are entirely alone in the vast expanse of the known universe. The implication of this conclusion was astounding to me – regardless of whether it's right or wrong. The point, which I had frankly never even entertained as within the realm of possibility, is that this puny little civilization on this backwater planet, orbiting a little star on the edge of one of the billions of galaxies in the known universe may be the only pocket of sentience, consciousness and awareness that ever has or ever will exist anywhere. The conviction that there are others, billions of others elsewhere in the universe, was an essential part of my imagined Narrative that had been with me since childhood. Even though I had never seen an alien or even any evidence of life elsewhere in the Universe, the existence of abundant life was a very real part of my Narrative. The Oxford team's recalculation of the Drake equation compelled me to reevaluate a big part of my future Narrative that had, to me, always seemed very real.

The Narrator and its ability to imagine has another important consequence. It gives rise to a distinctive feature of our experience of the Narrative – the sense of time. We ordinarily divide time into the past, the present and the future. It is the imaginative ability of the Narrator that enables such a division and which allows us to maintain the illusion that time is segmented in that way.

The past is a Reality that once was but is no more. It survives only as the stored Narrative – a memory. We once experienced that Reality directly with our senses, but the stimuli that caused the sensory experience have had their day and are now silent. I watched an absolutely beautiful sunset last night, with the sky aglow in flowing shades of orange that turned to crimson and finally to pink. Eventually, the sun set behind the mountains and the sky turned an inky blue before it faded to black. I experienced the sunset in real time, aware of the Narrative as it occurred. I was experiencing the present moment. As the Reality of the sunset passed, it was lodged in my memory and the experience was woven into the fabric of my past – the stored Narrative. What happened, from my perspective, was that the present (the beautiful sunset) shifted and became the past (a memory of the sunset).

The future Narrative is qualitatively different from the current or the stored Narrative. The future Narrative reflects a Reality that has not yet been experienced with any of the five senses, although it is experienced in some way through the ability to imagine. As the curtain was drawn on my experience of the sunset and darkness arrived, I enjoyed it so much that I looked forward to experiencing another like it on a future day. In that moment, I *imagined* what the future sunset would be like, where I'd be, what colors would dance in front of my eyes and how the experience would make me feel. I didn't experience the future sunset in the same way I experienced the sunset that had just passed; but I could project what the experience, the future Narrative, would be like – I could imagine it. This projection, the imagining of that which has yet to occur, is what we call the future.

The sense of time is therefore deeply connected to the different aspects of Self. For segmented time to exist, at least the way humans seem to experience it, imagination is necessary and the ability to imagine is solely the domain of the Narrator. Without the third-person perspective, the ability to speak and abstract thought, which qualities emerge only with the Narrator, imagination cannot exist. So, it is only beings with a Narrator Self that experience time as we do, divided into past, present and future. The other side of that equation is that creatures lacking a Narrator as part of their cognitive machinery cannot imagine and therefore do not experience the future. For them, time is limited to the past (if they have the capacity to store memories) and the present.

In addition to generating the sensation of time, the imaginative capacity of the Narrator – the cognitive ability to experience things and the relationship between things when they are not available to the senses – enables the Narrator to conceive of answers to the abstract questions it asks. The Narrator does that by imagining abstract answers. So, it's easy to see that the imaginative Narrator can entertain the abstract and existential question "what is the origin of all this" and can produce the answer: God. The Narrator has never seen God. It is a concept, an idea, an abstraction, born of the imagination of the Narrator to answer a hitherto unanswerable question.

We can ascribe qualities to the abstract concept of God, like omniscience, omnipresence and omnipotence. We don't really know what these qualities are because we've never experienced them. But we can, with the Narrator's imagination, speculate about what they would entail. We can imagine what a thing would be like that created all of Reality, that was all-powerful, that knew everything and that was everywhere at the same time. We can also imagine that God would be everlasting, without beginning and without end. That's another quality we've never experienced. But our imagination allows us to speculate, to conceive, what existence without beginning or end would be like – at least to a point. That our conception of God as the answer to the origin question is the product of imagination doesn't make it necessarily wrong. And it also doesn't make it necessarily right. We don't know that quite yet. All we can be certain of is that the answer is speculation, the product of imagination.

The ability to imagine is also the ground from which anxiety, but probably not fear, arises. Fear and anxiety are two sides of the same emotional response but have different causes. Fear is the emotional response to potential harm from a particular cause or stimulus, like a predator that begins an attack or seeing an oncoming bus as you step off the curb into traffic. The body's biological reaction to a threat like that is usually increased heart rate, greatly shortened breath and sweaty palms. This is the so-called fight or flight response. Anxiety may produce the same type of physiological and biological stress response, but anxiety usually doesn't involve an imminent physical threat. Instead, it involves the *idea* of something bad occurring in the future – a threat that is *imagined*. Sometimes anxiety arises from a non-specific cause, called Generalized Anxiety Disorder by psychologists, and sometimes anxiety is triggered by a specific object or circumstance, like enclosed spaces, heights or open spaces.

The response to stimuli that give rise to fear is mostly instinctual. It occurs without thinking. When you accidentally step off that curb into the path of the oncoming bus, your body will react automatically, either jumping back or catapulting forward to escape the danger. There's probably no time to weigh options, consider alternatives and then choose a course of action. The danger and potential for harm is so immediate that your sympathetic nervous system takes over the response. The Actor Self just acts. The Narrator doesn't have any role to play. There isn't much imagining that takes place with fear, at least not the kind of fear that results from an immediate threat. The response to conditions that produce anxiety is different. Anxiety-inducing stimuli don't usually produce instinctual responses. Instead, these conditions trigger the Narrator, who begins its commentary on the situation and ends up judging the anxiety reaction, often deciding that it isn't warranted, which causes even more anxiety. If you have a fear of flying, the Narrator will observe and evaluate: "Why are you feeling scared?" There's nothing to worry about. Planes are safe. Your anxiety is irrational."

Often the anxiety-provoked Narrator imagines alternate future Narratives. I was experiencing shortness of breath not too long ago and my regular doctor referred me to a cardiologist. The cardiologist scheduled me for a nuclear stress test. After I arrived at the testing facility, a technician injected radioactive dye into a vein in my arm. After the dye circulated through my body, I was brought into a room and seated in a contraption called a Gamma Camera, a fancy kind of imaging machine that detects gamma rays emitted by the radiative liquid I had been injected with. The images produced by the Gamma Camera allowed the doctor to "see" where blood was and wasn't flowing in my heart and the veins and arteries around it.

After the test, I asked what it showed and the technician told me the cardiologist would examine the results and call me "soon." I waited a day and then another, all-the-while imagining possible outcomes and what they might mean. Some of those future Narratives I imagined were desirable (everything is fine) and some weren't (there's a problem that will require surgery or some new medicine). At the end of the second day, after a yoga class where I had switched off my phone, I noticed a voicemail from the cardiologist. I felt anxiety just seeing there was a message, not even knowing what it said. I picked up the phone and played the voicemail. It said "Garry, this is Dr. Simon. Please call me back when you can." As you can imagine, that didn't lessen my anxiety. I touched "call back" on the message and waited to be connected. As I waited, I replayed the possible outcomes, the alternate future Narratives I'd previously imagined. I felt anxiety because of the lack of certainty because I didn't know what the outcome was going to be. In the midst of my imagining, the doctor picked up and told me the test results were fine, nothing to worry about. With that, my anxiety, my worry about what the future would be, dissipated and I was able to let go of the unfavorable alternate Narratives I'd imagined. At that moment, the present Narrative caught up to the future and the other possible futures were released. The anxiety vanished. The ability of my Narrator Self to imagine gave rise to all of this drama. Without the imaginative ability of the Narrator, I couldn't have had this experience.

* * * * * * *

The Narrator Self uses its imaginative ability to weave future Narratives. Sometimes the effort happens almost automatically, like with my imagining various different outcomes from the medical test, and sometimes the effort can be very directed and intentional, like when my wife and I imagined and designed the garden arbor. Directed imagining – the ability to picture something that has never been experienced before – is not frivolous or inconsequential. In fact, it is the basis of all that humankind has accomplished in the world, both the good and the bad.

Erected over a twenty-year period from 2630 to 2611 BCE, the Pyramid of Djoser in Egypt is believed to be the first step pyramid ever constructed. I've seen it in person and it's monumental, about 350 by 400 feet at the base and 200 feet tall. Someone named Imhotep is supposed to have been the architect. Neither Imhotep nor anyone else had ever seen such a structure before. So, Imhotep must have imagined the grand structure, created a future Narrative, and then worked out how to bring the imagined object into existence. To be sure, he didn't start completely from scratch. Imhotep was familiar with mustabas, rectangular structures with flat roofs that were made from mud bricks. Egyptian royalty had been buried in mustabas for quite some time. Imhotep's innovation was to stack successively smaller mustabas one on top of the other, like an enormous layer cake, forming the stepped pyramidal shape. When he started construction on the Pyramid of Djoser, neither he nor anyone else had ever seen anything like it. It was, at that point, merely imagined. Without the miraculous imaginative ability of Imhotep's Narrator Self, the Pyramid could never have been built.

The same can be said of all other monumental structures produced by humans. Think how Stonehenge, the Colossus of Rhodes, the Taj Mahal, the Statue of Liberty, the Eiffel Tower, the Empire State Building and Mount Rushmore came to be. Someone had the idea to build them. They had an image in their brain of what the structure would look like. Maybe they rendered the idea in two dimensions, a drawing of some kind, or maybe they fashioned a small-scale model in three dimensions. Perhaps they did both. The creator then worked out what materials would be needed and the processes that would have to be followed to create the giant object. Without the ability to imagine, it just wouldn't have been possible to produce these structures.

Buildings aren't the only things that owe their existence to the ability to weave a future Narrative. Works of art, paintings, drawings, statues, musical compositions, performance art, plays and movies, all owe their very existence to the ability of the artist, the composer or the writer to imagine that which has never existed. Pablo Picasso founded the Cubist movement in the early 1900s. The Cubist artists abstracted a form, such as a human body, isolating its individual pieces, and then reassembled the pieces in a different and novel way. This allowed the artist to show the form from different viewpoints on the same canvas at the same time. For example, the same drawing could show a face from both the front and the side simultaneously, giving the viewer two different perspectives of the same person. It was a radical departure from what had gone before. Picasso's cubism wasn't accidental. It didn't occur by chance. He was a gifted painter and had produced many works that showed Reality in perfect detail, exactly as it was. Cubism was a very intentional and deliberate abstraction of Reality in a way that created an entirely new expression of art. It could only have been done by the artist first imagining what the final work would look like and then blending line and color to achieve the intended result. In other words, the artist necessarily created a future Narrative in their mind, a mental depiction of an object that did not and had never existed, an object the artist had never experienced "in real life." This wouldn't be even remotely possible without the capacity to imagine.

The process of creating music or writing a play is no different. Mozart, Bach, Tchaikovsky, Schoenberg, and the Beatles didn't create music by randomly scribbling musical notes on a score or plucking away on an instrument until something pleasing emerged. They first imagined the music, or discrete pieces of it, and then built their compositions a note at a time. The plays of Shakespeare, the works of Proust, the stories of Mark Twain were not created by the random deposition of words on a page. They were conceived by the authors – they were imagined – and then eventually rendered in written form. The ability to imagine is not just a part of the creative process, it is the essence of creation. Without imagination – the capacity to hold in the mind a sight or a sound that has never existed and the creator has never experienced with their senses – creativity could not exist.

The indispensability of imagination to the creative process is of course not limited to buildings and monuments, works of art or stories. It applies equally to all human endeavors. When Washington, Jefferson, Adams, Franklin, Madison, Jay and Hamilton led the American revolution, they had a specific future Narrative in mind. The Constitution that was crafted at the Convention of 1787 outlined the vision of what the new Republic would look like, composed from the collective imaginings of all the delegates. The structure of the government of the United States is not random. It did not arise by accident. It is the consequence of the very deliberate intentions of those who created it. It was their future Narrative. Without the ability to imagine – to conceive of that which did not yet concretely exist – the experiment which is the United States could never have come to be.

By using the example of the United States I do not mean to hold it forth as the pinnacle of our collective imaginings or even as necessarily something good. The case can easily be made that this Republic has been guilty of many evil acts, if evil can be attributed to a nation, including mass eradication of indigenous peoples, global imposition of colonial rule, and support of brutal foreign regimes, to name just a few. I bring it up solely to illustrate a prominent example of creating something tangible that is not a physical object. Other imaginers, like Marx and Lenin, penned their own blueprints for a wise and beneficial State. Examples in the realm of religious practice, like Martin Luther, to whom the Protestant Reformation is normally credited, and Joseph Smith, the founder of Mormonism, can be recognized as well. The point is simply that the ability to imagine, to create a Narrative encompassing more than currently exists, has profoundly altered the course of human development in all endeavors to which the human brain has been directed. The capacity to imagine might be singled out as the defining characteristic of humanness.

Finally, I would be remiss if I didn't remind you of another of humankind's great creations, my favorite chocolate, a pleasure I learned from my Grandpa, honeycomb. Sublime is its core of crispy air-filled honey and sugar, coated in chocolate, dark chocolate of course. Honeycomb doesn't grow on trees. It didn't fall from the sky. It was created by some chocolatine magician, a wizard really, whose name we do not know. Whatever intuition could have led this ancient alchemist to add baking soda to honey and sugar and then dip the dried foam in chocolate, the imaginative process is the same as we have seen for other human endeavors (but with perhaps even more wonderful results). Without the human ability to imagine that which had never existed before, Reality would not be quite as sweet a place as it is.

Chapter 15

Return to the Castle

What we see and hear, smell, taste and feel – what we experience – is what we consider to be real and that Reality is the domain of the Narrative. The Narrative of the present is what we experience as it occurs. The Narratives of the past are our memories, experiences that once were but are no more until recalled. Because Reality consists solely of our experiences, it is entirely subjective. As we've seen before, the very idea of an objective Reality is an impossibility. It simply cannot be.

With our native inquisitiveness, we have explored everything around us and these explorations have greatly expanded the scope of our knowledge of Reality. With instruments of technology we have transcended the biological limitations of our senses and enhanced their capabilities.

Humans have observed the night sky and the pinpoints of light suspended in it for at least eight thousand generations. But it was only fifteen generations ago, in 1608, that Hans Lippershey, a Dutch spectacle maker, applied for a patent (which was denied) for his instrument "for seeing things far away as if they were nearby." Invention of the telescope vastly extended the reach of our vision. Galileo, whom we've encountered several times before, was intrigued by Lippershey's instrument, which he heard about in June 1609. Within a few days, Galileo had built his own instrument, which magnified objects about three times. By November of that same year, he'd perfected a telescope that could magnify objects twenty-three times. Pointing it to the sky, he discovered in short order hills and valleys on the surface of the moon, spots on the sun and satellites circling around Jupiter. Over the ensuing years, other technological innovations, like silvered mirrors, allowed telescopes to increase greatly in size and reach. By the early 1900s, Mount Wilson Observatory in California sported both 60-inch and 100-inch reflective telescopes that permitted astronomers to see deeper and deeper into the cosmos and simultaneously allowed them to peer further and further into the remote past. Radio telescopes, using non-visible light wavelengths, came along between the two World Wars, extending the reach of our vision even more and eventually we launched artificial satellites into space to serve as platforms for telescopes, like the well-known Hubble Space Telescope. The Hubble brought many new discoveries and images of stars and galaxies unimaginably far away. These wonders extended our vision far beyond what our ancestors eight thousand generations ago could have witnessed with the naked eyes.

While telescopes were trained to the heavens, our inquisitiveness also led us to peek more deeply into objects here on earth. Microscopes arose about the same time as telescopes and with them, our ability to see within was greatly augmented. By the 1670s, microscopes capable of magnifying an object 300 times were in use and biological specimens were a favorite object of study. Individual blood cells, spermatozoa and micro-organisms – structures that were present, but we had never seen before – all came into view. The practical magnification limit of light microscopes is about 2000 times. The development of the electron microscope in the 20th century permitted a much deeper dive, with magnifications up to the fifty-million range. At that level, we can see individual atoms within matter, giving us the opportunity to peer incredibly far within, nearly to the level of elemental particles.

Countless other inventions and technological innovations have extended the reach of all our senses. Devices have greatly extended what we can see, hear, taste, smell and feel. Artificial lights allow us to see in the dark. Little plastic boxes monitor inside air quality, warning of the presence of life-threatening carbon dioxide levels that our human noses cannot smell. Earthquake sensing devices detect low-frequency vibrations our bodies cannot feel. Sensor packages in the polar regions detect infinitesimally small movements of ice sheets. Inexpensive monitors detect fluctuations in the Earth's ionosphere caused by solar flares that our bodies cannot perceive.

Having an equally significant role in the expansion of our perceptions has been the development of electronic computing devices which have exponentially increased our ability to process and analyze the new data produced by all the sensory-enhancing devices. DNA is a chemical compound containing the genetic instructions that direct cells to organize into a particular plant or animal. The molecules of DNA consist of a paired strand of twisted chemical compounds called nucleotide bases – the well-known double helix shape. A genome is an organism's complete set of genetic instructions. It was just over a century ago that a young graduate student named Alfred Sturtevant was able to map the location of individual genes for certain characteristics, like eye and body color, on the four pairs of chromosomes of the minuscule Drosophila fly. Sequencing the much more complex human genome, with three billion base pairs on twenty-three chromosomes, took many more calculations and was far beyond

Sturtevant's reach. Even though he had worked out how to sequence genes, the ability to experience the promise of his insight was decades away. Seventy years after Sturtevant's first work on the little fly, in 2000, scientists successfully completed sequencing the entire human genome, allowing us to "see" the complete manual of instructions for making a human body. This momentous extension of our perceptual abilities would not have been possible without the explosive development of the digital computer at mid-century. Even by the 1980s and 1990s, computers were so sluggish that the first human genome took thirteen years to sequence. We can now do the same thing in as little as one hour. Such has been the incredible increase in the speed and power of our computing machines. With each exponential increase in computing power, we can process ever-increasing quantities of new data produced by our technologies and devices.

These twin developments in our recent past – the extension of perceptual capabilities through the use of devices and the electronically assisted capacity to process all the new data that's become available – have quite literally expanded Reality. We can perceive more, at deeper levels, with greater precision, than ever before. And the changes have not been merely incremental. No, our experiential capability has exploded, growing exponentially. And as our perceptions – our experiences of the world – have increased, we have been able to make many more connections and arrive at conclusions about how things work, how they developed over time, and why they are the way they are. Darwin spent years collecting experiences of the natural world and he then synthesized those experiences into a coherent theory of biological evolution that explained why plants and animals were the way they were. Nicolaus Copernicus spent decades observing the sun, the visible planets and the stars before completing his revolutionary work (in Latin of course) *De Revolutionibus Orbium Coelestium, The Revolutions of the Celestial Spheres*, which was published the same year he died in 1543. The work completely upended our view of the solar system, placing the sun at the center and relegating the earth to the lesser status of one of many objects orbiting the sun. In 1962, Francis Crick, James Watson and Maurice Wilkins received the Nobel Prize for developing the double helix model of DNA, based on experimental observations they and many others conducted.

When you sit back and think about it for a moment, you realize the great distance we've come, how far our understanding has progressed, the greatly increased subtlety of our knowledge of the world – of our Reality. It is almost breathtaking. We have made enormous strides in exploring our Castle. We've also come a long way in being able to describe why the Castle appears as it does and understanding all the rules that govern objects and interactions within the Castle. We've crept all around the Castle and illuminated the dark places. We've uncovered hidden rooms and opened them for inspection. We've learned so much.

But all the knowledge, all the understanding, all the experiences we've had have been within the Castle. Despite all our capabilities, our Reality remains necessarily endogenous. There are no windows we can look through to see outside. There are no doors we can open to step across the threshold. There is no rooftop we can climb to for an exterior view. We can't dig a tunnel under the Castle floor and emerge somewhere else. Our Castle, our Reality, however deeply we may probe it or however much knowledge about it we may acquire, is a closed system. There is and can be nothing "outside" of it because everything that exists is only within. Contrary to what we might believe, this is not some limitation on our ability that we can overcome through effort or technology. This is not a boundary in any sense that we know. The Castle walls do not divide our Reality from that which is outside our Reality. No – there is no outside to be discovered. There is no Reality beyond the Castle walls. The Castle is everything there is and the Castle is all that there is.

Think about it this way. The Indiana Jones character in the Raiders of the Lost Ark movies can run around in the movie all he wants. He can inspect every nook and cranny of his office at Marshall College, search every South American rainforest and tromp all through the deserts of the Middle East. He may increase his experiences and expand his knowledge of all the sites within the movie, but he can never peer out of the movie screen into the theater and see the audience. In his Reality, his Castle, there is no audience, there is no movie theater, there is no outside world. To Indy, those concepts don't mean anything. If that seems hard to accept, it's only because those things mean something to you. Your Reality includes a universe with a galaxy called the Milky Way and a solar system with a sun and a planet you call Earth and a country and a city in which you live. You have a movie theater or a video screen where you watch Indy as he moves around in his Reality. But your Reality, your Castle, is different from his. And even though your Reality encompasses his, your Reality is still a Castle and in your Reality, just like Indy's, there is and can be nothing beyond.

* * * * * * *

As I mentioned in Chapter 13, I experienced the beginnings of meditation when I was a young boy trying to squeeze my body through a wall. Although I dabbled in the practice for the next couple of decades, it took a while before it settled into my life as a daily practice. But eventually it did, and I have now practiced meditation daily for many years. I used to set a timer to signal the intended end of my meditation session. When cell phones got smart and we all began to store our lives on the little devices, I found a meditation timer App to install on my phone. The App has a wide choice of electronically reproduced gongs or bells that are used to signify the beginning of the session and three dings signify that the session has come to an end. For some years my preferred simulated sound effect has been that produced by the Dengze, a bronze bowl (named for a village in Tibet) that produces a deep and resonant tone.

When the first bell sounds, I close my eyes gently and follow my breath, in and out, flowing rhythmically, in and out, like a wave, in and out, in toward the shore and then back out to sea. The breath practice calms the active brain, providing something simple to occupy the thoughts. It allows everything to settle, to simplify, to release. Often alternate nostril breathing will follow, breathing in through the left nostril and then out through the right, then in from the right and out to the left. The side to side pattern repeats for perhaps seven or fourteen or twenty-seven rounds until a profound calmness abides. The breathing practices are both a prelude to and part of the meditative process.

Although my description thus far makes it sound a little like meditation is an activity, like making dinner or taking out the trash, that isn't really the way it is. Meditation is instead the opposite of activity – it is allowing all the activity to cease. Letting go of the need to do. That's hard for us westerners to comprehend, mostly because our culture is based on doing, the accomplishment of things, being productive. So we tend to transform everything into an activity. When I teach meditation to beginners, they often want to know what the steps are to meditate correctly, what the goal is they should achieve and how they'll know when they reach that goal. They are trying naturally to fit meditation into the box of an activity, to describe and understand its characteristics in terms similar to that which they already know. Small wonder they should think that way when you see meditation marketed most everywhere as a consumer product, a method to achieve everything from weight loss to relaxation to increased cognitive function.

Students also often ask to be taught the techniques to still their ever-present thoughts or tell me they can't meditate because their brain is just too active. All of this of course misses the point. Meditation isn't about forcing your brain (the Narrator) to stop bombarding you with thoughts. That would be much too hard. It's easier than that. It is about surrendering to the cacophony and thus leaving it behind. It's just about letting go.

After my breath practice, I usually invite myself to focus on something specific for a time. This is a technique that helps occupy the brain, the Narrator, and its need to comment, analyze and plan. Sometimes the object of my focus will be an imagined physical object, the gentle flame of a candle or a baseball floating and slowly rotating against a dark and unseen background. Sometimes I focus on a single word or a short phrase and repeat it over and over. And sometimes the object of my focus is an imagined sound, a single note or chord. In this phase of my meditation practice, concentration deepens until all that exists within my awareness is the object of my focus. I allow this to settle in for a time.

From this state of focused concentration, a profound shift can occur, certainly not every single time I meditate, but often enough. The volition that has held my attention on a single object dissolves and with it, the object dissolves as well. The remarkable part is what remains when this happens – nothing. It's not a nothing like a dark and empty room. Darkness isn't present. Neither is it light or anywhere between darkness and lightness. It's not a void either, because a void would be something. There's no fullness or emptiness. What's occurred in this state is that the Narrative, both of the present and the stored memories of the past, is simply gone. It is no more. It has vanished. There is no Narrative playing at all. There also is no imagining – no creation of a future Narrative or the playing out of alternate scenes of the future. And the Selfs are missing too. Gone. No longer present. There is no Actor dancing his un-self-aware dance within the Narrative. There is no Observer mutely watching the Narrative that is no longer on display. There is no Narrator commenting on a Narrative that has ceased to exist. There is nothing. Not nothing bounded within a room or container or even a universe. Just nothing at all.

It is in this . . . . . what do I call it? Place. Realm. Condition. Words don't really fit because words necessarily describe things and the world of things is not where we are. Let's just call it an experience. It is in this experience that Reality has vanished. The Castle is no more. We haven't moved outside the Castle. We haven't even transcended the Castle into some other place or dimension. It simply no longer exists and there is no we or me to need to locate anywhere because the Selfs have all vanished too. This isn't an out of body experience where I'm hovering near the ceiling and looking down at my body sitting on the floor. It's not a trance-like state. It's not like movies depict falling into a wormhole, with colored lights flowing by. There's no movement. I'm not viewing the Big Bang and the universe exploding or watching in time-lapse as the primordial stew on earth evolves over millions of eons into modern man. Here there is no time because time exists only within a Narrative and the Narrative has vanished. And just as there is no time, there is no space. And there is no matter. Because time has no existence, it doesn't make sense to ask how long this experience lasts, how many nanoseconds or hours or days or years.

This Nothingness is understandably difficult to imagine because I am trying to describe it and you are trying to conceive of it from within the Castle. We are attempting to apply the rules of time, space and matter which we are familiar with and that operate within our Reality to a phenomenon that does not exist within the Castle and therefore isn't subject to its rules. We can offer a description of Nothingness and we might be able to understand the construct in some way on an intellectual level. For instance, I can say Nothingness is the absence of anything, which is sort of what I've done so far. You comprehend what I'm getting at. But does that description really let you share the experience of Nothingness? Not really. I can also describe what it isn't — I can try to define it by directing you to its opposite. Some of that type of description is also woven into my narration. But that really doesn't convey Nothingness either. We've encountered this kind of issue before when talking about the experience of a sunset. I can describe the sunset and you will understand what it is. But that's not the same as seeing it for yourself. Nothingness is the same. The only way to really get it – to apprehend Nothingness, if you can excuse my *non sequitur* – is for you to experience it for yourself.

While there might be a variety of paths that will lead you to this experience, the only one I've found is the path of meditation. And what has worked for me is the particular meditative path I described in the prior few pages. It is the yogic path, encompassing the so-called fourth, fifth, sixth and seventh limbs of Yoga written about by the Sage Patanjali about sixteen centuries ago. Although others might disagree with me, I find nothing mystical in this method. It is simply a well-trod road of quieting the thinking process, letting go of what we have called the Castle and the Selfs. It is taught that following the yogic path of meditation leads to the last of the eight limbs of Yoga – Samadhi – enlightenment. Enlightenment is often conceived of as bliss, perfect awareness, perfect knowledge. I'm deeply dubious of those kinds of descriptions because they are all conditions, states of being, that are distinctly of and within the Castle. At least my experience has been that the Nothingness which comes from releasing Reality and the Selfs is not like that. Perhaps the descriptions of Samadhi merely reflect the inarticulateness that comes from trying to use language to describe the indescribable. Or perhaps the realm we're talking about may be experienced in different ways.

As I continue sitting on my meditation cushion, I am resting in Nothingness, this place that is not a place, this state that does not exist, this realm that cannot be adequately described. All the Selfs I know are still gone, not just hidden away, but no longer extant, and Reality too is still absent, it no longer exists. Nothing about the Nothingness has changed, except . . . . . . except . . . . . . there is something different. It's a very strange experience. Not like anything encountered before. It is the experience that there is nothing to be experienced. And then at once, I realize that the experience that there is Nothingness is something. This realm is not empty. It is filled with the experience of the Nothingness. Then a new type of awareness dawns. The new awareness is incredibly profound. It is sublime.

Just then, from impossibly far away, a barely perceptible vibration begins to resonate, intruding into the Nothingness. At first I can't tell what it is. It seems very much disembodied. And then I realize it's a sound, but not just a sound. It's also a visible wave I can see off in the darkened distance. I simultaneously watch and listen as the wave slowly approaches and I hear and see a tone that's growing louder and louder, coming closer and closer. Now I realize the intruder into Nothingness is the electronically synthesized tone of the Dengze bell from my phone. Just as that realization dawns, a second bell sounds and loudly reverberates throughout whatever domain I still partially inhabit. I notice how long the reverberation lasts, how it rings and echoes and I watch awestruck as the waves fold back upon one another.

There is more to the bell than just a sound calling to me from the Castle. It is an invitation for me to return, a request, a question, not a command. Before the third and final bell begins to resonate I realize a choice is present: to return or not. Then just as the third bell begins to sound, I make my choice. I watch as Reality starts to reassemble itself. But it's not like I'm seeing this in the usual way of seeing. I don't have a field of vision in front of me and peripheral vision to the sides. Instead, I can see everything all at once. I can see in front, to the sides, in back, below and above – all at the same time.

Gradually at first, in what seems like impossibly slow motion, I observe electrons as they materialize from nowhere and then fall into orbits circling clusters of protons and neutrons. That beautiful dance produces atoms and the atoms find partners and assemble themselves into molecules. The molecules then slowly begin to coalesce into substances. Eventually, objects begin to appear. I see the faint outlines of a room, a room that seems familiar, with shelves lining the walls, filled with books, a wooden floor, comfortable chairs and a table. I recognize the space as an echo, a gauzy image of the room where I began my mediation. Gently, without rushing, the process of reassembling Reality begins to accelerate as I observe, until finally my Castle is rebuilt. The Narrative returns, along with the Selfs and I find myself back where I began. My attention comes back to my breath as I bring my hands together and bow and my eyes open to greet the new day. I see that while I have been away the sun has just begun to rise above the eastern horizon and its soft rays are now glancing off the golden leaves of the trees fully dressed in their Autumn splendor just outside my window.

I am fully back now, nestled again within my Castle. Nothing is out of place. All is as it was. Except. Except. Except there is something brand new. Something that was not there before. Accompanying me upon my return to Reality is the new awareness I experienced in the Nothingness. This awareness is of a different kind from that which I possessed before. It is not an awareness or any knowledge of or about the Castle. It is not the kind of thing you can know from within the Castle. It is of a completely different order and composition.

Chapter 16

The End and the Beginning

In our long journey, we have arrived now almost to the summit. We've climbed nearly as far as we are able. There is but one more step to take before we reach the top of the peak. But before we do, let's take a moment to look around, to really see things from this new height, to reflect on our journey together. We have, you and I, traveled near and far on this grand adventure. We've explored Reality, Self and Soul from many different vantage points, including philosophy, science and religion. We've delved deeply. We've examined Reality, what it is, how it arises, where it comes from and why it appears the way it does. We've seen there are different aspects of Self, each with its own particular point of view and each with a different capacity for experience. We've assayed the Soul and found it empty of substance, the product of misplaced faith in a promise unfulfilled. Finally, we've become aware of a new presence. The new presence is not of the Castle, but it seems connected deeply to the whole riddle, the whole mystery we have pursued.

It may seem that in our travels together I have shared with you the stories of my life, my observations and insights, and that I've laid bare my Narrative for you to see. It may seem that in the course of these pages I have guided you through a tour of my Castle – the Reality my brain has generated and constructed throughout my life. But there is more to it than what it seems. Do you see the deeper truth?

You are the one who has had the experience of this journey, not me. The Castle, the Reality, we have explored is yours, not mine. It could not possibly be otherwise. I am just an illusion, a character roaming around in *your* Castle. This is your Narrative, not mine. The Garry Appel you think you have seen in these pages is no different from everything else in your Narrative, all the things, all the objects, all the characters that have come and gone, all the conditions, all the connections, all the feelings, all the emotions, all the thoughts, all the states of being. All your happy times and all your sad ones and all your memories of the past and your dreams for the future. These are all aspects of *your* Narrative. This is your Castle we have surveyed.

Give that a moment to sink in.

And maybe another.

Now, are you ready to take the last step, to make the final push to the top of the mountain?

What we brought back to your Castle from the Nothingness was a very special and unique kind of knowledge. It was not knowledge about the Castle. It was not knowledge about the things within the Castle. It was not knowledge about how the things within the Castle relate to one another. It was not even knowledge about anything beyond the Castle. It was instead knowledge about the nature of Nothingness completely disconnected from the Castle. It was the knowledge that when Reality dissolves and with it all that you think to be you vanishes and is no more, what remains is the experience of Nothingness. There isn't anything within the Nothingness. In any way that we know, the Nothingness doesn't exist. Yet, there was the undeniable experience of the Nothingness and there was a presence. But it was not a presence within the Nothingness. Instead, the Nothingness was the presence and at the same time the presence was the Nothingness.

Our natural inclination in this circumstance is to objectify that which was experienced – to give it a name – to call it something. We might say we have experienced god or the divine or oneness or universal consciousness. But that's a trap because in the naming we would do two things. As we've seen before, when we use language to name things, we manifest those things within Reality and by doing so we separate them from all other things we have named within the Castle. So, by the seemingly benign act of naming the experience we would create an object out of that which is not and cannot be an object or a thing. By naming, we contain and circumscribe that which cannot be contained or defined. When we engage in the quintessentially human act of naming, we tame the untamable and confine the newly-named object we have created in the cage of our Castle. We import it into our Reality. If we were to do that, we would negate the experience of the Nothingness, the glimpse we had, and transform it into an experience that is the same as any other experience within the Castle.

From our vantage point within the Castle, however, we can talk about the knowledge that emerged from our experience of Nothingness, the new awareness of a completely different kind, the presence that was the Nothingness. We can see that for us to have had the experience that we had, after all Reality, including the Selfs, was released and no longer existed, can mean only one thing. The presence – that which persists in Nothingness, that which exists in non-existence – is you. That which we experienced was you experiencing you. It is the only possibility. The experience was neither objective nor subjective because the presence that was experiencing Nothingness was the same as the Nothingness that was experiencing presence. Nothingness and presence were not separate. They were the same.

Because we dwell now in the Castle, where the Narrator Self is present with its ego characteristics and imaginative capabilities, it can be challenging to drink all this in and maintain clarity about it all. But perhaps it will help to recognize that the you we are talking about now is not the you that you think yourself to be within the Castle. This is not the you with the body you know. We are not talking about the you that has the cognitive abilities we've called the Actor, Observer and Narrator Selfs. This isn't the you whose magnificent brain has generated the Reality we call the Narrative or the you that resides within that Narrative. Remember, we let that all go. And still there was the presence. And there was the Nothingness. The presence is you. The Nothingness is you. This is who you really are.

You are everything and you are nothing. To paraphrase the mantra from Chapter 1, you are and you are not. Do you see now? What is experienced as the Selfs and the Narrative is a product of you. The Castle and the little Selfs that seem to inhabit the Castle – all that seems to be Reality – is just a reflection of you. You are the Castle Builder.

Your Selfs are a manifestation of you. The Reality you see "out there" is a reflection of you. It is you seeing the reflection of your newly realized Self, you. All the craziness, the suffering, the good and bad, the caring, the hatred, the joy, the anger the sadness, and everything else – it is all a part of you and a manifestation of you.

This book is also a manifestation of you. It is part of your exploration of the Reality that exists as a reflection of you. Recognize and accept all of this as an aspect of you, just as is everything else.

I know this is a lot to take in. A lot to accept. A lot to comprehend. While thinking about it and trying to work it out logically may be where you naturally are pulled, let me suggest that you let that go. While thinking is a wonderful capability that has brought you to this threshold, it cannot support you for the next step. Assembling nouns and verbs into sentences and applying the logic of cause and effect is the process that created your Castle and if you remain on that path you will be trapped, contained within the Castle you have created. It's a little like the Chinese Finger Trap.

The more you pull, the more caught you become. You can't extricate yourself from the predicament with effort. It's only by taking a completely different approach that you can free your fingers. With the Finger Trap, the only way out is to push the fingers together, expanding the bamboo sheath so the fingers can be gently withdrawn. If you continue to Narrate and apply the rules of Reality you've learned so well over your lifetime, you will just reinforce that Reality. It's only by letting go, taking a different path, that you can find your way to the truth.

What is this new path? Where do you begin? We've already seen one way forward when we experienced the presence and the Nothingness in meditation. There we got a taste, a glimpse, and you may be drawn to continuing along that path, particularly the kind of meditative absorption I described in the last Chapter. It is there, uniquely, that you will learn to surrender both your Self and your Reality and when you are able to completely let go you'll be reunited with that which you have forgotten – you. Get help with this path. You will find abundant resources in your Reality to guide you. You may find your teacher in a person, in a book, in nature or by looking deeply within. Do not be afraid to ask for help and to accept the help that will be offered.

Practice. Set aside the time you need every day to explore the meditative path. Some days it will be difficult. Some days it will be frustrating. Some days you'll feel distracted. Some days the tug, the lure, of Reality and its pleasures and sorrows may seem overwhelming. Some days you may think you can't get there from wherever your little Selfs are. Many days you may want to give up. But one day, if you're diligent, if you keep at it, I promise you will experience another little glimpse, then another and another. Eventually, they won't seem like glimpses at all. Eventually, you will know you are home.

Another way forward is through the portal that this Reality provides. Here are the steps:

Accept.

You will begin when you can acknowledge the truth of what you've learned so far. The Reality you experience is a product of your brain. It is a grand illusion cobbled together from bits of sensory data collected by the eyes and ears and nose and mouth and skin, processed by the brain, and assembled into a Narrative that you experience during consciousness. There are different perspectives from which you can experience the Narrative, different Selfs. In moments that lack awareness, you are the Actor Self. At other times, the Observer Self emerges. In yet other moments, awareness of Self dawns and the Narrator begins its commentary on the Narrative that's playing out. Let go of the idea that there's an objectively real world, an objective Reality, against which you can measure or compare your Narrative to see if it's "correct" or not. Reality is Reality. It isn't right or wrong or correct or incorrect. It just is. Accept it that way.

The essential illusory nature of Reality doesn't mean it's unreal. It is very real. You experience joys and sorrows and pain and those are real. The Narrative you experience exists. It is tangible and actions within the Narrative have consequences. If you step in front of a car traveling ninety miles an hour, your Narrative will come to an end. The you within your Narrative will cease to exist. It will die. The Selfs you know, which you experience and believe to be "you," were born in the past and will eventually die in a future that has yet to occur. All the laws of nature you've learned are real. Bodies in motion tend to stay in motion until acted upon by an outside force. Objects attract one another in inverse proportion to the square of the distance between them. Systems always evolve toward equilibrium. Accept the vast expanse of your Narrative as just what it is – your experience of the world – your Reality. That it is an illusion doesn't render it unreal.

Observe

Once you accept the Reality of your experience, begin to observe it. Pay attention. Notice all the aspects of the Narrative, including your Self. Recognize the different aspects of Self that you already experience, the Actor, the Observer and the Narrator. Notice what Self you are at the moment and notice the shifts from one to another. This is a way to gain deeper insight into who you are and how you interact with the rest of your Reality. Become as deeply aware of the Narrative as you can. Watch the Narrative as it unfolds, notice as you replay the Narrative that has passed and how you interact with your memories. What do you do with them? What do you use them for? Notice if they inform your actions or haunt you in the present. Pay attention when the Narrator speaks. What is it saying? What conditions does the language reflect? Do the Narrator's words reflect fear, anger, ego, hope? Become aware when you are generating a future Narrative, how you're using it, what pieces it's composed of and where you found those pieces.

Remember that although you seem to experience things in the world as separate from one another, the separation is an illusion, even within the Narrative. The truth is that one thing is not separate from another. Each thing is composed of and shot through with everything else. The boundaries you think you experience between one thing and another thing are illusory. In a very real and literal way, the boundaries between things are not there. You may be tempted to think about this as interconnectedness — noticing that everything affects everything else — and the ego likes that explanation because it's easier to accept those conditions. But after a while, you'll begin to notice that it's more than interconnectedness. The idea of Interconnectedness implies a separation that just isn't there at all. The illusion of separateness arises from language and your facility at naming things. When you name this and that, you give it a separate identity. While that's useful for communicating ideas from one person to the other within the Narrative, you make a fundamental mistake when you find yourself believing that the naming of things gives them a separate identity. Instead, you can, if you work at it, recognize that things are not separate, one from the other, and at the same time be able to employ language to communicate with others. Deep observation leads to a deeper understanding of the Self and Reality.

Remember that the false sense of separateness applies not just to inanimate objects. It applies to people too, including the Self. As with all things in the Narrative, this means something different from the simplistic notion that all beings are connected to one another because the idea of connectedness necessarily implies separation. The truth is there is no separation and so no need to connect that which isn't separate. The implications of this as you navigate your way through the Narrative are enormous. The world takes on a completely different texture when you realize the conditions other beings face are not separate from you but are part of you. When you recognize that one-fifth of the children in America wake up and go to bed hungry each day and you experience that hunger as occurring within you, not a condition occurring somewhere "over there," then the condition will begin to change. It's easy to think of the pollution of oceans and streams with toxic chemicals and waste as something that's happening "out there." What happens when you begin, even in the smallest way, to experience those conditions internally, once you begin to truly see that the separation between "you" and the ocean or the river is an illusion?

As you observe the Narrative more deeply, strive to get to know it better by experiencing it below the surface. If you try you can see all the little threads that have come together at any moment to weave the beautiful tapestry before you. Several years ago, a magazine published this piece I wrote, titled *Meditations on a Piece of Fruit,* that spoke to this issue:

Looking deeply at my food as I slowly and consciously consume it, I see and taste and hear and feel and smell a sweet morsel, lovingly produced through much kind work. I see the sun, the water and the nutrients that exist in this bit of food. I see all the beings who harvested the fruit, packed it, transported it to me, then cut it into pieces and placed it into a bowl in the kitchen next to the dining hall where I now sit so I could choose a piece to consume. I see that this beautiful piece of fruit and everything that went into making it nurtures my body and my mind.

I also see and taste a bitterness – the suffering my need to consume a tropical fruit in the mountains of Colorado has caused. I see this pineapple was picked by laborers in Central America who work for subsistence wages, that the corporate owners of the monocultural plantation where the pineapple was grown profit greatly from my consumption, but at the expense of the workers. I see the profits do not benefit the community where the fruit is grown but enrich the foreign owners of the plantation. I see my consumption is tied to clear-cutting precious forests to make room for the pineapple plantation and that this harms the earth, displaces indigenous peoples and enslaves them. I see that my consumption displaces animal and plant species and in some measure even contributes to their demise. I see pineapples shipped by air and then trucked to me, which unnecessarily contributes pollutants to the earth, air and water, and in some measure, I am consuming those pollutants along with the sweet fruit.

If, when I consume, I feel only joy and see only the sweetness, I do not truly see. For there is great suffering that accompanies the sweetness. I realize this is true of everything. If we look deeply enough, sweetness and sorrow, joy and suffering do not exist separately from one another. Each exists only with and because of the other. They are inseparable. As I return to the fruit in my mouth, my joy at the sweetness is balanced by my sorrow at the bitterness. Now I do not know if I should smile or cry as I eat this fruit. Perhaps I must do both.

On the surface, the pineapple was just a piece of fruit that tasted good. But there was a deeper truth to the fruit, a complex and nuanced tapestry that came together to form the experience I had at that moment. Everything is like that. Nothing exists in isolation. The street you drive on to get to work or some other place is infinitely complex and required that countless strands join together for the street to come into existence. A group of people planned the street, another group planned the many stages to build it. A group of workers laid the asphalt. The asphalt was produced in a plant where even more people worked. The asphalt plant was conceived by someone and built by others and operated by numerous others over the years. The plant is powered by energy produced by natural gas that was extracted from the earth by yet another group of people. Each of the many thousands of people who had some role in producing the street were someone's son or daughter and their parents and siblings and ancestors each have their own stories. Where they came from. What their struggles were. And none of those people could have existed without food produced by yet countless others, both here and abroad, on farms large and small.

When you make the effort, in each moment you find a bottomless depth to all of your experiences, a depth you largely ignore. But it is that depth that shows your inseparability from everything else. These are the individual threads that are woven together into the tapestry of Reality. When you see just the surface, you miss most of what's there. You can begin this process of seeing more deeply as an occasional intellectual exercise, thinking of all the threads that came together to produce your experience of Reality in that moment. The result of that kind of simple exercise will be profound. It will quite literally change your experience of the Narrative. It will change the way food tastes. It will change what you see and hear. It will change the way you act and the way you react. As you continue to practice experiencing things in this new and deeper way, you'll become more adept at it. It will become easier to do and it will come more naturally. Eventually, it will become not an intellectual exercise, but a different way of experiencing the world. It will lead to a deeper and deepening way of experiencing Reality, to a different way of seeing the Narrative.

Understand

As you become more adept and practiced at observing Reality in a deeper way and progress from Narrating about the new world unfolding before you to experiencing it in this new way, your awareness will begin to shift. In fact, a new type of awareness will dawn. You will progress from the kind of self-awareness we've discussed before, where you are aware that you are aware, to a much deeper understanding. Awareness will not be limited to the Self, at least not to the little Selfs we've identified. Awareness will begin to touch you, in little subtle, fleeting ways at first and then with more and more regularity.

Because Reality is a reflection of the you that is the Nothingness and the Nothingness that is you, all the knowledge and understanding you gain of the Castle and everything in it will give you a deeper knowledge and understanding of you. You and Reality are linked a little bit like the way a toddler sees her reflection in a mirror. When the toddler moves, the reflection moves. That is its nature. By observing the reflection, you can learn much about that which is reflected. The more deeply you examine the reflection, the deeper your understanding of the subject. But the mirror analogy is only half of the story. With the mirror and object, changes in the object result in changes to the reflection, but the process only works one way. You can't change the object by changing the reflection. If you warp the mirror so the reflection of the toddler appears distorted, it doesn't change the toddler. The you and Reality relationship, however, allows two-way interaction because of the fact that you have volition, agency, within Reality. Your actions affect Reality and cause it to change and if Reality, which is a reflection of you, has changed, then you have been altered too. You change Reality all the time. You can't help doing it. Every one of your actions necessarily affects Reality. Your actions have consequences. Altering you is one of those consequences. Make your actions count.

Act

Once you begin to accept that your experience of the world, the Reality you perceive, is a reflection of you and you begin to observe Reality on a deeper level, you will begin to understand that changes you experience in your perception of Reality mean that there have been changes to you and that changes you create in Reality necessarily result in changes to you. You can use that unity. This is the place where you can become actively and knowingly engaged in the world, where you can become an intentional agent of change. When you see anger in the world, recognize this not as something occurring outside of you and over which you have no control, as you do now, but instead recognize the anger as reflecting a condition, anger, within you. It's an illusion that the anger is "out there." All of the anger, like everything else, is within you. When you act to reduce the anger, regardless of where it seems to be located, the whole world, all of Reality, becomes a less angry place.

Perhaps you are moved to reduce suffering in the world. Examine it. Learn what's causing it. Then work to alleviate the causes of the suffering. A friend was deeply concerned about the plight of the hungry and homeless. She asked if I'd help some friends who volunteered at a facility that prepared and served free meals to the hungry. I joined the little group of people who helped make a meal once a week for a group of fellow humans who, for whatever reason, were unable to feed themselves. As I watched the diners eat the meals we prepared, I observed that the little action of preparing a meal for someone changed Reality. It lessened the suffering they would have otherwise experienced. Because the Reality we experience is necessarily a reflection of you, the reduction in suffering in the world, even in that small way, means that you had been altered too.

The little things you do add up. If you've had a day filled with unpleasant conditions, you can pass that on to others you come in contact with like a virus. Or you can choose not to. Once, after a day filled with conflict and challenges, I found myself in the checkout lane at the grocery store. I could at that moment have continued to stew in my negative emotions, continued to be the grumpy me, and infected the cashier with the same feelings. Instead, I stepped away from those feelings and asked the cashier sincerely how her day was going. She looked at me, paused and then said: "not very well." She'd gotten word her Mom in another State was sick and she was worried about her. While she scanned the contents of my grocery cart, we talked about the illness, which my Mom had once had too. As she handed me the receipt, she said "thanks for talking to me. It's silly I know, but I feel better just talking about it." It didn't cost me anything to talk to her. It didn't show up on my receipt. But it changed her life that day and mine as well. And she surely passed that on to others. Little changes we make in the world compound and eventually grow larger and larger. It is that way with you.

Accept, observe, understand and act. These are the four pillars that allow you to change the real you, the you that is the Nothingness, the you that is not of the Castle. This is the path from which progress within the Castle is possible.

The two paths, experiencing the Nothingness directly through meditative absorption and practicing the four pillars, are not exclusive of one another. Both can be followed simultaneously. They complement one another. You can practice them both.

* * * * * * *

My friend, we've come such a long way. From Dr. MacDougall trying to weigh the Soul, we've traveled so far. We've explored the mysteries of Reality and unraveled the truth about the Self. In the process, we've discovered the miraculous secrets of our existence. We've discovered our true Self, the one irreducible you, the you that is everything. Now you realize that you are not inconsequential. You are not unimportant. You are not a grain of sand on the shore that is the universe. You are Reality and Reality is you. What you do matters. Not just a little. It is all that matters. Now it's your turn. You have the knowledge. You have the understanding. You have the skills. It is time for you to lead. Where will you take us on this great journey?

Made in United States
Troutdale, OR
02/26/2024

18004463R00192